Management for Professionals

For further volumes:
http://www.springer.com/series/10101

Stephen R. Balzac

Organizational Psychology
for Managers

 Springer

Stephen R. Balzac
Stow, MA
USA

ISSN 2192-8096   ISSN 2192-810X   (electronic)
ISBN 978-1-4614-8504-9   ISBN 978-1-4614-8505-6   (eBook)
DOI 10.1007/978-1-4614-8505-6
Springer New York Heidelberg Dordrecht London

Library of Congress Control Number: 2013944761

Printed on acid-free paper

Springer is part of Springer Science+Business Media (www.springer.com)

To my wife Aimee and my children Adira and Ilan: thank you for your support and patience as I disappeared into another book!

Preface

When I was a competitive fencer, I was always told that the person who won the tournament was the one who wanted it the most. I always figured that would be me, since I really wanted to win. Somehow, though, there was always someone else there who wanted it more than I did.

One of the most valuable lessons in competitive sports is that feedback comes very rapidly, at least to those who have the sense to understand it. It took me a while to figure it out, but eventually I realized that "wanting it" didn't mean what I thought it meant. Wanting is more than a desire to win, no matter how burning that desire might be. Wanting to win means more than training and practice, even though training and practice are critical. Wanting to win means learning strategy, understanding when what seems obvious is an illusion that only distracts, and developing the ability to perceive success.

How hard can it be to perceive success? Well, if you haven't yet succeeded, it can be very difficult indeed. Even when you have succeeded, that doesn't mean you'll believe it.

A certain company was experiencing explosive growth. Their hot new product enabled them to dominate the niche they had created. As their product became more and more successful, the senior management team became more and more concerned about the future. They focused on the consequences of failure and the decisions they made were based on protecting their turf, not continuing to innovate and expand. Despite their successes, they viewed themselves as fighting a doomed battle against encroaching competitors. Over time, just as they envisioned, their competitors chipped away at their market share and they saw their revenue decline.

Perception can become a reality.

The company was seriously stuck. They knew they had a good product, but they couldn't get any traction. Engineering teams were spending all their time arguing over minute details; everyone was so afraid of making a mistake that making a commitment to any course of action was seen as high risk behavior. Even when they did make a commitment they made almost no progress: every decision had to be reevaluated and rejustified at every meeting.

Rather than focusing on what could go wrong, the management team had to learn to focus on what could go right. Rather than viewing every decision in terms of avoiding failure, they had to plan for success. The only way to never fall off a bicycle is to never get on one in the first place. If you want to ride, though, you have to risk falling over. This company needed to stop being afraid of falling off the bike and simply start pedaling. They needed to perceive success around the corner. Once they did, their attitudes started to change and their fortunes followed.

Far too often, I am called in by businesses that don't really believe that they can do better. Some are successful, but not nearly as successful as they could be. Some are comfortable, and don't want to upset the applecart. Some are in trouble, and afraid to make things worse. Sooner or later, and it's usually sooner, doing nothing catches up to them: change nothing and nothing will change.

This book is about understanding and building the skills necessary to create a world class organization. It is about building the organizational mindset to perceive success before you reach it so that you can take the actions you need to take without constantly second-guessing yourself. And it is about not being distracted by illusions along the way.

If you have questions, feel free to visit my website, www.7stepsahead.com. I'm also always interested in hearing your stories about how the techniques and principles in this book helped you, how you applied them, and how I could have explained them better.

Stow, MA   Stephen R. Balzac

Acknowledgments

Portions of Chap. 1 appeared in slightly different form in *Corp! Magazine* under the title, "Put the Candle Back."

Portions of Chap. 2 appeared in slightly different form in *Corp! Magazine* under the title, "No Escaping That For Me."

Portions of Chap. 3 appeared in slightly different form in *Corp! Magazine* under the title, "Help Star Performers Ramp Up The Whole Team."

Portions of Chap. 6 appeared in slightly different form in the *Journal of Corporate Recruiting Leadership* under the titles, "Hire Slow and Fire... Slower?" "The Taboo of the Bananas," and "Storming the Black Gate: Recruiting With Confidence." Reprinted with permission from ERE.net.

Portions of Chap. 7 appeared in slightly different form in *Corp! Magazine* under the titles, "The Blame of Phobos Grunt," and "Why It's So Hard to Deal With Office Jerks."

Portions of Chap. 8 were published by the American Management Association under the titles, "The Blofeld School of Management," and "The CEO and the Holy Grail."

Portions of Chap. 9 were published in slightly different form in *The Imaging Executive* under the title, "The Efficient Light Bulb," and on The Business Sensei blog as, "Who Needs Strategy?"

Portions of Chap. 10 were published in slightly different form in *Corp! Magazine* under the title, "Real Science Fiction."

Portions of Chap. 11 were published in slightly different form in *Corp! Magazine* under the title, "Of Cats and Unwanted Prizes."

Endorsements

Praise for Organizational Psychology for Managers

Balzac combines stories of jujitsu, wheat, gorillas, and the Lord of the Rings with very practical advice and hands-on exercises aimed at anyone who cares about management, leadership, and culture.

> Todd Raphael
> Editor-in-Chief
> ERE Media
> http://www.ere.net

Riveting! Yes, I called a leadership book riveting. I couldn't wait to finish one chapter so I could begin reading the next. The book's combination of pop culture references, personal stories, and thought providing insights to illustrate world class leadership principles makes it a must read for business professionals at all management levels.

> Eric Bloom
> President
> Manager Mechanics, LLC
> Nationally Syndicated Columnist and Author

Organizational Psychology for Managers is an insightful book that reminds the business leader of basic principles of leading a successful organization in an engaging style. As a business owner for over 25 years, I am aware of these principles; however, I need reminding of how these principles work together and impact the energy and success of my company. Throughout the book, the author demonstrates these concepts into a clear perspective by citing examples within other companies which is always a helpful technique and is often eye opening. These are situations that I may not have thought about before. This book holds the reader's interest from start to finish. I look forward to his next book!

> Elizabeth Brown
> President
> Softeach, Inc.

"Author Stephen Balzac has written a terrific book that gets into the realpolitik of organizational psychology—the underlying patterns of behavior that create the all important company culture. He doesn't stop at the surface level, explaining things we already know like 'culture beats strategy'—he gets into the deeper drivers and ties everything back to specific, actionable stories. For example, he describes different approaches to apparent "insubordination" by a manager; rather then judging them, he shows how each management response is interpreted, and how it then drives response. Balzac preaches real engagement with one's own company and a mindful state of operation, especially by executives—who must remember that culture "just happens" unless and until they learn to recognize that their behaviors play a huge part in creating and cementing it. It covers the full spectrum of corporate life, from challenging bad decisions to hiring, training, motivating teams— and the secrets of keeping people engaged and learning—and/or avoiding actions which do the opposite. I highly recommend this book for anyone who wants to participate in creating and steering company culture."

Sid Probstein
Chief Technology Officer
Attivio—*Active Intelligence*
@sidprobstein

I had the privilege of meeting Stephen Balzac at the 2011 International Computer Measurement Group (CMG) Conference. He was one of our keynote speakers at the Conference that year. His presentation was amazing. It was the first presentation I had seen at our Conference in which the speaker not only gave a non-technical presentation that left the audience captivated and hungry for more, but he did it without using PowerPoint, or other visuals and simply with the strength of the story and his oratory skills. As Director of CMG Publications I asked him to contribute some articles for our publications. He has been doing so now for 2 years and is one of our most popular authors. I was thrilled to learn Steve was having a book, *Organizational Psychology for Managers*, published, and was honored when he asked me to read it and for my opinion.

Organizational Psychology for Managers is phenomenal. Just as his talks at conferences are captivating to his audience, Steve's book will captivate his readers. In my opinion, this book should be required reading in MBA programs, military leadership courses, and needs to be on the bookshelf of every Fortune 1000 VP of Human Resources. Steve Balzac is the twenty-first century's Tom Peters.

Stephen R. Guendert, Ph.D.
CMG Director of Publications

Contents

Chapter 1
The Vortex: Organizations as Systems

In the classic comedy, *"Young Frankenstein,"* Frederick Frankenstein and Inga, played respectively by Gene Wilder and Teri Garr, are seeking the hidden entrance to a secret passage. As Dr. Frankenstein checks out a bookcase, he asks Inga to hand him a candle. As she lifts the candle, the bookcase spins around, trapping Dr. Frankenstein behind it. Attempts to put the candle back only cause the bookcase to spin wildly, first pinning Dr. Frankenstein and eventually trapping Inga.

There is, of course, absolutely no logical reason why moving a candle should cause the bookcase to spin. There is also no apparent connection between the candle and the mysterious mechanism that moves the bookcase. There is, however, a very real connection between these events and comedy. It is the utter absurdity of the scene, to say nothing of its parodying hundreds of horror movies, that makes it so hilarious.

Unfortunately, when the same thing happens in a business, the feelings are more like the horror films rather than the parody.

Okay, there are rarely candles in an office and even more rarely does moving a candle cause a bookcase to start spinning wildly. However, the experience of changing something in one part of the business causing an apparently unpredictable reaction in another part of the business is, sadly, far too common.

At one company, the engineering department made an apparently minor change to the way they were formatting specifications for certain jobs. Suddenly, a whole raft of errors cropped up. The people following the specifications were convinced they were doing the job exactly as instructed. No one could figure out how the two things could be connected, but suddenly people were running off in the wrong direction while utterly convinced they were reading the map correctly.

At another organization, it became possible to deduce the supposedly secret positions different vice-presidents had on various issues by observing the behavior of people in offices hundreds of miles away.

In both of these examples, and others like them, the assumption is that the metaphorical candle and bookcase are not and cannot possibly be connected. However, as the results demonstrated, that was simply not correct. They were connected: because the people involved were all part of the same organization,

S. R. Balzac, *Organizational Psychology for Managers*,
Management for Professionals, DOI: 10.1007/978-1-4614-8505-6_1,
© Springer Science+Business Media New York 2014

changes in one part of the organizational system were manifesting in different parts of the organization. The system responds to information and events like any living organism or, if you prefer, like a very complex computer program. How information moves through the system varies according to the roles people play, the way communication is handled, and the unwritten, implicit assumptions that people make.

Systems, Silos, and Spaghetti

Traditional systems engineering argues that we identify the key systems and then decompose them into progressively smaller systems. Thus, a helicopter might be decomposed into a flight subsystem and ground subsystem. The fight system can be further decomposed into a drive system and navigation system, and so forth. Eventually, we get down to the smallest possible subsystems and then start building them up again. Each system communicates with other systems through a pre-defined interface. This approach is quite common in engineering disciplines, from aeronautic to software. It is also a common approach with human systems.

Unlike mechanical or electronic systems, however, human systems rarely maintain clean interfaces. Human systems are porous. In small organizations, this can work very well, but can become hopelessly chaotic when the organization grows. The lines of communication between different organizational systems start to look like a plate of spaghetti. While it's great that everyone is talking, the lack of discipline in the process leads to confusion and lost information.

On the flip side, when systems are tightly controlled, they can easily transform into silos. In this case, each group retreats behind its own metaphorical moat and interacts with other silos only through very limited channels. Organization members will typically express great frustration with the "bureaucracy." The key is to develop loosely coupled interfaces, allowing for flexibility in communications without either chaos or rigidity. Accomplishing that requires understanding a number of different organizational components.

Consider a typical business: Marketing, Sales, Engineering, Human Resources, QA, and IT. The litany of departments goes on and on. Every organization, be it a business, a non-profit, a church or synagogue, a school, a sports team, and so on is composed of a variety of moving parts, of departments and teams that themselves can be viewed as smaller organizations. The larger organization comes to life out of the interactions of the smaller organizations.

As anyone who has ever been part of a large organization, be it a corporation or a club, well knows, each subgroup in the organization is constantly struggling for resources, constantly trying to demonstrate its importance to the organization as a whole. Just as the larger organization is a complex system, each subgroup is itself a system, taking in information and resources and, we hope, putting out value to the organization as a whole. These systems all interact with one another, sometimes in very elaborate ways.

Even more important than the obvious and visible departments within the larger organization, though, are the hidden systems: how and why the organization does things, attitudes about success and failure, how the organization hires, fires, and promotes, beliefs about how mistakes should be handled, problem-solving and innovation versus blame, and so forth.

To understand the vortex of interactions between these systems, we first need to understand the organization's DNA: its culture.

Understanding Organizational Culture

J. J. Abram's 2009 *Star Trek* movie featured, as a major plot point, a good deal of back story to explain how the iconic Captain James Kirk became the person he was in the original series. What is interesting, however, is that when *Star Trek* first went on the air in 1967, the character of James Kirk was immediately recognizable to viewers: he was an exaggerated version of another famous military figure known for his heroic feats, charisma, womanizing, and connection to outer space. That famous figure was, of course, John Kennedy, and *Star Trek* was a product of the culture of the space race inextricably linked to the assassinated president.

How did James Kirk come to represent John Kennedy? What does that have to do with the vortex in your company or, indeed, organizational psychology?

Culture is an odd beast, most often described as "the way we do things around here." This description has just enough truth in it to be dangerous. There is truth in the definition since culture is, on the surface, what we do and what we see. These obvious components of culture, what MIT social psychologist and professor of business Ed Schein referred to as artifacts of the culture, are also the most trivial aspects of culture. When we focus on the artifacts, we are missing the depth of the culture's influence. Furthermore, we foster the dangerous illusion that organizational changes can be accomplished simply by making a few alterations to the way things are done.

For example, a company we'll call "Red, Inc," had a policy of rating employees each year and always firing the bottom 10 %. This policy worked for many years, and RED developed a very highly skilled, extremely competitive workforce.

Then something odd happened. Managers at RED started to notice that more and more often new employees, defined as those who had been with the company one or two years, were appearing in the bottom 10 %. RED was also gaining a reputation as a company where new people were burned out and tossed out and it became increasingly difficult to hire top people; indeed, some apparently highly qualified people were being given a thumbs-down from existing employees during interviews. Although managers made several attempts to change the interviewing process or come up with other ways to make things easier for new employees, the problems did not go away. Eventually, RED Inc started bleeding red ink.

Although RED was changing the way it did things, the underlying reasons why they were getting the results they were seeing did not change. All that changed was the superficial processes. This brings us to the deeper levels of organizational culture.

Layers of Culture

Moving beneath the layer of what we do, we have the deeper question of why we do it and what we believe about why we do it.

Understanding the Why

Culture is a very deep, very powerful force. It is *why* we do things far more than it is *what* we do. The choice of what is simply a vehicle for the purpose to manifest. You can change the *what* all you want; if the *why* doesn't change, neither will the results. This will require some explanation.

For example, there is a possibly apocryphal story about an experiment involving four gorillas. The gorillas are placed in a cage with a large ramp at the top of which is a bunch of bananas. Hidden around the cage are high pressure hoses. Whenever one of the gorillas attempts to get the bananas, the water is turned on. The gorillas are all knocked flat by the water, and left soaking wet. Eventually, the gorillas learn to not go near those bananas. At that point, one of the gorillas is removed from the cage and a new gorilla is put in. The hoses are secretly removed.

Well, what does that new gorilla do? He sees those bananas and he heads straight for them. The other gorillas promptly jump on him, drag him off the ramp, and beat him up. They know what happens if you go after those bananas!

Eventually, the new gorilla learns to not go after the bananas. At that point, another gorilla is replaced.

This continues until none of the original gorillas are left in the cage. Even though all four gorillas now in the cage have never been hosed, none of them will go after the bananas. The *why* is long forgotten; what is left is The Taboo of the Bananas, passed down from generation to generation.

Humans are no different. We learn quickly what works and what doesn't. We figure out how to avoid getting burned, and we make a point of not letting ourselves get burned. We figure out something that appears to lead to success and we engage in that behavior. So long as it is intermittently rewarded, the behavior is reinforced. We pass on the lessons we learn and we look for other people who are open to those lessons. We attribute values and beliefs to those lessons, and those values and beliefs become part of the lesson. The encapsulation of those values, beliefs, and lessons becomes the culture: not just what we do, but why we do it. Like our gorillas, though, the *why* is often forgotten or ceases to be relevant: the hoses were removed, but the gorillas never knew that. The automatic desire to avoid being soaked prevented them from finding out: actions are carried out at an almost reflexive level. In a business setting, not realizing that the *why* has changed can lead to missed opportunities or wasted time and resources.

Let's now go back to RED and understand what happened there.

RED was a competitive, high pressure company. The policy of always firing the bottom 10 % meant, in theory, that everyone would always be on their toes and pushing to constantly improve. It also led to a subtle pressure on each employee to always hire people less competent than they were. If Bob could hire someone less competent than he was, then Bob could relax: there was always someone available to take the fall. Again, this didn't work all the time. It didn't need to: whenever a newer employee on a team was the person fired, the perception that firing the newer people protected the older people was reinforced. Changing the mechanism, the recruiting process, didn't work because the underlying motivation to hire less competent people was a *why* not a *what*. Moreover, it was not something consciously planned or thought out. Rather, it was the result of behavior being shaped and subtly reinforced a series of accidental successes: in this case, the success was in people keeping their jobs. Existing employees truly believed they were hiring the best people they could! It's just that a lot of faith was put into the interviewing process, and if enough employees felt they couldn't work with a given candidate, or felt uneasy or uncomfortable with that candidate, then the candidate wasn't hired.

Understanding Purpose

There are times when someone's actions might appear to us to be senseless. In fact, it is rarely, if ever, the case that actions are truly senseless. Actions, as psychologist Peter Ossorio, observed, are always purposeful. They may be incorrect or confused, but they have a purpose.

In cultural terms, we are looking at not what is being done or even why, but rather the beliefs about why it is being done. In other words, what is the purpose behind the actions?

Understanding the ostensible purpose behind the actions helps make sense of behavior that otherwise might seem irrational or incomprehensible.

For example, at Digital Equipment Corporation, meetings were best described as intense. There was a great deal of argument back and forth with little sense of formality. Who was right was determined by who could make the best case for their position based on the available data. If agreement could not be reached, the company was comfortable with the idea of putting out different versions of a product and letting the marketplace decide.

Conversely, as Schein observes, at Ciba-Geigy, meetings were much more formal affairs. People waited their turns to speak. Who was right was determined by titles and degrees held.

In both cases, management professed the belief that holding meetings in this way was the best way to make sure that every voice was heard and that all employees contributed to the product development process.

Sometimes, however, purpose is assigned or assumed after the fact. In other words, observers will assume a reason when one does not exist.

For example, in one large martial arts organization, the requirements for black belt were set to include a subset of a specific list of techniques. Why those particular techniques? When asked, people provided a variety of explanations, all of which boiled down to a belief that the particular techniques chosen embodied certain key concepts. Students needed to master those key concepts in order to progress further. When I subsequently spoke to the man who had made the decision, his response was, "I needed to break the list somewhere and that seemed as good as any."

In other words, it was an arbitrary decision, made as much to get things done and move on as for any other reason. The assignment of purpose and the beliefs around it came later.

Over time, each department in a business will develop their own reasons for doing things and build up their own set of beliefs around those reasons. Their actions will reflect those beliefs. If different departments develop beliefs that are at cross-purposes, friction will develop and the system will become less able to respond to competitive challenges. In Chap. 2, we'll look at how to build the framework that enables the company to maintain a consistent belief structure.

What is Culture?

At this point, we can now answer the question, "what is culture?"

Perhaps the best definition is that provided by Schein, who argues that organizational culture is, at root, the residue of perceived success. In other words, it is the accumulated lessons that members of the culture have learned about how to do business, how to build products, how to treat clients, how to treat one another, and so forth. If something appears to work often enough, even if working means avoiding a problem, then that action, behavior, or belief becomes a part of the culture. Eventually, the reason is forgotten, only the behavior remains and the beliefs that are built around that behavior.

Culture, in other words, is an accumulation of purposeful behaviors: behaviors that are intended to produce certain results in the environment. These results might be personal, such as more interesting projects or increased status, or they might be corporate, such as successful products or enhanced reputation.

Every one of these behaviors was, at least at one time, correct in its purpose, or at least it seemed that way at the time. This is an important part of understanding culture: what matters most is that the behavior seems to work at the time. In other words, a rain dance, done long enough, "produces" rain. It worked!

To understand how this plays out in a business setting, consider the following case study:

Once upon a time there was a company known as Robotic Chromosomes. Don't bother Googling it; it's no longer in business and besides, that's not the real name.

Robotic Chromosomes had a way of hiring programmers that isn't all that unfamiliar to folks in the software industry: logic puzzles. Like Microsoft, and various other companies, Robotic Chromosomes put every potential engineer through a series of logic puzzles in order to determine if those engineers were qualified.

There is, in fact, no actual correlation between programming ability and the ability to solve logic puzzles. This did not stop the folks at Robotic Chromosomes, who were convinced of the validity of their methods and were not interested in allowing facts to get in the way.

Even within the logic puzzle method, though, there were some definite oddities and idiosyncrasies that distinguished Robotic Chromosomes from other companies.

For several years, no one skilled in visual presentation or user interface development was ever good enough to solve the logic puzzles, or at least they could never satisfy the solutions that the existing engineers believed were correct.

Also for a number of years no one with an actual computer science background was hired into the engineering team. There was always something wrong with their solutions: some were not elegant enough, others were too elegant.

Over time, the engineering department at Robotic Chromosomes developed a certain homogeneity of thought and approach to problem solving and presentation of information.

Also over time, Robotic Chromosomes' flagship product developed a rather intricate codebase and a user interface that felt like a very complex logic puzzle. Members of the QA department, and the customers, frequently found the interface to be more than a little opaque. Customer feedback, though, never quite seemed to penetrate.

When, after much arm-twisting, the company eventually hired a graphic designer to redo the interface on one of their products, the senior engineer on the team claimed that he couldn't see the difference, even though that difference was strikingly obvious to many other employees and to the customers. It was, unfortunately, a little too late. Not long after they finally began to improve their products, they started seriously losing market share to competitors with cleaner interfaces and easier to use software. Robotic Chromosomes was suddenly playing catch up in the market it had created!

How did they get to this point? They were guided by success.

The founder of Robotic Chromosomes was an extremely smart, very technical guy who loved logic puzzles. Although he had a string of degrees, none of them were in computer science. His visual aesthetic sense was mediocre at best, to the point where he could not see the point of many of the visual interface issues that users care about. When he recruited his first engineers, he hired people with a similar skill profile. He did that because his example of a successful programmer of the type of software he wanted to write was him. The people he hired were smart, knowledgeable guys who agreed with his approach to graphical user interfaces and to programming in general. None of them had computer science degrees but they all loved logic puzzles. They quickly produced a saleable product: in other words, success!

This, then, became the model of the ideal employee: smart, technical, loves logic puzzles, and no computer science degree. Indeed, this model of the successful engineer was so strong that someone who did not fit the model in any way would not be hired. Thus, computer scientists who solved the logic puzzles were routinely not hired.

The recruiting process was shaped by the model of the early employees, and then that process tended to pass only those people who supported that model. Each time that happened, the belief was reinforced. Since most of the failures were in not hiring qualified people, disconfirming evidence was minimal. Remember that since we're talking about intermittent reinforcement, the occasional bad hire would not be sufficient to force a reevaluation of the hiring metrics. Even when changes were made to the recruiting process, the profile of people being hired did not change: the way recruiting was being handled was merely a vehicle for finding people who fit a certain profile. Changing the mechanism did not change the beliefs of the people already there about what sorts of people would make good engineers.

Robotic Chromosomes is no long around. Their early successes helped shape a culture that was not able to respond effectively to changes in their market. One of the dangers of short-term successes is that, when not guided by good long-term strategy, they can lead you over a cliff.

Where is Culture?

It's easy to talk about culture as if it were some sort of physical entity. While we can see the manifestations of culture, its artifacts, all around us, those elements are not culture. They are simply the ways we do things, the why we do them, and our beliefs about why we do them.

Culture itself exists in the minds of the people who make up the organization. Indeed, if you put any group of people together, culture will develop provided the group can stay together long enough. We'll look at the lifecycle of a group in more depth in Chap. 3. In brief, though, the process of perceived successes is key: exploration of the environment, experimentation, efforts that either succeed or fail, give people information about what is and is not working. We naturally repeat what worked and, over time, discard things that don't work. Behaviors, and thought patterns, are thus shaped over time.

This process helps explain why culture is so hard to change: once we have something that works, we don't like to change the formula for success. Indeed, attempts to do so typically generate immense amounts of pushback and frequently end in failure. Culture is a habit and habits are very hard to break. Effective organizational change is a process of teaching people a new map for success and then helping them develop the new habits necessary to be able to read that map.

What are the Benefits of Culture?

From the examples and case studies presented thus far, it may seem that culture causes problems. Culture is a powerful tool, and like all power tools, if you don't use it carefully you may find yourself cut off at the knees. Although culture can, and does, lead organizations into trouble, it is also the glue that holds your organization together. Quite simply, when you put people together and ask them to work together, they look for common ground: how are we similar to one another? A shared organizational culture helps build that sense of similarity and community, accelerating the process of enabling people to build effective teams.

Culture also helps focus and direct resources. If we go back to our gorillas, we can see that, at least in the short-term, they have learned that pursuing those bananas costs far more in time and caloric resources than they are getting. Thus, they learn to not expend resources where there is no return. By learning what works and what doesn't, we start to reflexively ignore what doesn't work and spend our time and energy on what does.

To draw an analogy to sports, athletes develop skills to make it easier for them to train and focus their minds in competition. Those skills are practiced until they become reflexive: the athlete carries them out automatically, still keeping the majority of her focus on the other team. Similarly, cultural behaviors are like habits: reflexive behaviors carried out across the organization.

IBM's culture was one that fostered the belief that problems could be and should be fixed. When something didn't work, the response was to figure out why, determine the solution, and then implement that solution even if the medicine did not taste good. Thus, in 1992, after losing money for the first time in its corporate history, Big Blue's culturally reflexive behaviors enabled them to recognize and accept the idea that the solution was to bring in an outsider to run the company. That marked a major change to what they'd done before, and it wasn't easy; the strength of the problem solving elements of their culture meant that IBM could identify and implement that solution.

Each unit of an organization will develop its own cultural habits. The key thing is to guide that development so that you create the culture you want.

Good Culture, Bad Culture

Cultures are neither good nor bad. They are, however, functional or dysfunctional.

A functional culture is one that can obtain resources from its environment. A dysfunctional one cannot. Dysfunctional cultures either change or die. Functional cultures may become dysfunctional if the environment changes out from under them.

Cultures can also be symbiotic or parasitic with their members. A symbiotic culture provides members with benefits that go beyond just working for an organization that provides a salary. Parasitic cultures burn out members or otherwise use them up. Symbiotic cultures are harder to create but are more successful.

Transmitting Culture

"You have to haggle!"

Fans of Monty Python's *Life of Brian* might recall the haggling scene: desperate to escape from pursuing Roman soldiers, Brian attempts to buy something to use as a disguise. The merchant, however, won't simply sell it to him; instead the man insists that Brian haggle, forcing Brian to bargain loudly as the Romans close in.

Walking through the bazaar that is the Old City of Jerusalem, I found that Monty Python had, if anything, understated the aggressiveness of the merchants. At one point, my wife glanced at a camel leather bag. Immediately, the merchant opened with, "This bag is wonderful. Only 600 shekels."

For reference, that's about $150.

My wife wasn't particularly interested, and the merchant kept insisting on haggling, much like the scene in *Life of Brian*. In this case, though, there were no Romans, and before long the merchant had bargained himself down to 90 shekels, or about $22. Even at that price, though, the bag wasn't worth buying.

No matter which part of the city you might be in, Jewish Quarter, Muslim Quarter, Armenian Quarter, or Christian Quarter, merchants were loud, aggressive, and quick to haggle. You might find it frustrating, or you might view it as part of the entertainment. Either way, though, the behavior never ends. Indeed, anyone who opens a shop soon falls into the standard pattern of behavior.

This is culture in action: although the bazaar may not have an obvious corporate structure, it is still an organization. When you put people together for long enough, culture forms and is passed on to the new people who enter the organization. It doesn't much matter whether the organization in question is a corporation or a bazaar.

Changing the behavior of a merchant in the bazaar is almost impossible, if for no other reason than each merchant sees what the others are doing and imitates them. In a business, new employees see what the existing employees are doing and imitate them. New employees also hear the history and stories about the company. In young companies, employees might hear directly from the founder what the founder believes to be the best way to get work done. Finally, employees and managers act according to the way other companies in the area act: at one Silicon Valley technology startup, the expressed mindset was, "We're a Silicon Valley company, therefore we work long hours." Performance was measured almost entirely by how many hours someone was in the office, not by how productive they were, how rapidly they met their milestones, or even whether their software worked!

The great strength of culture stories is that they reflect an exaggerated view of the cultural values and images. Their great curse is that they reflect an exaggerated view of the cultural values and images. This is why John Kennedy became James Kirk, and why many other 1960s fictional heroes fit the Kennedy mold. Stories exemplify the values of the culture, but they also tend to accentuate the positive elements and gloss over the defects. Kirk thus is portrayed as an idealized version of a fictional John Kennedy, all the warts airbrushed away. New employees hear the stories of the company's past, and learn from those stories how they are supposed to act today.

Over time, those stories will become more and more idealized, eventually creating role models that are simply too perfect for effective imitation. It is human nature to embellish stories, to add little extra details: the minnow that got away eventually turns into a whale.

Essentially, what you have is a feedback loop that keeps accentuating certain elements and minimizing others. This will eventually lead the company into a state where it's no longer responding appropriately to its environment, even if the environment were standing still (which it never does!). As Schein observes, a big part of why IBM got into trouble in 1992 was that over the years the engineering elements of the culture were being exaggerated while the marketing elements atrophied. In a very real sense, Lou Gerstner's biggest contribution was to bring them back into balance. It's important to keep creating the new stories about the company in order to maintain a grounding in reality.

Culture is also transmitted through imitation of those higher up the organizational hierarchy. The more senior the employee, the more likely he is to be a role model to others. "She's worked here for years, she must know what is going on!" is the mantra.

One Boston technology firm had serious problems with decision making. Teams would debate things incessantly yet never actually come to a decision and choose a course of action. Naturally, managers argued that this problem was purely at the lower levels and that's where it needed to be fixed. However, when it came time to move forward on a plan to resolve the situation, the people in charge kept putting things off. In the end, no one could make the decision to move forward. Cultural transmission was alive and well.

Leaders, Villains, and Opportunities

It's not enough to just think about how culture is transmitted. We also need to consider what is being transmitted. Because cultures are the encapsulated guide to the world, what is being taught is the guide to how that organization works. The information is often accepted uncritically, particularly by newer members of the organization who are eager to fit in. That uncritical acceptance actually contributes to the reflexive nature of cultural behavior. This is fine to some degree, but too much uncritical acceptance can blind people to opportunities later on.

Some of the key elements taught by cultures are what leaders and villains look like. The memory of a charismatic leader or company founder can shape the expectation for what future leaders look like. When I worked for IBM right after college, one of the executive assistants took me to one side and advised me to never grow facial hair if I wanted to move into management. Why not? She didn't really have a good explanation, it was just that managers were usually clean-shaven. It turns out that so was IBM's founder, Tom Watson. He and his son shaped the image of IBM's managers for years after they were gone.

These cultural images of what a leader looks like can propel unqualified people into the job or prevent qualified people from being recognized as leaders. If people just don't think you can lead, you won't be given the chance. We'll look at ways of dealing with this in later chapters. The key point here is to recognize that part of being seen as a leader in a culture is espousing the values of the culture; indeed, sometimes being the anointed standard bearer for a particular ideology or culture is enough to cause someone to be viewed as a leader independent of all other qualifications.

Conversely, cultures also teach us what villains look like. In the 1960s, for example, this was the Soviets and the Chinese, who became, respectively, the Klingons and the Romulans in the original *Star Trek*. In many high tech startups, the engineer who spends long hours working is highly regarded while the person who leaves at 6 pm is seen as not being serious. This happens despite the ironic truth that the person spending all night working is often putting out the fires they caused, while the person leaving at 6 pm is doing much more solid, careful work and not causing fires in the first place. In this case, the culture was valuing the easily observed and easily measured aspects of hard work, not the actual results. The view that long hours and working weekends shows dedication is, itself, a holdover from the industrial age when simply putting in more hours meant turning more bolts or tightening more screws. In modern businesses, where the emphasis is on highly skilled work, those long hours actually reduce productivity, motivation, and innovation while increasing errors. We will return to this in Chaps. 7 and 9.

Cultures also teach us how to make decisions, whether formal or informal interaction with the boss is appropriate, what constitutes expertise, what is a reward and what is a punishment, and so on. Thus, some companies, such as DEC, determined expertise and who is right based on argument and debate. Ciba-Geigy, on the other hand, made the determination based on degrees and titles. Some organizations insist on the use of titles such as "Doctor," while others are determinedly informal. In one culture being assigned a windowless office is considered low status, while in another it's something actively sought after.

In the next chapter, we'll look at ways in which cultural beliefs shape organizational stories, and how to rewrite those stories to better serve the organization.

How Cultures Form

No organization, no group of people starts out as a complete cultural blank slate. Everyone in the group is bringing themselves to the table: in other words, their own values, beliefs, assumptions about how the world works, lessons they've learned over time, and the cultures they belong to. Each person is bringing, in short, their cultural heritage.

In thinking about cultural heritage in this context, we're not just talking about religious beliefs, nationality, or ethnic background. While these are certainly factors, people today are part of a great many cultures: a student with an engineering degree has undoubtedly internalized elements of the engineering culture, a physicist is likely to be part of a larger scientific culture, and so forth. These cultural values can transcend ethnic and national boundaries: consider that during the Cold War, scientists on either side of the Iron Curtain often felt more in common with one another than with their political leaders.

Part of the development of an organization's culture is the interaction between these many different value sets and beliefs as the group seeks to come to common ground. This can be frustrating. As one senior manager at a Boston area high tech company once complained to me, "I'm from India. I've hired a lot of Indian engineers. They're great, but they won't argue. They won't push back. If I screw up, they're too polite to bring it to my attention. I was brought up the same way, but this is America! We argue here."

Please recognize that this is not a question of who is right and who is wrong; rather, it is a question of developing the appropriate behaviors to enable the system to function. Behaviors depend on values, or the why, and values are driven by beliefs.

Over time, assuming the organization stays intact, people gradually reach agreement over values, or at least they manage a truce. In the former case, the agreed upon values start to be taken as given, and new members of the organization are taught those values. Eventually, the agreed upon values become organizational norms. Norms, in turn, are packaged into ideologies, or collections of belief structures and values. The values, norms, and ideologies are subsumed into the culture. The danger here is that ideologies can be very powerful: as the old saying goes, "Reality recedes as ideology emerges." General Motors in the 1990s reacted to competition from Japanese imports by retreating behind an ideological belief in the superiority of their cars and ended up withdrawing from markets along the coasts were they couldn't compete effectively. It took the economic collapse of 2008 bringing GM to the edge of destruction to penetrate the ideological bubble the company had entered.

Sometimes, however, we have the second case: rather than one value or set of values predominating, both are accepted into the culture. In this situation, different behaviors can result depending on the context of a question or a given behavior. The culture has effectively developed multiple habits or procedures for certain situations and figuring out which ones are going to be activated when can be extremely difficult.

Subcultures

As anyone who has travelled around the United States has noticed, there are a great many regional cultures. Organizations are just the same. Each organizational unit forms its own subculture in response to its specific needs, geographical local, customers, and circumstances. In addition, subcultures will also form across units: thus there is an engineering subculture, a management subculture, a sales subculture, and so on. Engineers separated by thousands of miles will still view themselves as engineers, and still act according to the dictates of the engineering culture. Many of the difficulties that arise between different departments in a company stem from their different cultural assumptions and narratives.

Counter-Culture

"Take off that tie!"

Many years ago, while attending MIT, I interned for several summers at various IBM locations. This was very much in the heyday of IBM's blue suit and tie image. In those days, everyone wore a tie, even the interns. It didn't matter that we never saw a customer or were even allowed near them. Computers were very sensitive in those days, and would be offended if the programmer wasn't well-dressed.

Then I landed at IBM's Watson Research Center in Yorktown Heights. I walked into my manager's office. He took one look at me and told me to take off my tie. He also suggested that I'd be much more comfortable during the hot summer days in a pair of shorts rather than slacks. He was wearing a t-shirt, shorts, and flip-flops.

At a typical IBM location, if you tried to follow someone in when they opened the door with their ID badge, you'd be asked to show your badge. At Research, this only happened if you were wearing a suit: that was the signal that you didn't belong.

Many organizations form subcultures that ostensibly reject some aspect of the main organizational culture. These counter-cultures take great pride in so demonstrating their uniqueness, even while being loyal to the main culture. The way in which the counter-culture chooses to rebel is often critically tied to their function in the company.

One of the great organizational sagas in IBM is the story about the source of the blue suit and tie dress code: one day, Tom Watson, Sr., was visiting a customer, the president of a large bank. As they rode up the elevator, a man in a garish lime-green suit jacket got on, rode up a few floors, and got off. Watson made a joke about it to the bank president, who replied, "Didn't you recognize him? He's one of your salespeople." The story is that as soon as Watson got back to the office, he announced the new dress code. Research division has a counter-myth: one day Tom Watson, Jr., was taking a senator on a tour of IBM's main research lab. As they stood in the computer room, an unshaven man with wild hair, wearing a t-shirt, shorts, and flapping sandals, pushed past them and went into the depths of the room. A few minutes later, he came back carrying a large printout, shoved past them again, and flapped off down the corridor. Watson turned to the senator and said, "That's one of our top scientists." Where most of IBM was hierarchical, organized, and conformist, research division created its own counter-culture which de-emphasized hierarchy, promoted difference, and more to the point, promoted the idea that "we break the rules." That has a subtle effect on a cutting edge research facility: it says that we don't let problems or the belief that it can't be done stop us. Although this appears to be a rebellious subculture, in fact, it is much more an example of one in which people accepted core aspects of IBM's culture, but rejected those aspects perceived as unimportant or silly in order to create an environment where they could perform their jobs effectively.

The Roles We Play

We've already seen how culture shapes our perception of heroes and villains. More broadly, it shapes our images of other roles as well. We see this in our larger, national culture in arguments over gender roles and the like. Organizationally, culture shapes what it means to be a leader, to be a follower, to be an expert; it shapes how we behave when we are granted a certain title as part of a role. Thus, in one technology company, engineers generally dressed in t-shirts and jeans, but managers did not wear t-shirts. If you were an engineer given a management title, you were expected to stop wearing t-shirts the next day.

How we approach roles we are given is then a part of the culture. The lessons of the culture tell us what to do and how to do it. A black belt in a martial arts organization behaves differently from a brown belt, a post-doc is different from the doctoral student, and a professor is different from the post-doc. Along with the changes in behavior come changes in our perceptions of the person: as someone increases in status, other attributes of the person are accentuated or minimized according to the culture's rules about what is valued. Thus, we find that a person's height is estimated ever higher based on the title observers were told that person possessed.

Conversely, the roles that exist within an organization are also drawn from the culture. It is quite common for large companies like IBM or Raytheon to have multiple levels of a job: junior engineer, engineer, senior engineer or maybe Engineer I, II, III, etc. Other companies will follow this model because "it's how things are done," even when it doesn't make sense. In one case, a five person company attempted to impose levels such as junior and senior on its staff, despite the fact that there was minimal difference between the people. It was simply how things were supposed to be done, and that came about because the early engineers came from giant companies.

Because none of us are blank slates, we come in with certain assumptions and beliefs about how different roles should be played. In the absence of other information, we will tend to fall back on our pre-existing role expectations based on the cultural values we have most deeply internalized. Someone who frequently acts as a leader might therefore attempt to take charge of a group in a new organization, much to the annoyance of the designated leader. In one rather dramatic situation, an MIT trained scientist who entered a psychology program approached the new academic environment with the same level of ruthless inquiry that MIT demands of its students. In the psychology program, however, this was not seen as positive behavior! Part of how we judge the authenticity and accuracy of someone's performance of a role is how closely their behavior matches our cultural beliefs about what that behavior should be.

One of the most common behaviors that suffers from this sort of role definition confusion is that of the leader: images of leadership abound in our culture, in books, movies, TV, etc. As we've already discussed, these images are often distorted in some way, emphasizing some traits and minimizing others. As a result, people often attempt to act like a fictional leader instead of a real one. Fictional leaders can get away with this because they have a script. Real leaders, on the other hand, do not.

As we can see, entering an organization and attempting to bring in our outside role assumptions can be problematic. This is one of the reasons why organizations often prefer to promote from within and often find it difficult to bring in outsiders into leadership roles. Because of this, organizations seeking fresh blood will often look to hybrids.

Hybrids

Subcultures provide a valuable training ground for future generations of managers. Because subcultures partake of the main culture and also add their own twists, managers who come up through the ranks in a subculture tend to have a wider perspective while still being sufficiently part of the culture to be recognized throughout the organization.

Similarly, a manager who leaves the company to work elsewhere and then returns may also have gained a wider perspective while still being recognizable as a part of the culture. Steve Jobs, for example, was thrown out of Apple in the early 1990s. His experiences helped him mature as a leader and gave him a wider perspective. At the same time, having founded the company years before and being part of its culture made him credible when he returned as CEO in the late 1990s.

Schein refers to these people as hybrids.

The Cultural Immune Response

"That person might destroy our culture."

I hear that line often in organizations, usually to explain why a potential new hire was rejected. The logic of it is somewhat dubious since cultures are extremely robust and do not accept change easily. Indeed, far from being damaged by a new person joining, the culture is more likely to change that person or drive them out.

When someone joins an organization, they need to come up to speed on appropriate behavior fairly quickly. A good orientation program can help with this, as we'll discuss in Chap. 8. The good news is that people tend to be tolerant of newcomers, provided they respond to feedback. In fact, what typically happens is that other employees will informally inform newcomers when their behavior is inappropriate. Provided the person appears to be attempting to respond to the feedback, their occasional lapses will be tolerated. However, should someone not respond to feedback, the intensity of the feedback escalates into a more formal process which may involve disciplinary action. If all that fails, ostracism often results. At that point, the person may then be fired or may quit because they feel they "just don't fit in." The culture has rejected them.

When a senior person doesn't fit, however, the consequences can be more severe. Recall that leaders are viewed as exemplars of the culture; thus, when a leader fails to embody the values of the organization, this creates a great deal of confusion and cognitive dissonance. Cognitive dissonance is the unpleasant feeling we get when our actions and values do not match: for example, when the person who does not believe in violence loses his temper and punches someone, he may then feel a great deal of confusion and guilt along the lines of, "How could I have done that?" This will often happen even if the violence was objectively justified, for instance out of self-defense. Similarly, when employees are asked to follow a manager who violates cultural norms, they will often feel guilty or uncomfortable.

They might seek to avoid that manager, passively resist instructions, perceive their job as inherently less interesting, and hence less attractive, become less loyal to the company, or even become depressed.

If the person who doesn't fit the culture is the CEO, the problems are considerably worse. In this case, the reaction will spread throughout the company. Mistakes increase, motivation and loyalty decreases, and many top employees may leave. It also becomes harder to attract new people who quickly find the atmosphere oppressive: an organization filled with unhappy people is painfully obvious and not a fun place to be. Apple under John Scully and Digital Equipment Corporation under Robert Palmer are classic examples of this immune response in action. Apple, of course, eventually rejected Scully and brought Steve Jobs back in. DEC went out of business and was eventually bought by Compaq as employees rebelled against Palmer's efforts to dramatically change the culture.

Combining Cultures

In 1998, the world was treated to the merger of two giant auto companies: Daimler Benz and Chrysler. The combined firm, DaimlerChrysler, was predicted to become the world's largest auto behemoth. It was going to revolutionize the auto industry. It was going to be unstoppable. In fact, it was going to become a joke.

A few years later, DaimlerChrysler became Daimler and Chrysler. In the end, their organizational cultures went together about as well as oil and water.

As is hopefully clear by this point, combining two cultures is not just a simple matter of taking what each of them do, choosing the best, and implementing the results. It's not enough to agree on what you do. You also have to reach agreement on why it's done that way and the underlying beliefs about why it's being done that way. Without that agreement, what you have is a train wreck waiting to happen.

How an agreement might be reached boils down to three fundamental cases.

The Fiefdom

This method works best and is fairly common when one member of a merger is much larger than the other. In the fiefdom approach, the smaller company exists within the larger organization as a self-contained fiefdom. The senior management team now reports to people higher up in the acquiring organization and paychecks get a new logo. Beyond that, the acquired company is allowed to operate pretty much the way it always has. Over time, some of the borders may eventually become more porous, until the smaller company is absorbed or the fiefdom may endure for many years if economic conditions are favorable.

When the fiefdom adopts elements of the larger organizational culture, it can become a powerful launching point for the next generation of hybrid managers.

The Borg

In this case, one culture simply dominates and absorbs the others, much like *Star Trek's* Borg. The culture of the acquired organization fades away over time, leaving possibly a few small artifacts behind. Although the process may not be obvious at first, after a relatively short period the combined company culture is effectively indistinguishable from that of the original parent company. Many of the car brands associated with General Motors, such as Oldsmobile, Pontiac, Chevrolet, and Cadillac, were once separate companies acquired by GM early in its history. Rational Software's acquisition of SQA Software in the late 1990s started out as an apparent fiefdom arrangement, but morphed over time into absorption. Rational was subsequently acquired by IBM and appears to have been absorbed in its turn.

The Blend

Almost, but not completely, totally unlike blending paint. The theory is that the cultures integrate, taking the best from each one. The reality is that this almost never works: one culture ends up "winning" over the other. That victory can destroy the very thing the acquisition was intended to create: incompatible beliefs result in one culture destroying the other and the proponents of the losing culture leave.

Daimler and Chrysler were attempting to create a blended culture. Due to their incompatible beliefs, they were unable to successfully blend. Because the two cultures were both large and well-entrenched, neither one was able to dominate the other. The net result was that the two organizations split apart again.

Organizational Change

At this point, it should be clear that culture is an extremely powerful force. Human belief about what we do and why we do it is enough to make or break corporations. Thus, it is hardly surprising that making lasting changes to an organization can be extremely difficult: unless the change is just addressing what we do, it's going to run up against why we do it and our beliefs about why we do it. If we don't address those underlying issues, the change will fail. People simply do not like to change something that they believe is working and they particularly do not like to make a change that goes against their underlying beliefs.

To make matters worse, organizations frequently approach change much like a season of *The Amazing Race*.

The Amazing Race is a popular reality show in which contestants have to race around the world accomplishing various tasks along the way. The trick is that they never know where they are going or how they are supposed to get there until they open the right envelope. Contestants lug around large backpacks containing everything they think they might need. On the principle that adventure is something dangerous and unpleasant happening to someone else, *The Amazing Race* is a fun adventure show. As a way of accomplishing organizational change, however, it leaves something to be desired: remember that most teams never make it to the end.

When organizations approach change by treating it as a race to unknown destinations with hidden obstacles along the way, people respond with a certain degree of reluctance. Not only are you trying to alter deeply held cultural beliefs about the organization, you're also triggering their concerns about their job and the future of the company. Move too fast and you trigger the cultural immune response. In the end, change is not about how fast you start; it's about how smoothly you accelerate.

The key to making change work is to show people from the beginning how they will benefit from the change, address their specific concerns, and build their enthusiasm and involvement. You'll need to develop a clear narrative or cultural story about the change and how people will benefit; we'll look at that process in the next chapter. You also need to allow people to convince themselves that change is needed, change is good, they are capable of change, and they know how to make change happen.

Start by asking people questions that will let them see the problems with the status quo. What's wrong with our current situation? What would happen if we did nothing? What barriers are preventing you from getting your work done? Don't rush through this process. Until people feel unhappy with the way things are, they won't be interested in or eager to change.

Once you've made people unhappy with the current situation, then you can start asking people questions designed to get them thinking along the lines of how they'll benefit from change: How will you benefit from change? How will the team benefit from change? What new opportunities will change bring for you? For your group?

Next, you need to let people convince themselves that they can change. You do this by letting them remind themselves of other successful changes they've made. This may be in their professional life, it may be in their personal life. The key thing is to get them talking about how they've successfully handled difficult changes in the past.

After you've gone through the process of making them unhappy with the current situation, gotten them thinking about change as a good thing, helped them develop the confidence that they can change, only then you can start brainstorming with them on how to best make the changes work.

Since cultural routines are effectively powerful habits, once you've built the motivation to change, you need to harness that motivation to create new habits. This is an important distinction: never try to break habits; rather, create new ones. It's hard to break out of a rut, but easy to slip into a new one. We'll look at how to do this when we discuss training in Chap. 8.

At this point in the process, the more senior you are, the more you are on display. If senior management doesn't, as the saying goes, walk the walk, neither will anyone else. Leading means just that: being out in front showing the way. We'll discuss this in more depth when we get to leadership.

As your change goals are realized, you need to be telling the stories about the successful change and how the new world is a better place. You want the cultural values you've changed to be constantly reinforced. If you go back to the old stories, the old ways will also come back. If you don't replace the old stories with new stories, then, by default, the old stories are what people will repeat.

Finally, remember that you are dealing with a system. The bigger the change, the more systems will be affected. If you don't address the change with each system involved, then those systems will act as anchors, pulling back against the change you are trying to make.

We will look further at change when we discuss organizational learning in Chap. 8.

The Vortex

Cultural forces and the interactions between systems can seem overwhelming at first. It's easy to simply decide to ignore all this stuff and charge forward. This can be a great solution if you have unlimited time and resources at your disposal. For those in the real world, however, if you take the time to look at your organization and observe people's behaviors, you'll start to see the different forces being played out in front of you. With sufficient practice, the vortex becomes obvious.

Questions to Consider

1. What are some of the taken for granted behaviors in your organization? Ask others in your organization why things are done that way. What sorts of responses do you get?
2. What are the systems in your organization? How to they interact with one another?
3. What are the artifacts of your organizational culture? Compare them to the artifacts in other organizations you belong to (e.g. Church, Synagogue, clubs, etc.). What similarities and differences do you observe?
4. What do your organization's stories tell you about the organization? What stories are typically told to new hires?
5. What forces might cause an organization to change?

Chapter 2
Telling Your Story: Organizational Vision as a Driver of Success

Returning for a moment to *Young Frankenstein*, we learn that Gene Wilder's destiny as Dr. Frederick Frankenstein is to follow in his grandfather's footsteps and create the monster. Of course, this being a comedy, things do work out somewhat better than they did in the original story. Destiny, it turns out, can be changed with sufficient effort. Indeed, it is exactly because Frederick Frankenstein realizes that he's following in Victor Frankenstein's footsteps that he is able to turn things around and bring about a happy ending.

In my consulting projects and in conducting leadership training with various groups, from college students through executives, I've frequently observed that perceived destiny plays a significant part. People play out the roles that they believe they are supposed to play out. It's rather like the fact that if I say I'm going to tell a funny story, then at the end of the story most people will dutifully laugh, only on a much larger scale. Organizationally, we act as our organizational culture teaches us to act in our various roles: CEOs are expected to behave in one way, managers another, engineers yet another. As we mentioned in Chap. 1, in some companies it's perfectly normal for engineers to show up to work in jeans and t-shirts, but totally inappropriate for a manager to do the same.

At a much broader level, as we've already discussed, organizations learn lessons about how to deal with a variety of issues, including conflict, negotiation, challenges from subordinates and peers, threats from other organizations, and so forth. Those lessons are incorporated into the organization's culture and become the stories that are passed down over time. IBM founder Tom Watson driving to a train wreck in the middle of the night to organize and supervise the emergency crews is one such story. At another company, how the board dealt with a challenge from an employee who eventually left to find a competing company became the stuff of organizational legend. Decades later, the then president is remembered by different groups within the organization as both the hero who stood up for the company's values even at the cost of creating a competitor and as a tin-pot dictator whose egotism cost the company many of its most creative people.

S. R. Balzac, *Organizational Psychology for Managers*,
Management for Professionals, DOI: 10.1007/978-1-4614-8505-6_2,
© Springer Science+Business Media New York 2014

What makes these stories particularly interesting is that they become the model for how future situations are handled: this is culture in action. In one organization, the developing conflict between two senior managers is becoming increasingly intense as each one takes on the roles of the people in their departments who fought similar battles a generation ago. Each one is making assumptions about the motives and goals of the other and simultaneously doing their best to avoid any face-to-face conversation: that might just interfere with the narrative they are telling themselves. They are each creating their own monster and the final resolution is not yet clear. Fortunately, organizational stories can also be powerful tools to focus the organization and propel it toward success. It all depends on what stories are told.

What is Organizational Narrative?

Humans are pattern-matching creatures. We are built to try to make sense of our environment. Indeed, as more than one psychologist has observed, we see patterns even when they aren't there! This tendency toward pattern-matching is a very powerful tool, though, because it enables us to impose structure on our environment. If we've done a good job of imposing structure, we can not only make sense of what is happening now, we can make reasonably accurate guesses about what will happen in the future. In fact, our ability to impose order and identify patterns is a big part of what enables us to think and plan strategically.

Culture, you will recall, is a device for making the world predictable. It tells us what to do when. Structurally, what we have is a narrative: in a certain situation these actions led to these results or these actions expressed these values, and that's why we do things that way today. Quite simply, we impose a narrative structure on our own experiences and those of the organization. Consider how many of our metaphors reflect this view: "turning over a new page," "starting a new chapter in our lives," "taking a page from his book," and so forth.

This narrative structure is so powerful that many people will ignore information that doesn't fit the narrative: for example, there are still many people who believe that Humphrey Bogart said, "Play it again, Sam," in the movie *Casablanca*. He didn't, but he should have. It's a much better line than the one he actually says.

This narrative structure helps us understand, or at least explain, our own lives: Elizabeth Loftus, a psychologist and Harvard professor, is also the world's expert on memory. She believed that this stemmed from her experience of repressing her memories of discovering her mother's drowned body in the family swimming pool. She later recovered her memory of the event and, over the course of a few years, the rest of the details came back to her. It made sense; it explained her fascination with memory. Then one of her relatives told her that she hadn't discovered the body, her aunt had. Other relatives confirmed this. The memory expert had, herself, created a false memory and believed it because it made sense.

Organizational stories are most obvious in older organizations, be they corporations, religious institutions, professional groups, and the like. However, even small organizations, including start up companies, quickly develop their own organizational narratives. Indeed, the question is not whether you will develop a narrative, but who will do it. Will you define your narrative or will others define it for you? If you don't define your own story, you can be certain that your competitors will be only too happy to do it for you. All too often, companies allow themselves to accept default stories about their business and then wonder why they are seen as "just like everyone else."

Think about how often you've heard someone talk about your company's "story." We assemble incidents into chronological events and draw lessons from those events. The following three snippets play out in organizations all the time:

> Bob ignored his assignment to deal with what he felt was a serious problem and the boss fired him even though Bob was right.

> Bob ignored his assignment to deal with what he felt was a serious problem. The boss saw what Bob did, and thanked Bob for saving the company money.

> Bob stood up to the boss, the boss was going to fire him for insubordination, but the boss's boss said, 'Hey! Bob just saved the company a ton of money! What is wrong with you?

Each of these stories teaches a different lesson about how to behave. The first says never argue with the boss. The second says you should bring up problems. The third says that if you bring up a problem and your boss doesn't appreciate hearing it, don't worry, his boss will see that justice is done. I saw this one play out in just my first few weeks at IBM after I graduated from college. When Bob's boss was subsequently reassigned to a remote branch office, that cemented the lesson that employees should act on serious problems.

The problem with most organizational stories is that they just happen. Events occur and are assembled after the fact into stories that current employees tell one another and pass along to new hires. These stories become part of the background, repeated often without really thinking about it. Frequently, the lessons taught to new employees are not the lessons management thinks are being taught. Taking control of the process, however, can dramatically improve organizational performance in all areas.

In Chap. 1, I discussed IBM's culturally reflexive behaviors that enabled Big Blue to pull out of the tailspin in which it found itself in 1992. Where did those behaviors come from? How were they spread throughout the company? The behavior, the culture, was spread through the stories about Tom Watson Senior and Tom Watson Junior, and countless other stories of how IBMers overcame seemingly impossible problems. That narrative carried IBM through what may politely be called an extremely rough patch. Helix Systems, on the other hand, told very different stories: stories of one-upsmanship and non-cooperation. Stories of how other people didn't pull their weight. Stories of broken promises and impossible deadlines. When Helix ran into problems, the downhill slide was mercifully swift.

How Do We Create the Organizational Story?

There is a sport psychology technique used by many top athletes which involves imagining yourself looking back from the future at an upcoming competition and then writing yourself a letter describing how you won. This may sound silly, but it works. It has the effect of focusing the athlete on the desired outcome and also makes them think strategically about how to attain that outcome. The technique of building an organizational story is similar: we start with the end in mind, something better known as the organization's "vision."

Business books, psychology texts, classes, all talk at length about vision. They do not, however, agree on just what vision is. Indeed, I've observed that if I ask ten people what vision is, I get eleven different answers! Thus, it should come as no surprise that when I ask employees, even senior managers, at corporations what the company's vision is, most of them can't answer me. Those who can are, by an amazing coincidence, those whose companies are doing the best.

The reason there is so little agreement about what vision is, is that it is too often looked at in isolation. Unconnected to anything else, it is all too easy to fall into the trap of arguing how many visions can dance on the head of a pin. In other words, vision by itself is nice, but of limited utility. To be effective, the vision must fit into and tie together the organizational story. It is the element that provides focus and meaning for the organization's goals and enables the development of effective strategy for accomplishing those goals. Whether we are talking about Microsoft's famous "A PC on every desktop," Google's vision of a world in which all information is easily accessible, Starbuck's vision of nurturing the human spirit one cup at a time, or Walt Disney's vision of a park where "families could experience and enjoy the wonders of nature and technology," a vibrant vision combined with a strong organizational narrative is extremely powerful.

How powerful? As the NY Times reported back in March 2011, when Google did a detailed analysis of employee and management behaviors, they found that one of the biggest reasons people quit is lack of connection to the vision or goals of the company; conversely, a strong connection to the vision dramatically increases loyalty, commitment, and motivation.

Building the Vision

Building a vision means looking at what the organization dreams of accomplishing: A PC on every desk? Accessible and usable information? The key is to not focus on the mechanics of what you are doing, be that writing software, making coffee, or building theme parks, but on what your actions mean to the world and why that matters. At this point, how you're accomplishing your goals is not nearly as important as being able to succinctly state the outcome you expect.

In other words, your vision must answer a few simple questions, starting with:
Who are we?
This may sound like a philosophical point. It's not. You have to ask yourself what your organization will look like. What will it be like? What principles and values do you hold? How will you stick with them when it's difficult? It's easy to make grand statements when things are going well, but how about when conditions are terrible? During the Great Depression, Tom Watson refused to fire anyone at IBM. When investors and board members put pressure on him, his response was that it was his job to build men, not destroy them. One of his values, and, for many years one of IBM's values, was that you built a strong company by building strong people; that you show loyalty to get loyalty. Watson was uncompromising in his principles, and his attitudes suffused IBM.
How will we change the world?
How will we know we're making progress?
Some companies change the world in a big way: think Google or Apple. Others change the world in very small ways that only matter to a few people. In this case, size really doesn't matter. What matters is that you can quickly and easily tell people how the world will be different. Along the way, you need to be able to measure your progress toward the realization of that vision. Whether you're looking at cups of coffee sold and stores opened, or visitors to your theme parks, you need to be able to see that the change is happening.

Feedback on how our vision is coming to life is how we maintain enthusiasm and focus. It gives the organizational narrative direction and draws people into a cycle of increasing performance. Feedback also tells us if something isn't working. Conversely, if the vision is constructed such that we can't really see progress, then it no longer serves as a focal point for effort and organizational resources. Goals are less focused and resources are not concentrated well. For example, Microsoft's current vision, "to help you realize your full potential," is basically meaningless. You can never know if you've reached your full potential, or even what that is. Indeed, it can be argued that to reach your "full potential" in one area, you must forego achieving it in another. It's extremely difficult to build a narrative around something that vague, and deeply unsatisfying as well. Vague focus yields vague goals; vague goals and an unsatisfying outcome lead to wasted effort and a lack of engagement.

The next question your vision needs to answer is:
Why does anyone care?
It's not enough to change the world. People have to care about the change. In other words, your vision must get other people engaged and excited: it must appeal to them on an individual, emotional level. If it doesn't, you're going to have a very difficult time convincing people to fund you, recruiting people to help you, and finding people to buy your products or services. This is a perfect example of the "what's in it for me?" principle at work.

Starbucks, for example, did a superb job of getting people to care about its coffee. By creating a whole jargon around ordering coffee, to wit, Tall, Grande, and Venti, they built a sense of inclusion. Knowing the code made people feel special. It was

A Thing to bring someone to a Starbucks and show off your insider knowledge. By further providing comfortable chairs, tables, and WiFi, they managed to create the atmosphere of a cozy, neighborhood coffee shop. Starbucks not only built a successful culture, they drew people into that culture. They got enough of us to care about their products that they became extremely successful.

In thinking about how your vision reflects a change in the world, you need to consider what this means to other people. How will they benefit? What about your vision will make your company an exciting place for people to work? What will make others want to support your products? The people who care about that change will become your employees and/or clients or customers.

This is an important point: you are crafting your vision so that people will care, and the people who respond to your vision are the ones who care. Not everyone is going to care. Some people don't like Starbucks or won't touch an iPhone, a Mac, or, conversely, a PC. That's okay. You can't appeal to everyone. Quite frankly, you don't want to. A vision that appeals to everyone is also going to be so broad and vague that it's worthless: we're back to helping you realize your full potential.

It's worth noting at this point that "making money" is not a good organizational vision: it's surprisingly hard to get people to really care. While it may be personally very satisfying and I certainly consider it a fine thing to do, as a vision it is seriously lacking. Why should anyone else care about you making money? Maybe if you can convince some people that they will share in the profits then those people will help you. What about your clients? Why should they be interested in making you rich? What's in it for them? People will work for a cause about which they deeply care far more intensely and with far greater effort than they will for money alone.

When it comes to vision, money is one of the ways you know you're succeeding: if you're making money, you are getting feedback that something is working correctly!

The Limits of Vision

The best thing about having an exciting vision is that you might just accomplish it.

The worst thing about having an exciting vision is that you might just accomplish it.

A good vision is ambitious, often extremely so. When Microsoft started out, the idea of a PC on every desk and in every house was a distant, impossible dream. To the extent that anyone imagined it could happen, it was kind of like waiting for Godot. Then, by the year 2000 or so, Microsoft's vision was essentially reality. They hit their dream and, like the canonical image of the dog finally catching the truck, didn't quite know what to do about it. They came up with this "helping you achieve your full potential," vision. While Microsoft has certainly done some interesting work in recent years, the company hasn't had the same level of intense, laser-like focus that it did before. Sure, other factors contributed, but if you don't have a clear destination in mind, distractions become much more powerful.

An important part of understanding your vision and organizational narrative is thinking about what the next story will be. When you achieve the vision, the first reaction is satisfaction, a sense of victory, and a great sense of control. Like the athlete who wins a major event, the organization feels invincible. Athletes who become complacent at this point start losing. Athletes who recognize that if you don't keep pushing yourself to higher levels of performance you become stuck, quite frequently manage to move on to higher peaks. Companies, as well, often become complacent at this point: some examples include IBM, Polaroid, Microsoft, to name just a few obvious examples. IBM recovered and created a new vision, Polaroid vanished, and the jury is still out on Microsoft.

In a sense, athletes have it easy: no matter what your sport, there's always a bigger competition, or the opportunities to beat world records in the Olympics or win multiple medals year after year. You know what you have to do. For organizations, it can be much harder. It pays to devote some time to considering what you'll do if you finally catch that truck.

Not All Visions Look the Same

For the most part, effective visions are short and to the point. If it takes more than a few minutes to convey the vision, as opposed to the surrounding story, you've probably lost your audience. However, some organizational visions do something a little different. As befits a company that whose motto is "think different," Apple is famous for its non-vision vision.

Rather than a traditional vision statement, Apple lists its history of successful products and the changes it created through those products. Thus, Apple talks about how it is leading the digital music revolution through the iPod and iTunes, and how it revolutionized smart phones, and so forth. While unorthodox, Apple's approach does have something going for it: a focus on past successes is one of the best way to get people dreaming about, and excited about, future successes. As we'll see when we get to motivation and leadership behaviors, a focus on past success, when handled well, can be one of the best ways to predict future success.

How Do I Create the Rest of the Story?

In creating the rest of the story, we need to recognize some basic facts: people operate in their own perceived best interest and people preferentially choose higher status over lower status. The problem is that we don't always know what they perceive their best interest to be, and we don't necessarily know how someone measures status. However, we do that there are certain things people seek in a job, be that volunteer work or their careers. To paraphrase psychologist Peter Ossorio, when people value a concept or an ideal, they will value and be attracted to specific instances of that ideal. The goal, therefore, is to understand what you offer along the dimensions of things people value. Understanding what you offer along each of these dimensions is critical to being able to construct an organizational narrative that will attract the right people to the organization, provide the framework in which motivation can occur, and maximize your chances of creating a highly motivated, loyal, productive work force: it's not enough to merely provide opportunity; you have to make sure people both know that the opportunity exists and believe it's worth chasing.

We need to start by recognizing that everyone is the hero of their own story. We all have dreams, hopes, and aspirations for the future. When the job we are doing fits into our self-narrative, we feel connected and excited. The work matters, it's helping us get where we want to go. Note that this doesn't mean that you need to hire a college graduate straight into the role of CEO in order for them to feel heroic; that would be foolish on many levels. Rather, people will work hard at even menial jobs provided those jobs provide a path to something bigger. Conversely, high profile jobs with lots of perks won't hold someone who feels that, even in such a role, they are relegated to being a bit player or an interchangeable component. Nobody likes being the sidekick forever. People want to feel important, as if they matter as individuals. People who feel like cogs in the machine disengage.

Next, the story has to be exciting, or at least interesting. It has to hold our attention, particularly in today's distraction filled world. What we are doing has to matter sufficiently that it's what we'll choose to do because it matters, not because we'll get yelled at by the boss or fired. Remember, you might find writing software to be the most boring thing imaginable, but most software engineers find it incredibly enjoyable. In building your narrative, you need to understand at least a little bit about the people you want to attract so that you can speak to them in their language. That means that you will have multiple overlapping stories for different parts of the organization and different jobs within it. Generic stories attract generic people.

In building the story, there are then six key elements that we have to consider: the variety, or lack thereof, of the skills a person will be called up to use; the visibility of a task; the importance of a task; how much autonomy or supervision the person will have; how they will receive feedback; opportunities for growth; and safety. Frequently, we will have to balance different competing values of at least some of the first five elements. A lack of a path for growth, however, never goes over well. A lack of safety, itself a rather complex subject, can undermine everything else.

Skill Variety: The Exercise of Vital Powers

Aristotle once said that happiness is "the exercise of vital powers along lines of excellence in a life affording them scope."

Organizational psychology tells us that one of the key elements of creating an environment in which people feel motivated and excited is giving them the opportunity to exercise their skills. Simply put, people like doing what they are good at. In a very real sense, the reason our strengths are strengths is because they are things that we enjoy doing so we keep doing those things. As a result, we get better and better at them.

When people work in your organization, will they have the opportunity to develop their strengths? Will they get to experiment and discover new strengths? Will tasks restrict people to the use of only a few skills or will they get to stretch and use their full spectrum of skills? For example, engineers are often viewed as introverted and assumed to be uncomfortable standing in front of an audience. But some very excellent engineers also happen to love to teach: will they be pigeon-holed into specific engineering tasks, such as writing code or designing circuits, or will they be able to expand their job to include teaching or mentoring others? What story does your organization tell about how different jobs can change or grow over time? Some people will be attracted to the job where they can do a few things, but get the opportunity to do them very well, while others will prefer the opportunity to do many things. So long as both routes provide paths for growth, neither is inherently better than the other.

Task Visibility: What's That?

Some people prefer to work behind the scenes, quietly doing their jobs, comfortable in the knowledge that they are contributing to the company. So long as their manager knows what they've done, they're happy. Other people want their work to be visible, something they can point to and say, "I did that!"

Different tasks are more or less amenable to being visible or not. The key is to understand which is which and talk about it. The person who wants to work in the background will be happiest on the less visible tasks, while the person who wants to point at their work will be happiest when they are involved in tasks with high visibility. Again, one is not inherently better than the other; rather, they will often attract very different people. Even when the same person is happy in either space, it's wise to make it clear whether, and how much, say they have in how visible the task will be. Not everyone wants visibility thrust upon them.

Which tasks are visible and which are not? How much room will people have to experiment and figure out which they prefer? How easily can they switch projects over time?

Task Significance: Does It Really Matter?

Distinct from how visible a particular task may be, is how important it is. Some tasks may be visible and important, some may be extremely important but not very obvious, and some may be extremely visible but not very important. For example, the graphical user interface of a software program is both visible and important: if it doesn't work, you can't interact with the program effectively.

I've been told that the inside of an iPhone is a thing of beauty, a miracle of engineering design. I don't know; I've never seen the inside of an iPhone. What I do know, however, is that my phone works. The inside is not visible, but it is extremely important.

Working at IBM in the late 1980's, I did work that seemed to be very visible in that we talked about it, presented on it, wrote papers, and so on. However, after that, each project vanished into IBM's equivalent of the warehouse at the end of *Raiders of the Lost Ark:* put on a shelf somewhere and forgotten. The rare project that did make it to market was never more than a rounding error on Big Blue's balance sheet. After a while, the work no longer seemed important.

One of the key factors around the importance of a task is not just how important it actually is, but how important it appears to be for the person doing it. Many years ago, a cousin of mine told me about work he did for NASA. It was so secret that he didn't even really know exactly what part of the shuttle he was designing; all he knew was that it was important. In the end, it turned out to be the lock on the door. While this is an extremely important part of a spacecraft, in that the consequences of your door flying open when you're in orbit are extremely unpleasant, he didn't see it that way. He claimed that was the last time he ever worked for NASA.

What does your organization tell people about the importance of their tasks? Do employees feel that their work matters? If employees start on projects that are not important, how do they move to more important projects? When the work is important, how is that communicated to the employee? It's important to find out what they actually believe, not what you think they believe or what you wish they believe.

Autonomy: I Did It My Way…

A key element of how interesting and exciting a job appears to someone is the amount of control they have over their actions. While people may seek advice, instruction, or supervision early in a task, as they become comfortable with their duties and develop better understanding of their jobs, they naturally seek greater autonomy. This desire for, and expectation of, autonomy, is a normal part of the life story of an adult in Western society: children have little autonomy, teens more so, adults still more. Unfortunately, the other common cultural story is the one that says that people seek autonomy before they are ready and must be stopped lest something terrible happen. It is very easy for employees and managers to inherit those stories from the surrounding culture, setting the stage for conflict.

This, however, also represents a misunderstanding of what autonomy means. Autonomy is a function of organizational structure: the need to hit deadlines, the need to work with others, satisfy customers, attend to regulations, and so forth. Too much structure, of course, will stifle autonomy, but lack of structure also creates less room for autonomy. We'll look at this in more depth when we discuss leadership in Chap. 4 and motivation in Chap. 5.

In terms of understanding and shaping your organizational narrative, the question is more about how members of the organization develop autonomy. What do employees have to do to be given more freedom in how they work?

For example, how a company handles the question of whether an employee can work from home, presuming it's a business where that makes sense, says a great deal about the company. I've encountered technology companies that don't allow employees to work from home on the grounds that having everyone in the office fosters team development. While that may be true in a general sense, the devil is in the details: everyone is working in offices behind closed doors or sitting in cubes with headphones on the whole time. No teamwork there. Instead of sending a message that team development is important, the company was actually telling a story of how management did not trust employees to work if they couldn't be observed.

Building autonomy is a large component of employee job satisfaction and productivity. Consider how your organization approaches autonomy and look closely at the elements that block it. What are the stories managers tell one another? What are you worried about? If necessary, get an outsider to help you identify the factors that are interfering with giving people as much autonomy as possible within the constraints of the organization's business.

Feedback: A Sign, A Sign!

When we're driving along the road to an unfamiliar destination, how do we know we're on the right track? We look for signs or landmarks, or at least directions from our GPS. A critical part of our ability to get from point A to point B is that we receive feedback from our surroundings. Without that feedback, we feel lost.

Of course, to be able to receive feedback, we have to know what that feedback looks like and be able to interpret it. This may seem obvious, but consider it this way: a trained hunter can track an animal through the forest, while an untrained person would have no clue what to look for and probably wouldn't recognize the signs even if someone told them what those signs were. An expert software engineer can deduce the likely cause of a bug in the program by observing the behavior of the program under different conditions, while most of us would simply be frustrated that the program wasn't working.

In an organizational setting, feedback is another key component of how much people enjoy their jobs, and, hence of your organizational story. Feedback gives us a sense of progress, critical to maintaining motivation and, indeed, interest in the task. Feedback allows us to figuratively and emotionally orient ourselves: we know where we stand, we feel more in control of the task. It is, for example, easier to write a book when Word is constantly showing word and page counts, when you can check off chapters as they are completed: all forms of feedback. Feedback is also critical for growth to occur.

Part of your organizational story has to include feedback mechanisms: not just how the individual gets feedback on their progress, but how the organization gets feedback on how employees are perceiving the organization, how employees experience their jobs, how the organization is doing in the market, how competitors are doing, and so on.

A canonical story about General Motors pre-bankruptcy is that an employee there was trying to convince a VP that people weren't buying enough GM cars. The VP took him to the window, pointed at the parking lot, and said, "Look out there. What do you see?"

"GM cars," said the employee.

"Exactly," said the VP.

"But that's our parking lot!" exclaimed the employee, his words, however, falling on deaf ears.

Whether or not this story is literally true, it sent a very clear message about how open GM was to feedback. Employees hearing that story would be less likely to bring problems to the attention of their managers. Potential customers would form an impression of GM as a company indifferent to feedback. Potential employees might well choose to go somewhere else, where feedback is appreciated.

What is your story about feedback? How do you give it, how do you receive it? If your organization has trouble getting or giving feedback, what are the stories people are telling that get in the way? There is always a story; you just have to find it.

Growth

Most people seek to grow in their careers. Indeed, the desire for growth is hardly limited to one's job. In any activity to which we devote any substantial amount of time and effort, we naturally expect to expand our capacities. Students in a martial art, for example, expect to progress from white belt to black belt. Fencers seek ever higher ratings and national competition. When growth appears impossible or when there appears to be no further place to go, we lose interest. Our focus shifts elsewhere, to other challenges and activities. Students who feel they aren't progressing toward that black belt quit. In many religious organizations, most congregants are fairly loosely connected; those who are more seriously committed also pursue growth in a variety of ways, be that becoming educated in the religion, volunteering in the community, fund raising, or other activities that confer status.

At a fundamental level, growth typically equates to an increase in status and opportunity; conversely, an increase in status is a form of growth. As Peter Ossorio likes to say, people always choose more opportunity over less. Granted, that doesn't mean we seek to grow constantly; even the most creative person needs downtime to recharge, a point we will come back to in later chapters.

When speaking to people who worked at IBM in the 1960's and 1970's, one of the consistent themes I heard from them was that there was always a place to go. No matter how good you were, IBM would help you find ways to increase your abilities. IBM did very well in those days; individual growth is a central factor in organizational success.

What are the paths for growth in your organization? Are they open or restricted? Does someone have to move into management in order to grow, or can they grow in their field of expertise? What do members of your organization believe about growth? Do you see people choosing higher status over lower status, or the other way around? If people are choosing lower status or less opportunity, that's alerting you to a problem: either their perception of growth and status is incorrect, you are not providing the growth opportunities you think you are, or people are not finding out about them. Remember, it's not enough to just provide the opportunities; you also have to have the stories in place that tell people those opportunities exist and are worth pursuing.

Safety

Safety is a complex issue. It's easy to get caught up in the image of safety as meaning only physical safety. Physical safety is important, of course, but is also only one component of the safety equation. Safety also means job security, emotional and intellectual safety, freedom from being insulted, belittled, or embarrassed. In many ways, these aspects of safety are much more salient than just physical danger.

MIT's Ed Schein observes that the desire to prevent loss of face is extremely powerful. Fear of loss of face is often enough to squash conversation, questions, innovation, or brainstorming. For all the movie images of the Japanese as being mortally afraid of losing face, Americans and Europeans are no different. It's only a question of what constitutes loss of face in each culture.

While attending a bar-mitzvah one Saturday morning, there came the point in the service where the rabbi was about to speak. As he stood up, the packed room quieted. As he opened his mouth, the silence was abruptly shattered by a cell phone going off. This was particularly embarrassing when one considers the many large signs posted around the temple reminding people to not bring cell phones into the service, or to at least turn them off.

The ringing continued as the person whose phone it was realized that as soon as he, or she, turned it off, it would be immediately obvious to the entire congregation who the guilty party was. This fear of loss of face paralyzed the person. Thinking quickly, the rabbi asked every person to reach into their pockets as though they were silencing their phone. This way, no one would know whose phone it was. Most of the people present reached into their pockets and purses and the ringing stopped. I will admit that I took advantage of the moment to make sure that my phone was off. No more phones went off that day.

How do people perceive safety? What will be done to make sure that people do not lose face? If someone does lose face, under what conditions does that occur? If people know the risks and can choose their behavior, that's a lot better than having it feel random. When people are focused on the lack of safety, it's hard to get them to listen to anything else. We'll come back to this when we discuss organizational stress in Chap. 11.

Change Narratives

I live in a small town west of Boston. Halloween is a big deal here. It doesn't matter which night of the week Halloween falls, that's the night the kids are out trick or treating. Naturally, the kids prefer it when Halloween falls on a Friday or Saturday night so that they don't have to worry about going to school the next day, but the idea of celebrating Halloween on the nearest Friday or Saturday night is anathema. Witches have more flight capability than the idea of moving Halloween. It just doesn't happen.

My son, though, came up with a different approach: he asked me what would happen if there was a snow day on Halloween. Would that mean a full day of trick or treating?

"What are the odds of a snow day in October?" was my response.

I've always heard that it's not nice to fool Mother Nature. The converse is apparently not true. In 2011, we got a Halloween snowstorm. Not only did schools close on Halloween, they closed for the next two days as well. So much for the odds.

But Mother Nature's little treat quickly revealed itself as a trick: due to downed trees and power lines, Halloween was postponed, and ended up being the evening of a school day after all. Halloween moved and no one objected: when Mother Nature makes a change, it can be best described as, well, a force of nature.

A year later, we had Hurricane Sandy. Some towns kept Halloween on schedule, some moved it. The force of the story is very strong: Halloween is supposed to be on October 31st. Although there was still storm damage, the cultural habits produced different results in neighboring town. The kids, of course, made out like bandits: they got to go trick-or-treating twice!

This is the problem most organizations face when it comes to implementing effective and lasting organizational change. So long as enough force is applied, the change will happen. As soon as the force is removed, people revert to their old behaviors. They might not even wait for the force to stop. Sometimes a crisis can force permanent change, as happened at IBM when Lou Gerstner took over. A crisis can also force the sort of permanent change that happened at DEC: they were acquired by Compaq. Waiting for a crisis to force a change to occur is a very risky way to approach organizational change.

In Chap. 1, we discussed the process of unfreezing a culture in order to make change possible. What we are going to look at now is how change affects the narrative of the organization and how to frame the changes in the context of the existing narrative. Not only does change reactivate all the issues we've already discussed, it introduces a whole new set of cocnerns that need to be addressed if you want people to become active agents of change instead of opponents of it. While these new questions can manifest in a variety of ways, the seven canonical versions are:

- What will this do to the organization?
- How will my place in the organization change?
- How will this affect my job?
- Will I still enjoy working here?

- Will this hurt our product quality?
- Will I still measure up?
- Would I be able to get a job in this new organization?

Let's look at each of these questions individually.

What Will This Do to the Organization?

In other words, "I have an image of the organization, based on the vision and the stories and my experiences here. What is going to happen to that organization? Will I still be proud to work for the new organization?"

Fundamentally, people base their perceptions of the organization on their experiences. The organization is as they have found it to be. The longer they've been there, the more deeply immersed they are in the culture of the organization. It's become something solid, something predictable. Now that is all changing! Like living in California during the Loma Prieta earthquake, it's very disconcerting to have the solid ground under your feet suddenly not feel quite so solid. For several weeks after the quake, whenever the cat jumped on the bed, I would awaken bolt upright. Don't make change in your organization feel like that!

In constructing the story for why change needs to occur, we have to connect the existing values of the organization to the new values. It's a sequel, not a completely new story. People need to be able to see that at the end the values of the organization and the underlying culture they are part of will still be there. They may be different, but they'll be there. By connecting the dots, by telling the story of how the current values and vision are transforming into the new values and vision, people can feel comfortable with the change, rather than worried or anxious. Anxious people resist; comfortable people join in the process. Resistance is a sign that you're going too fast.

If there are organizational values or processes that are going to disappear, again, connect that to the story. You'll recall that in Chap. 1, we discussed the process for getting employees to convince themselves that change in necessary. In inviting people to talk about why the current situation isn't working, include those things that are changing: "How is this process getting in the way?" "What are two or three better ways of getting this done?" Your goal is to have people telling you why the values or processes need to change or disappear, rather than you fighting to convince them.

In conducting serious organizational change, sometimes a few sacred cows need to become hamburger. The less sacred they are when that happens, the easier it is for everyone to swallow.

How will My Place in the Organization Change?

In other words, "I know my place in this organization. I know what I'm doing. I know how to grow. I have status and I know how to continue to gain status. If we make this change, will I still know what to do? Will I still have paths for growth? Will I retain my status? Will I be able to gain more status?"

Recall that people preferentially seek to increase their status. Given a choice between actions which appear to decrease status and actions which appear to increase status, people choose the latter. If that's not available, then they will attempt to at least preserve the status quo.

In one large martial arts organization, it is extremely difficult to introduce anything substantially new into the basic curriculum. Senior members of the organization, high degree black belts all, are resistant to the idea of having to learn the new material and simultaneously do not want to seem ignorant of it. The solution is, for the most part, to not let it in. The areas where new material is being allowed in are also those areas where everyone can agree that there exists a teacher who is of such high status that it is an honor to be allowed to learn from him. They reframed the status equation so that admitting that they didn't know the material was no longer embarrassing.

In formulating change, questions of role and status need to be directly addressed. Employees need to see how their existing status will transfer to the new world, and they need to understand how they will continue to gain status once the changes are complete. Part of how this is done involves training, a topic we'll cover in Chap. 8.

How will this Affect My Job?

This may seem to be nothing more than a version of the previous question. Not quite. Whereas the previous question was focused on status and growth, this one is asking a more basic question: "Will I still have a job I care about? For that matter, will I still have a job?"

Change and layoff come together so often that it's very hard to talk about the first without people thinking about the second. Again, the most important thing is to address the question head on: if you are evasive or refuse to discuss it, you only send the very clear message that there really is something to be afraid of. Barring a sighting of Great Cthulhu, the thing we can't see is always more frightening than the thing we can see.

If jobs are going to be eliminated or even significantly changed, it's important to get that out in the open early in the process. Show people how they can successfully make the transition so that they will have a job in the new organization. If, on the other hand, the changes are really a cover to implement layoffs, well, you'll have a hard time regaining trust if you don't play it straight. When layoffs appear random, people do not feel safe. At that point, it becomes very hard to maintain motivation and productivity.

Will I Still Enjoy Working Here?

To put this another way, "Will the things that make this job fulfilling still exist after the change?"

In other words, this question is expressing anxiety about the key elements of the organizational narrative we discussed earlier: skill variety, task visibility, significance, autonomy, feedback, growth, and safety. Remember that members of an organization are, by definition, the people who have accepted and bought into the organizational culture. They are used to things working a certain way, and they've learned the ropes. Their involvement, be that a job or a volunteer position, is providing them at least some satisfaction or they wouldn't be there. They are concerned that after the changes those lessons will no longer be valid; the elements that made the job fulfilling will be gone.

As part of describing the change, you must address this question as it goes to the root of your entire organizational story. You need to connect the dots from the old ways in which people experienced job satisfaction to the new ways, and be prepared to help people see those connections. It will be tempting to just say, "Look it's there! Shut up and change already!" Don't yield to that temptation. It only makes things worse.

Will I Still Measure Up?

When you hear this question, it's telling you that the people asking it are afraid that they won't be viewed as competent in the new organization. Again, it's important to address this concern directly: if you are evasive, they'll assume you really are hiding something. Similar to addressing the question about, "How will my place in the organization change?" you need to show people how competence will be measured and demonstrate that those people viewed as competent will have the opportunity to continue to be viewed as competent. This may be by highlighting similarities in the job descriptions or through training and accreditation ceremonies. We'll look more at that in Chap. 8.

Will This Hurt Our Product Quality?

It doesn't matter whether you are producing a physical product, a service, or a piece of software. Questions of this nature reflect a deeper fear that the change will threaten the viability of the organization. People are afraid that once the changes go through, clients will abandon the business and it will fail or at least be forced to lay people off.

One of my early clients was a non-profit organization teaching rape prevention to women. When their new Executive Director announced changes to how they delivered training and how they trained the trainers, existing staff went ballistic. The ED was accused of not being a "real leader," trainers claimed their competence was being questioned, and so forth.

Once I was able to sit and talk with each of the parties involved, it quickly became clear that the real issue was that existing members of the organization were deeply afraid that the changes to how the trainers were trained would lead to substandard rape prevention courses. Not only did such a prospect violate their sense of professionalism, they were deeply concerned that some woman would end up insufficiently prepared and be raped as a result. Once these fears were identified and brought out into the open, the organization was able to effectively address the issues and move forward with the proposed changes.

Questions about product quality in this context are almost really about organizational viability. In talking about change, you need to make sure that everyone can see how the change will produce a stronger, more vibrant organization. Review the unfreezing techniques in Chap. 1 if necessary.

Would I Be Able to Get a Job in This New Organization?

In other words, "It's time to panic! I'd never be able to get a job in this new organization! They're trying to get rid of me and replace me with some kid just out of school!"

If you're hearing this sort of question often, it's telling you that people are scared. They don't believe the changes are for the good of the organization; rather, they believe that the changes are merely an excuse for layoffs or some other dubious form of cost-cutting that will leave qualified people out in the cold. Now, you might argue that layoffs are for the good of the organization; I assure you that your employees won't see it that way and will do everything they can to undermine the process. After all, what do they have to lose?

If you get to this point, you need to slow down and review what you've been doing to this point. Have you connected the dots from the old organizational story to the new one? Have you taken the time to unfreeze the situation, as discussed in Chap. 1? Have you built the belief that change is necessary, focused them on the benefits of change, built confidence that change is possible, and involved them in the process of coming up with ideas for change?

When you find the breakdown point, it's relatively easy to adjust and move forward. If you just try to force things along, the changes will unravel when you stop forcing.

Wrapping Up The Change Narrative

It's important to remember that these questions may not come up exactly as written here. Be assured, though, that they will come up. If you are attentive to your organization, you will become able to identify the variations and permutations. The secret is to listen for the underlying concerns.

Change works best when you address the issues we've discussed right from the start. The longer you wait, the more you allow people's imaginations to work against you. This is why it's important to set the stage by unfreezing the situation first. When you don't prepare your employees for change, the normal, reflexive response is to resist. Remember, it's easier to move through water than ice.

As we discussed in Chap. 1, the final step of change is cementing in place, or refreezing. Highlight victories and emphasize successes. Talk about how challenging it was and how people overcame those challenges to make the changes.

Connect those stories to the future vision of the organization. The changes are not really complete until they become the new status quo.

The Never-Ending Story

Organizational stories never really end, at least so long as the organization remains viable. The members of your organization are always learning new lessons and repeating the stories about their experiences. Your stories, and hence your culture, are changing and growing all the time. The real question is how well you are managing the process. Are you always focused on the short-term or are you taking a more strategic perspective? Do you have lofty goals or pedestrian goals?

Questions to Consider

1. Think about your organization. What stories do people tell? What stories do you tell?
2. What are your organization's examples of top performers? Poor performers?
3. How do people know how to behave in your organization?
4. What changes has your organization attempted? What happened?
5. What fears does change elicit in your organization?
6. What does your organization believe about change? How does that match with the success or failure of any change attempts?
7. What questions would elicit a desire for change in your organization?
8. How can you praise your employees and provide them with feedback on change?
9. What example are you setting through your behavior?

Chapter 3
The Life Cycle of a Team: Developm(Problem Solving, and Decision Makin

Once upon a time, the late and unlamented Soviet Union decided to grow wheat in Siberia. Their logic was simple: by growing wheat in the inhospitable conditions of Siberia, the wheat would become stronger. The wheat, however, was indifferent to Soviet philosophy. Despite speeches, threats, and promises from the government, the wheat stubbornly refused to grow.

In the 1990s, a group of Nobel Prize winning economists developed some very interesting theories about how financial markets should work. Their theories were brilliant and attracted billions in investment dollars into the hedge fund they created. Long-term Capital Management almost took down the entire US economy when it collapsed in the summer of 1998.

In both cases, a belief about how the world *should* work was trumped by the way the world does work.

To bring this a little closer to home, I worked with one high technology company that decided to create a set of coding standards for its software development team. While not an unusual occurrence in software companies, in this case, the manager in charge wrote up a fifty (that's right, 50) page standards document. Naturally, everyone was overjoyed and memorized everything; at least, that is what the manager thought. In fact, no one read more than a page or two and most of the engineers ignored even that.

Another company was trying to manage information: design decisions, notes from discussions, and so forth. They had the very good idea that they could manage all their accumulated wisdom as a Wiki. Unfortunately, the Wiki swiftly ballooned into an unmanageable morass of data in which no one could actually find anything useful. The problem was not so much getting people to remember to update the Wiki; it was organizing the information in a manner useful to everyone who needed to use it, and in convincing people to take the time to keep it organized. Indeed, even agreeing on how it should be organized generated controversy and bad feeling.

In both of these cases, beliefs about how people *should* do their work were trumped by the way people actually do work. Like Soviet wheat, it can be remarkably difficult to motivate or threaten people into doing something that they really do not want to do. Unlike wheat, people can be forced. It is merely a

S. R. Balzac, *Organizational Psychology for Managers*,
Management for Professionals, DOI: 10.1007/978-1-4614-8505-6_3,
© Springer Science+Business Media New York 2014

on of how much time and energy you want to spend: pushing people takes a great deal of effort and tends to result in significant amounts of anger and frustration for all parties involved. Not, in other words, a conducive atmosphere for creating a strong, collaborative team.

Of course, sometimes it is necessary to have people do things they don't want to do. Code does need to be commented, information needs to be documented, and so forth. Fortunately, unlike wheat, people can be convinced. Instead of pushing them, the key is to get them to pull: the best teams are the ones that know where they should go and will trample anyone who gets in their way.

So what are teams really? Why are some teams a marvel of camaraderie and high performance, while others burn out their members, leaving them exhausted and depressed? Why do people go from loyalty to opposition to the leader? What is the relationship between the leader and the team? We will start by looking at how teams develop over time. In the next chapter, we will look at things from the perspective of the leader and, in Chap. 5, we look at motivation.

The Life Cycle of a Team

In 1965, a psychologist named Bruce Tuckman first proposed what is now known as Tuckman's Model of Team Development.

According to Tuckman's model, teams go through five distinct stages of development. Team performance and member behavior varies with the stage the team is in. Leadership style also varies with the stage: an effective leadership style at one stage may be counterproductive in another!

Tuckman's model floated around psychology texts and management courses for decades, as much as a topic of debate as a useful tool. In the early 2000s, another psychologist, Susan Wheelan, expanded and extended Tuckman's model. Her results have since been verified in thousands of teams in dozens of countries from the United States to Japan. Although the specific manifestations of different stages may be culturally bound, the stages turn out to be culturally invariant. In other words, where American businessmen might be screaming at one another, Japanese businessmen will be adopting the icily polite mannerisms that is their culturally equivalent method of expressing rudeness or anger.

Tuckman's stages are Forming, Storming, Norming, and Performing. This is also a Terminating stage, but this chapter will focus primarily on the first four stages as they are the ones that most people experience. Each stage has distinct psychological characteristics. There also appears to be a minimum time required for a team to navigate each stage. It is not entirely clear why these minimum times exist, however, they hold true in every team that has been observed. While it entirely possible that a team might be able to progress through the stages faster than current research indicates is possible, to date all efforts to do so only make the process take longer!

The minimum time for Forming and Storming are two months each; one month for Norming. The only exception to this appears to be when a group is formed from an existing group. In this case, the new group starts at the level of the parent group.

A team can remain in Performing arbitrarily long. The challenge, however, is keeping it there.

It is quite possible for a team to become stuck at any point in the process, remaining in a given stage for years. Fully half of all teams never make it out of the Forming stage, or are trapped cycling between Forming and Storming. More than half of those remaining get stuck in Norming, with scarcely more than one team in five reaching Performing.

Stage 1: Forming

Imagine that first day on a new job working with a group of strangers: there you are, staring at your partners, wondering what to do. You don't want to admit that you don't know; after all, perhaps you're in this group by accident. Sure, they said that the selection process was careful, but they must have made a mistake in your case. If anyone realizes just how little you know, they'll surely ask you to leave!

The good news is that everyone else feels the same way!

If you're lucky, a manager or team leader has already been assigned. They'll clear up your confusion and get things going. If there is no formally appointed manager or leader however, that can be a problem. It is truly amazing how long it can take to get nothing done. Often enough, though, the mounting pressure of an impending deadline will force someone to take charge or perhaps simply do the project themselves. The latter case, in particular, tends to trigger more than a little resentment!

The dominant characteristics of Stage 1 groups are dependency and inclusion. Members are primarily concerned with their place in the group; the greatest fear is banishment. Consider that exile from the community was, for much of history, seen as a fate worse than death. Indeed, even today with all our technology, survival completely apart from the group which is civilization is extremely difficult!

Thus, members of Stage 1 groups have a very strong focus on appearing competent. Making a mistake is perceived to be tantamount to risking membership in the group. Unfortunately, with many of the companies I work with, that is also the reality (that's why I'm working with them! It's not easy to change.). As a result, members are afraid to take risks or admit to mistakes, preventing effective error correction from taking place. The unwillingness to make mistakes or appear less than competent also means that members will often fail to ask questions, leading to confusion about objectives, and are unwilling to accept help lest that be seen as a sign of weakness.

Another characteristic of Stage 1 groups is that the group does not know how its skills match up with the task at hand. Indeed, in a very real sense, the group does not know what its skills are as a group. It takes time and exploration for the group to discover their strengths and weaknesses and how they can support one another to maximize their strengths. There's a reason the Red Sox have Spring Training, and even then they sometimes never get it together.

Communications in the group will tend to be polite, distant, sometimes appearing formal, or at least extremely careful, in nature. Because group members do not really know how they stand with one another, no one wants to offend anyone else. Conflict is seen as disruptive to the harmony of the group, proof that members are not committed or loyal. There is a great deal of "go along to get along" taking place.

It's been argued, granted somewhat sarcastically, that to know oneself is the ultimate form of Freudian aggression. By contrast, in a group, the person most people wish they could work with is themselves. Since that's not actually possible, similarity is the next best thing.

Groups seek common ground. This commonality may be physical, stemming from gender, skin color, size, etc. It may be based on background, nationality, education, or culture. The more diverse the group, the more likely the group will demand conformity as a way of building similarity. The conformity may be based around dress, time spent at the office, where and when to eat lunch, or buying into some particular ideology. IBM's blue suit and tie dress code was part of the effort to create similarity in the company and became a cultural icon; a political party's efforts to require all members to buy into a particular orthodoxy is another way of building similarity. Conformity can also be based around dislike of an outside group or a member of the group who does not buy into the group's values. Stage 1 groups are quick to punish such deviants, initially with the goal of bringing them back into the fold. Should that fail, they are usually shunned or exiled. Conformity works best when it focuses on issues that actually help the group get the job done. When conformity focuses on trivial or irritating topics such as requiring everyone to eat lunch together or always show up at the same time, it tends to stifle creativity and individual expression. This causes resentment and reduces group performance.

A strong leader can often be enough to provide the focal point, or at least a focal point, of similarity for the group. Members are usually extremely loyal to the leader, and will rarely question his judgment. When there are questions, they are usually relatively polite and restrained, at least as defined by the cultural norms of the organization. Think of the image of the 1950s manager who takes care of his employees and to whom the employees will go with work or personal problems.

Lacking a strong leader, the group may not coalesce at all. If the group does coalesce, it is often around something trivial or inappropriate: a particular style of dress, eating lunch at a certain restaurant, or in opposition to the schedule, mannerisms, or style of a particular team member. These early attempts at similarity actually produce conformity. Some conformity is necessary for the group to function; too much is stifling. Lacking leadership, the group will not be productive until a leader emerges. As distressing as this fact is for many people, leaderless groups simply don't function.

The more diverse the group, the greater the need for conformity: the less the members appear to have in common, the more they need to create common ground. On the flip side, the higher the intelligence and self-esteem of the members, the more they resist conformity. As you might imagine, a diverse group of highly intelligent, competent, confident individuals is going to be struggling with two opposing psychological imperatives. Skillful leadership is particularly important here!

Decision Making in a Forming Group

Western civilization has a cultural bias toward democracies. We routinely make decisions by voting. As a result, it is culturally normative to use voting systems to make decisions. Unfortunately, voting is an absolutely awful method of decision making in an early stage group.

One of the problems in early stage decision making is that in the short term, voting will often appear to work. This is because the desire to avoid disagreement and the lack of deep engagement or emotional investment means that initially no one really cares that much about the outcome of the vote. Everyone goes along with the outcome because no one wants to rock the boat. Furthermore, people will often tend to overestimate just how much everyone else on the team shares their views. Thus, when people do start to engage more deeply, the group is committed to a voting system, but doesn't yet have the capacity to use it effectively. Another problem with voting systems coming too early in the life of the group is that the vote itself causes people to commit to a position before all the issues are fully identified. This early commitment can then interfere with both problem solving and innovation.

Consider that the hallmarks of a Forming group are goal uncertainty, role confusion, an inability to argue effectively, and a profound ignorance of how group members fit together and exactly what the real skills of the group are. Group members are focused more on safety and inclusion in the group than on the big picture; indeed, members are often too preoccupied to even pay attention to the big picture! For a voting system to be effective, members need to be able to argue and debate without fear of reprisals or having the other party storm out of the room. Voting is a relatively mature method of decision making and requires a group to have already developed a solid communications and social structure.

When voting systems are applied over a long period of time in Forming groups, the process will usually degenerate from a debate over ideas to a battle over votes. In other words, the losers did not lose because their ideas were rejected; they lost the vote because the Other Side did a better job of rallying the voters. The goal then becomes making sure the Other Side (or sides) fails so that Our Side can win the next vote. The losers will often seek to change the voting rules or disenfranchise voters in order to win the next time around. In other words, voting in Forming groups leads to coalitions, which will often unite around ideology and opposition to the other coalitions. Modern American politics circa 2012 is an excellent example of this phenomenon in action.

Along with voting, the two other most common, and dysfunctional, methods of early stage group decision making are the Plop and Minority Rule. Yes, "plop" really is the term.

With the Plop method, a group member proposes an idea. Before anyone can comment on it, or even think about it, someone else proposes another idea, leaving the first idea to figuratively plop to the floor. This process continues until exhaustion sets in and the group agrees to go along with the last idea proposed. As Schein observes, many a boardroom floor is covered in plops.

Minority Rule takes several forms. In the most common form, an idea is proposed and members go along with it because they assume that's what everyone else wants. No one wants to rock the boat or be the lone voice of dissent. This particular phenomenon is popularly known as the Abilene Paradox, named by Jerry Harvey. He describes a family collectively agreeing to have lunch in distant Abilene because each person assumes that's what the others want, only to discover when they get there that no one actually wanted to go.

Another common form of Minority Rule is when someone proposes an idea and then quickly follows it up with, "Any objections? No? Good, let's go."

If the person does this forcefully and confidently enough, the rest of the group will often go along. Sometimes, a coalition will work together, with one person proposing the idea and someone else making the immediate call for action.

Finally, a minority might attempt to subvert or undermine a group as a way of reversing a decision that the minority did not agree with. For example, a minority might use procedural tactics to effectively hold the group hostage until their demands are met. I've attended many a meeting where an encyclopedic knowledge of Robert's Rules of Order was the weapon of choice!

So if we can't go with voting, or majority rule systems, and minority rule doesn't work, how should a Forming group make decisions? In Forming groups, in turns out that the most effective means of decision making is rule by formal authority, which is a nice way of saying "directive leadership" or sometimes "dictatorship."

As ideologically unpleasant as it is for many people, directive leadership really is the only effective decision making method in a Forming group. Initially, the group is too lacking in structure to be able to make their own decisions. The challenge for the leader is to patiently request feedback and input from the group, even though it will often take quite some time before anyone will engage at a non-trivial level. Once the group begins to engage, that's a signal to the leader that it's time to help the group develop more sophisticated decision making capabilities. Leaders who are unwilling to do this are blocking the group from further development. Unfortunately, more sophisticated decision making also requires that the leader surrender increasingly greater amounts of power, which many people are loathe to do. In a very real sense, the difference between a directive leader and a dictator is that the former will surrender power as the group matures. We will look at this in more depth in the next chapter.

Groupthink

Groupthink, first identified by psychologist Irving Janis, is that well-publicized but generally misunderstood phenomenon that leads to groups making apparently bizarre decisions, often leaving outsiders wondering about the sanity of the group members!

In groupthink, decisions are made seemingly without consideration of external reality, frequently being based more on ideology or wishful thinking. In fact, groupthink occurs primarily in situations where the group has a highly directive leader, limited or no disputation or debate skills, a strong desire to avoid conflict, and a belief that a decision must be made Right Now. The group will often be quite convinced of its own invulnerability and the absolute moral rightness of its cause. The group will punish dissent, leading to a high degree of self-censorship. IBM's board, in the late 1980s, viewed their market position as unassailable and criticism as disloyal to the company, leading to a major catastrophe for the company a few years later. As we touched on earlier, in the early 1990s a vice-president at GM famously pointed to the lack of foreign cars in the GM parking lot as proof that the company's marketing was successful, eventually leading to the GM crash of 2008. The attacks on Medicare by the Republican party in 2011, and the punishment meted out to presidential candidate Newt Gingrich for disagreeing, demonstrate that groupthink is hardly limited to corporate boards, but can occur in organizations of any size. As revealed in several articles that came out after the 2012 election, even Mitt Romney's presidential campaign suffered from groupthink: they were unable to even accept the possibility that their internal polling methodology was inaccurate and the much maligned "lamestream media" had it right. As a result, Romney never saw his defeat coming.

Groupthink itself is an extreme example of group polarization in decision making. The tendency of group members to be, for example, risk-adverse or risk-taking often manifests as more extreme risk-avoidance or risk-taking on the part of the group. Quite simply, when the group limits outside input and views loyalty in terms of conformity and adherence to group ideals, communications become an echo chamber. Members of the group hear the words that reinforce their own ideas, and then seek to demonstrate loyalty by taking on ever more extreme positions. The symptoms of groupthink, in their less polarized form, are often healthy and necessary beliefs of the successful group: groups have to believe they can succeed, believe that what they are doing is worthwhile, and have some degree of cooperation. It is when these values become extreme that the problems come in: thus, the belief that the group can succeed if it works hard enough turns into a conviction that success is inevitable unless prevented by the villainy of others.

The faulty decision making that leads to groupthink occurs most commonly in Stage 1 groups. Although group polarization can occur at any time, it becomes less likely as the group develops and approaches Stage 4. Improved decision making, disputation skills, and an increasing tolerance for non-conformity sharply reduce the conditions that lead to polarization.

Stage 2: Storming

The team has been functioning smoothly for at least a couple of months. The leader is getting comfortable with the status quo: he gives instructions, the team executes them. If it's not functioning quite like a well-oiled machine, at least the gears aren't grinding too much. One day, the unthinkable occurs: instead of nodding and heading off to follow the instructions given out by the boss, one of the team members responds, "That's stupid. Here's how we can do it better."

What's a leader to do?

Unfortunately, when I pose this scenario to management students or business executives, the most common answer is, "I show him who's boss!"

Just because it's the common answer doesn't mean that it's the right answer, or even a particularly good answer.

That pushback is the first sign that real engagement is taking place. In Stage 1, group members are too concerned with fitting in and not losing face to really engage with the project. As the feelings of security start to develop and group members start to become personally invested in the project, the natural and logical next step is to become more involved. Group members now want to have a voice in the direction of the project and help shape the outcome. The first manifestation of this is asserting autonomy by pushing back against the leader.

In fact, the primary psychological characteristics of a Stage 2, Storming, team are Counter-dependency and Fight. Quiet acquiescence gives way to passionate, sometimes vituperative, argument. How well the team leader manages this transition determines whether the team continues to Stage 3, remains in Stage 2, or slides back into Stage 1. The more intense the conflict, the more likely the team will slide backwards as members seek to return to the relative comfort of Stage 1.

Where leadership in the first stage needs to be highly directive, in Stage 2 the leader needs to become a diplomat. Telling no longer works. Instead, she has to sell her ideas to the team. The hardest thing for a team leader to do at this point is resist engaging in the conflict. Smacking down the "opposition" only sends the message that engagement is not wanted. Rather, the leader must harness and direct the burgeoning passion.

Further complicating the issue is that those leaders who slap down their opposition are often seen by outsiders as more powerful, tough, and effective than the leaders who co-opt the passion and build an atmosphere of mutual respect. At Pfizer in the 1990s, Hank McKinnell was chosen over Karen Katen as the new CEO exactly because of his tough, no nonsense, abrasive manner. Katen, by comparison, built respect and fellowship and was viewed by analysts as too soft. Five years later, the board forced McKinnell into retirement after his management style led to a severe brain drain and declining revenues and profits (discussed in the Harvard Business Review article, "Why Fair Bosses Fall Behind," by Batia M. Wiesenfeld, Naomi B. Rothman, Sara L. Wheeler-Smith, and Adam D. Galinsky). Knowing when to avoid using power is at least as important as knowing when to use it.

It is very common during Storming to see the group divide into two factions, one supporting the leader and one opposing. The former continues to view the leader as the source of safety and the guide who will lead the group to success. At least at first, the opposing group does not so much view the leader as the problem as they view the way things are being done as the problem and the leader symbolizes the status quo. This is not surprising when we consider that at this point in group development loyalty to and identification with the group is often synonymous with loyalty to and identification with the leader: "This is Bob's team," or "This is Sarah's department."

Depending on how the leader handles that nascent conflict will determine the future of the group. It is quite possible for a group to become so mired in conflict that it cannot progress to Stage 3 or retreat back to Stage 1. In that case, the only option is to disband the group and try again. Being a member of a conflict frozen group is highly stressful and exhausting for all concerned. It is a great way to burn out your team in short order.

Sometimes, the group will turn on the leader so viciously that the leader is forced out. Each time the group symbolically kills the leader, it becomes that much harder for the next person to take charge. Once a group tastes blood, they become increasingly less willing to accept leadership. Unfortunately, this doesn't mean that the group becomes able to function without a leader; rather, the group remains non-productive, uniting only to oppose each leader assigned to it.

Decision Making in a Storming Group

Decision making in a Storming group is no longer the relatively easy process of directive leadership. The increasing engagement of group members and the natural desire to assert autonomy by pushing back against the leader means that directive leadership is more and more likely to be met with opposition. At this point, for the group to continue to advance, the leader must recognize the growing capabilities and engagement of the group and start bringing them into the decision making process. This requires a shift from "telling" to "selling."

During the Forming stage, a leader might request input and feedback and never get it. Leaders then become used to not getting a response and stop asking. Alternately, leaders may not even bother asking for feedback or input into decisions. While the group is in Forming they can usually get away with that behavior.

As the group enters Storming, the leader needs to make a point of requesting input and feedback. Questions and challenges need to be co-opted instead of opposed: "This will never work!" should be met with, "What problems do you see?" rather than, "Of course it will." Opposition only cements opposition and refusing to discuss something only sends the message that it must be a really big problem if it can't be talked about.

As unpleasant as it may feel at first, these questions and challenges are the leader's chance to encourage discussion and shape how the group will argue and debate amongst themselves. While leaders need to avoid getting drawn into open conflict with group members, they are human and will make mistakes. How they handle that mistake is extremely important to the development of the group: if the leader can admit the mistake and correct it, that sends one message to the group. If the leader denies the mistake or tries to pretend it never happened, that sends another. Just as a broken bone, if allowed to heal properly, is stronger at the site of the break, so too is a ruptured relationship stronger if it is allowed to heal properly. Indeed, the act of rupture and repair is essential to forming strong relationships and bonds of trust, provided, of course, that the rupture is not too severe.

As the group develops and refines its communications, it potentially becomes able to adopt a more democratic form of decision making. Whether this happens successfully or not depends on a great many factors, including the skill of the leader, self-efficacy, intelligence, and education of group members, and the nature of the problems the group is facing.

Storming Traps

The two most common traps in Storming are the extremes: not allowing conflict or engaging in it with gusto. In the first case, the group's attempts to enter Storming are constantly shut down, keeping the group trapped in Forming. The Board of Directors of one corporation has been in trapped in this cycle for 50 years. The original board followed the charismatic founder until his death. Conflict was not permitted, and those who disagreed would leave, in some cases to found competing companies. His successor made an attempt to not be The Man, but was constantly pushed back into that role every time the board ran up against any sort of conflict. Rather than address the conflict, they waited for him to make a decision. After his death, a new Chairman was appointed by the board, and then deposed a year later and another Chairman appointed. Although the Board is loosely divided in almost textbook fashion between the two men, the strong relationship between the two has thus far kept the situation stable. This marks a significant step forward for the organization and holds out hope that they will finally be able to successfully enter and navigate Storming.

In the second case, leadership allows itself to be drawn into the conflict. It is an unfortunate fact that conflict can take on a life of its own, blinding the participants to the longer term goals of the company. This can shatter the group completely. In one company, the disagreements between two senior members of the executive team swiftly escalated into a personal conflict. Other members of the leadership team were drawn in, some supporting one of the original two and some forming their own factions. The departments lined up behind their leaders, creating a great deal of interdepartmental rivalry and nastiness. Attempts to resolve the conflict appeared to be making headway until the Camlan Field moment occurred: fans of King Arthur might remember that the final battle between Arthur and Mordred is triggered by a knight carelessly drawing his sword to cut at a snake, leading the other side to believe that a betrayal was occurring. In this case, what would normally have been a minor incident between two people from different departments was seen as an attempted power grab and the fragile peace was shattered.

The problem here is that none of the leaders were ever trained to be leaders. The most difficult lessons in the Japanese martial art of Jujitsu are learning to not rely on force and learning to trust in the technique. The difference between leadership and jujitsu is that in jujitsu it is extremely hard to become a black belt without at least beginning to learn those lessons.

"Violence," Salvor Hardin famously stated in Isaac Asimov's *Foundation*, "is the last refuge of the incompetent." Violence, or force, is also the natural refuge of the untrained.

Stage 3: Norming

After at least two months of darkness and storms, suddenly the clouds break, the sun shines, and everyone is walking around with big smiles on their faces. Okay, maybe that's not literally true, but when a group makes the transition from Storming to Norming, it can feel that way.

For a group to make it through the storming stage, it's done a great deal more than just learning how to argue. The topics of those arguments are the things that people are passionate about: the goals of the group, how the group should work, how accountability will be measured, how decisions will be made, how problems will be solved, how status will be recognized, what roles each person will play, and so forth. In short, the group has developed a social structure and culture. Whereas in Forming only the leader has a clearly defined role, by Norming all group members have clearly defined roles. Norming is, therefore, also known as "Trust and Structure."

Conformity, which drops off strongly in Storming, returns in Norming. Unlike the forced conformity of Forming, however, by Stage 3 conformity is based on a considerably more realistic assessment of the needs of the group and a high desire to identify with the group. In Stage 1, conformity is the means by which the group members create common ground and defend against the anxiety of possible public embarrassment and loss of face. In Stage 3, members conform because they've agreed on the best ways to work and to demonstrate their pride at being in the group. Because Stage 1 conformity is based on binding anxiety, deviation is not tolerated. In Stage 3, because group members have learned to trust one another, deviation is starting to be accepted as a necessary part of exploration, growth, and problem solving.

Approximately half the groups that make it this far get stuck here. Norming feels, quite often, like an island of calm after the recent tempests the group endured. Now that things are working, no one wants to rock the boat. Norming is thus also sometimes referred to as a period of enchantment.

Decision Making in a Norming Group

By the time a group reaches Stage 3, it is capable of adopting more sophisticated methods of decision making, typically some form of voting or consensus driven approach. If the group fails to do this, it is unlikely to progress further and may well regress back to Stage 2 or Stage 1. Even in cases where it appears that the leader is still making all the decisions, a closer examination of the process will usually reveal that the leader is effectively ratifying the consensus of the group.

Leaders, by this point, have lost the quasi-magical aura that they possess in the lower stages. Even though the leader may have the trust of the members once again, dictatorial leadership will not be tolerated by the group. Leaders are now very much participants in the group's activities; conversely, the group is now handling many of the functions of leadership. Decision making can no longer be the province of one person. Instead, it needs to involve the group.

Consensus, it is worth noting, does not mean unanimity. Consensus means that each person feels they had their fair chance to influence the decision and is comfortable supporting the decision of the group.

One might ask at this point, "But wait! Military organizations are very hierarchical. How does that fit?"

As Ed Schein points out, the military command structure is highly relational: it is rare for someone to reach high rank if they are not capable of forming strong relationships with their unit. The military is hierarchical because it needs to execute precision operations and perform rapid decision making. Schein, a retired MIT professor and social psychologist, worked extensively with the US military for many years.

Even in a hierarchical organization such as the military, units which achieve Stage 3 or higher and adopt a more consensus-based decision making process make better decisions than those which do not.

Stage 4: Performing

This is the holy grail of team development, an achievement that fewer than 25 % of teams ever accomplish. Many people will go through their entire careers without ever experiencing a Stage 4 team.

In a Stage 4 team, productivity increases exponentially. Development teams produce higher quality products in less time and with less failure work. Surgical teams save more lives. Military units accomplish their missions with fewer errors and less loss of life (well, at least amongst members of the unit). A Stage 4 team is the quintessential well-oiled machine.

Stage 4 teams have achieved what Schein describes as a network of mutual helping. Consider how difficult it is for most people to ask for help or, for that matter, to receive help. In many businesses, particularly in the high-tech industry, asking for help is seen as a sign of weakness, an indication that you can't do your job. Contrast this to the Boston Red Sox in the years they've won the World Series. If members of the Sox were unwilling to help and be helped, fans would still be talking about the legendary "Curse of the Bambino." It is a significant accomplishment when a team achieves this level of performance.

Stage 4 teams have achieved an almost intuitive awareness of each member's strengths and weaknesses. Because they are functioning in a helping network, the team automatically rotates the right combination of members into position to deal with whatever problems the team is facing.

The exact mechanism by which the team functions so smoothly is not entirely clear. Based on Sandy Pentland's work at MIT on social signaling, it is quite likely that the team has unconsciously synchronized their body language and social signals. Social signals spread through group relatively slowly, which might explain why it takes several months for a team to achieve Stage 4. We do know that when people are added to the team relatively slowly, they are rapidly brought up to speed, but if too many people are added at once, the team can be disrupted.

The leader of a Stage 4 team is now a respected advisor and coach. Many leadership behaviors are now distributed throughout the team. The job of the leader is to focus on long-term strategy and keep the team operating at peak levels.

The biggest risks to Stage 4 teams are boredom and burnout. Our brains are built to seek novelty, and it isn't long before that metaphorical beautiful weather becomes just another boring day in paradise. Operating at a high performance level is also both incredibly enjoyable and exhausting. The most important task for the leader of a high performance team is to periodically shake up the routine a bit and make sure that members take breaks. Although a Stage 4 team can maintain its intensity for longer than any lower stage group, exhaustion will eventually set in. If not addressed, that exhaustion will destroy the group. We will come back to strategies for maintaining peak performance and preventing exhaustion in Chaps. 10–12.

Decision Making in a Stage 4 Team

Perhaps the best word to describe Stage 4 decision making is "intense."

I find when I work with businesses or teach college classes that most people imagine that a Stage 4 team is a sort of idyllic environment in which members seem to telepathically know what the other is thinking.

It is true that members of a high performance team will exhibit an almost preternatural level of coordination under certain conditions. This is particularly easy to see in top teams in sports, the military, and medicine. However, there is nothing idyllic about it.

In the original *Star Trek*, we periodically see scenes of brief, intense argument between Captain Kirk, Mr. Spock, and Dr. McCoy. Note the structure of the interaction: a problem is stated, information is sought, information is shared, opinions are sought, and opinions are shared. Then a decision is made. Despite the military command structure, the decision making process is highly consensual. This is, it turns out, an extremely accurate portrayal of how high performance teams make decisions.

Rather than being conflict free, high performance teams experience a great deal of conflict. However, because the team learned to argue effectively in Stage 2 and developed a high degree of trust, social structure, and decision making capability in Stage 3, conflicts are generally extremely brief. However, what they lack in length they make up in intensity. Members are extremely good at working together to rapidly analyze a problem, determine a course of action, and mobilize the resources to execute their plan.

Unbaking the Cake

Once you've baked a cake, you can't unbake it. The same is not true about teams.

Although it takes months for a team to progress through the stages of development, a team can regress in a heartbeat.

It's easiest to see this at Stage 2, where the conflict so upsets management or the group members that the group retreats to the comparative safety and peace of Stage 1. This can leave the group trapped in an approach-avoidance loop for months or years. Such an environment is extremely draining for group members, and can leave them feeling exhausted, burned out, or physically ill.

As I intimated in the section on Stage 4 teams, exhaustion and burnout can also cause a team to regress. Boredom and exhaustion cause a degradation of function on the individual and the group level. If it gets severe enough, team synchronicity will dissolve and will have to be relearned almost from scratch.

Adding too many people to a team, adding people too rapidly, or replacing too many members can also cause a team to regress to Stage 1. At a 51 % change or increase in membership, you virtually guarantee the team will regress. Members may not recognize that this has happened. The first clue is often the unexpected experience of conflicts spiraling out of control. This is what happened to Digital Equipment Corporation: by growing too rapidly, their tightly knit team structure regressed to Forming and then swiftly entered a prolonged conflict period.

Replacing the leader of a team with a new leader who does not buy into the team's way of working or who attempts to make rapid, radical changes can also destroy the team's cohesion. This is the "cultural immune response," which we discussed in Chap. 1. New leaders are well advised to take the time to understand how the team works and get to know the members before attempting to impose their own stamp on the team.

Why Teams Fail

Even the best looking teams can fail, sometimes dramatically. Just look at the 2012 Boston Red Sox. Failure, however, does not have to be dramatic. It can simply mean never achieving close to the level of performance of which the team is capable.

Recall that fewer than one in four teams reach the high performance stage. Many more could get there but fail to do so. The biggest problem is that far too many people fail to realize just how strong their teams could be. Of those who feel that their teams could do better, many of them don't really know how to make that happen. By reading this far, you're already ahead of probably 90 % of the people out there.

Common Issues Blocking Team Development

Inflexible Leadership

While we will look at leadership in more depth in the next chapter, there are a couple of points that are important to consider in the context of team development.

First of all, the leader and the team are symbiotic. Neither can exist without the other. The right way to lead depends on how mature the team is. This means that leaders need to be constantly adjusting their leadership style as the needs and abilities of the team change. Unfortunately, there is a strong belief that leadership is somehow independent of those being led. One has only to imagine the late Steve Jobs attempting to run the US Military or Colin Powell attempting to run Apple to realize how ludicrous that is (even apart from the minor fact that Steve Jobs is dead).

Second, leaders need to become comfortable with the idea of giving up power. The process of team development is one of a group developing increasing ability at self-determination. That process requires a leader to give up many of the trappings of leadership as the group progresses: group behavior in Forming is very much leader-determined, while in High Performance it is self-determined. If the leader views giving up power as a sign of weakness, that spells trouble ahead. When a leader responds to challenge by slapping down the challenger, the group learns that the safest course is to go along.

Remember, the best teams are not built just by the leader. Having members who support and build the team is at least as important.

Impatience

The next thing that gets in the way of team development is impatience. Early in my consulting career, I had a manager tell me that he needed his team performing Right Now. He didn't have time to wait six months or three months or whatever I said it would take. He needed results NOW. When I asked him how long he'd been having performance issues, he told me, "Three years."

Baking a cake takes time: you can't put the batter in the oven and have it done sooner than the recipe says just because you want it that way. You'll end up with a mass of batter or a burned mess. Similarly, teams take time. People are not robots:

we need time to learn to work with others. While people who know one another may start out with some advantages in that regard, even they need time to learn how each other works.

There is an old saying that a couple isn't really married until they've had their first fight. Teams are the same: people need to know they can argue with one another without destroying the relationship. This learning takes place in Stage 1. Trying to rush through Forming means that you don't have the foundation necessary to navigate the later stages. This is particularly evident in groups that communicate primarily through e-mail: because people tend to be less inhibited in their tone and use of language in e-mail, arguments will start before the group has the structure to manage them. If those arguments get out of control, the group can be frozen before it really gets going.

Handling Conflict

Another issue is managing conflict. Forming groups are highly conflict averse. That is fine, and even necessary for a time. However, as a permanent state of affairs, it's a recipe for mediocrity. Questioning, argument, debate is how we solve problems and test ideas. This behavior needs to be carefully moderated in Stage 1, but still needs to happen. The job of the manager is to make sure that it doesn't get out of hand, not to prevent it. As the group starts to approach Storming, you want them to already be developing the habits of effective debate. If the group is too afraid of conflict, then the moment Storming rears its head, the group will retreat back into the illusory safety of Forming.

Conversely, too much conflict is also a recipe for disaster. Once the debate becomes about personalities, motives, or character, you're done. When I hear someone saying, "Oh, you're just arguing that because you don't want to work late," or, "Well, of course *you* would say that," I know I'm hearing a team in trouble. Redirection is necessary. If a team member fails to respond to redirection, then you need to speak to them privately and possibly take additional actions. Conflicts that spiral out of control destroy teams.

Decision Making

Conflict, to be useful, needs to end in a decision. That decision may be that you need to obtain more information, but no matter how you look at things, there must be a way to move forward. The exact decision making method you use will depend on the stage of the group. Remember that early stage groups have a lot of trouble making decisions; if you leave it to the group to vote, you're going to be there a long time. The leader needs to moderate the discussion, and help the group reach a working consensus which she can then validate. While simply making the decision for the group can be effective in the short term, it doesn't enable the group to develop their own decision making skills.

It can help to assign someone to the job of "Devil's Advocate." This person is charged with raising questions and asking, "What could go wrong here?" By making this someone's job, it makes it easier to ask the tough questions and forces the group to address concerns. It's important, though, to rotate the role so that no one gets typecast. Even when someone is told to argue a contrary position, it's common to assume that's what they really believe.

Problem Solving and Mistakes

Teams that don't work when the manager isn't around are legion. It's a common problem, and common wisdom suggests that the team members lack motivation or are trying to goof off: when the cat's away, and all that.

Common wisdom may sound good, but is often wrong. This is no exception.

Groups can get stuck when the leader becomes the chief problem solver. While it may seem efficient for a leader who is also an expert in the domain to quickly solve problems and instruct the team on what to do, this approach again has the drawback of not enabling the team to develop the necessary skills and confidence in those skills. If the team doesn't think it can do the job, or isn't willing to try, then it doesn't matter how skillful they are at decision making and it doesn't matter how clear the goals are. It'll merely be that much clearer to them that they cannot do it. It may be necessary for leaders to walk through the problem solving process in front of their team and it will certainly be necessary for leaders to moderate the process.

Basically, teams need to solve problems as a team. This includes making the inevitable mistakes along the way. It is the act of making mistakes, learning from the experience, and moving on that enables the team to truly develop not just confidence in its skills but resilience as well. Without that experience, team confidence is brittle and team members considerably less willing to explore innovative solutions to problems. The broader organization's cultural attitudes toward mistakes is going to play a significant role here.

Understanding Hierarchy

While I was writing this, I was asked the question, "How important is hierarchy on a team? I've been told it's a problem. I'm responsible for 160 people, and I don't know what I'd do without a hierarchy."

Hierarchy is a tool. Whether it works for you or against you depends on how well you understand your tool and the situation in which you are using it. For my friend who has to manage 160 people, some sort of hierarchy is essential: without it, he'd swiftly be overwhelmed.

Hierarchy is a way of organizing and structuring a system. In a typical martial arts school, the hierarchy of belts provides each student a quick visual assessment of who knows what. This can make it easier for students to ask questions or know whom to imitate: learning is enhanced when we can imitate someone we see as similar to us. That person who is one belt ahead is easier to see as "like me" than the person who is many years and belts advanced. The hierarchy also provides visual feedback of the student's progress, a key component of maintaining motivation.

One of the key roles of the military ranking system is providing a method of coordinating precision operations. It does this by, amongst other things, providing clear rules for whom to listen to and under what circumstances and managing transitions of power should a leader be abruptly removed or cut off from the team. Like the belt system in martial arts, it also provides visual feedback of progress.

In a large organization, hierarchy provides a structured way to know where you are in your career, an easy way to identify nominal skill levels, and a means of coordinating different business activities.

However, when hierarchies become inflexible or bureaucratic, they can easily turn into obstacles. Small companies that attempt to impose rigid, large company hierarchies are asking for trouble: they don't need the overhead and lack of flexibility that hierarchies can create. A small business's biggest strength is that it can shift course quickly. A large company, on the other hand, is slower to change but has more resources. It is silly and counterproductive for a small business to impose large company hierarchy and thereby give up its flexibility when it doesn't have the resources to take advantage of that hierarchy.

Even in larger organizations, the structure needs to be flexible enough to permit good information flow up and down the hierarchy. Too rigid an adherence to hierarchy will reduce productivity and motivation and stifle innovation.

Hierarchy needs to be built out carefully, in accordance with the narrative, goals, and needs of the organization. Make sure you clearly identify what each level of the hierarchy means and how people move up. Periodically review your hierarchical structure and make sure it is still serving you, and not the other way around.

Hidden Assumptions

Teams also need to learn to examine the hidden assumptions that are preventing them from solving problems. This is not easy, since hidden assumptions are, by definition, hidden. However, as Harvard professor Ellen Langer observes, they can be extremely powerful. To give an example of this phenomenon in action, I was running a particular management training exercise. As part of the exercise, participants were each given a stack of items and had to trade around to obtain the things they actually needed. Each person involved saw me handing out bags containing the items.

As the exercise progressed, certain items, in this case, apples and leaves, turned out to be in short supply. Some participants quickly became convinced that other people were holding out on them, and refused to trade their items. The entire economy ground to a halt.

Here's the punchline: the exercise took place in a room with an open window and a tree next to that window. Anyone could have gotten a leaf by pulling it off the tree. There was also a cafeteria down the hall. Anyone could have gone and bought an apple. But because they had seen me hand out bags of items, they made the assumption that all items must be in the bags. This type of hidden assumption can be hard to spot, but it can halt your team in its tracks.

Internal Competition

This can be thought of as the "hot hand" question.

A hot hand in basketball is when a player is shooting better than normal. A star player with a hot hand is, therefore, going to be shooting incredibly well. Many players claim that it happens, and many statisticians point out that it doesn't. The argument against basically says that when you look at the frequency that a missed shot follows a successful shot, you find that the whole "hot hand" thing is just an illusion. It may feel like something is happening, but the results don't match.

The statisticians, however, are missing a key point: a basketball player is not on the court by himself. In other words, he's not playing in isolation. When a player is shooting extremely well, the other team is going to put more effort into guarding him. Of course, if that's correct, the extra effort expended guarding that star player should leave less available to guard other players on the team. In other words, the increased performance of a star should have the effect of increasing the performance of the entire team.

Once someone actually thought to ask that question and look at star performance in that context, the answer turned out to be that hot hands exist and that true star performers don't just perform well on their own—they increase the performance of everyone on the team.

Star performers in a business setting are the same, or at least they can be. The trick is to set up your team so that star performers increase everyone's productivity rather than just their own.

If you're only rewarding team members for their individual performance, you've got a problem. You've told your star performer to make herself look as good as possible, even at the cost of other team members: Imagine a basketball team where each player was only concerned about his own personal record and not about whether the team won or lost. The fact is, such a team wouldn't be all that successful. I've seen any number of software development teams, for example, structured in just that way, with exactly the expected results.

Internal competition fragments the team and prevents trust and cooperation from fully developing.

More Serious Issues: The Four Horsemen

No, not War, Famine, Pestilence, and Death. Nothing so melodramatic. These four horsemen are smaller, more mundane, but no less dangerous. First identified by psychologist John Gottman, they can show up wherever people are working together. Their names are personal criticism, contempt, defensiveness, and withdrawal.

Personal Criticism

When criticism is personal rather than objective, that is, it attacks the person and not the idea, it undermines trust and creates anger. The natural response to feeling attacked is to attack back. Internal combat destroys team cohesion and leads to defensiveness. Be wary of the person who makes everything a personal attack: "I'm not sure if this will work" is met by, "Are you questioning my competence?" or something similar. Transforming objective criticism into personal criticism prevents discussion, analysis, and effective problem solving. As a dominance game, it can be quite rewarding to the individual, but highly destructive to the group.

Contempt

Contempt, scorn, disdain, call it what you will, destroys trust and cooperation. As soon as one member of the team treats another as worthless, it closes the team off to their ideas, and makes it clear to them that their input is no longer welcome. Once that happens, the team steadily reduces the resources it has available to solve problems and accomplish its goals. Once the habit of contempt is established, it is very hard to break.

Defensiveness

When people feel they have to defend, problems don't get solved. Fingers may be pointed, blame may be assigned, but the actual problem? That gets forgotten or hidden. Defensiveness causes mistakes to compound on mistakes. Defensiveness and personal criticism feed off one another, destroying constructive communication.

Withdrawal

Working at home is one thing. Withdrawing is another. When your employees won't even engage with one another that tells you that they don't care. Once they no longer care about the team, the product, or one another, they're not going to try. About all you can hope for is that they'll work hard enough to keep getting a paycheck. Once a better opportunity comes along, they won't even do that. Employees who care don't look for better opportunities, and it takes an amazing opportunity to lure away employees who care. Quitting is the ultimate form of withdrawal and contempt for the company.

Argument, debate, questioning, all these need to be part of the life of your team. The best teams are those that know how to fight well. But when the four horsemen join your team, the arguments are personal, the debate endless, the questioning ineffective or non-existent.

Final Thoughts on Team Development

As I often remind my jujitsu students, if it was easy, they wouldn't need me and they wouldn't need to practice. The process of leading a team from formation to high performance is difficult. Mistakes are inevitable. The real secret is learning from those mistakes and building on them. The more you understand about what is normal and what is not the easier that process will be.

Questions to Consider

1. What are you doing to help your team improve?
2. Why might showing them who's boss be counterproductive?
3. What stage is your team in? How can you tell?
4. What are you doing to help your team help you help them?
5. What are the advantages of taking the time to help your team progress through the stages of team development? What's stopping you?

Chapter 4
Leadership, Power, and Emotional Intelligence

James Bond movies always follow some very predictable patterns. The movies always open with Bond involved in an extremely dangerous mission, which he single-handedly accomplishes to the tune of numerous explosions. Bond then shows up in M's office in London to be briefed on the mission that will be the focus of the current movie. That done, Bond picks up his arsenal of tech toys from R (formerly Q), and is off. M, meanwhile, remains behind trying to keep track of what is going on and presumably coordinating other agents and missions.

James Bond is, of course, the ultimate individual contributor. While various people might help him from time to time, he is basically on his own. Because Bond has a script writer, he is never going to become a manager: that would spoil all the fun. Of course, we can imagine what might happen were Bond to end up behind a desk running the operation. SPECTRE would hatch some sort of dastardly plot and the agents sent out to stop them would all be killed, except for the dying guy who escapes to tell Bond what happened. Bond would then have to go back into the field and foil SPECTRE himself.

Unlike James Bond, many individual contributors do end up in management. Perhaps it has something to do with their jobs not being as exciting as Bond's, or maybe it is just that that's the only promotion path in the business. Either way, it's not unusual to see excellent salesmen becoming sales managers, excellent engineers, engineering managers, excellent marketers, marketing managers, and so forth. Like our hypothetical Bond scenario, however, many of them unsuccessfully fight the urge to do everything themselves.

Being an individual contributor means being in the trenches getting your hands dirty. While it is very frustrating at times, it can also be very rewarding. Perhaps more important is the fact that you get to be the person taking action. You don't have to sit around and wonder, you know what's happening. You're in the middle of it. You are like James Bond, only without the explosions, deadly tech toys, and, of course, the sex. On the other hand, odds are pretty good that no one is trying to kill you.

Now, like Bond's boss, M, you are a manager. Being a manager means not being in the thick of things. It means not doing the work yourself. It means going

S. R. Balzac, *Organizational Psychology for Managers*,
Management for Professionals, DOI: 10.1007/978-1-4614-8505-6_4,
© Springer Science+Business Media New York 2014

against years of training because now you have to work through others. Now you have to give instructions to your team of individual contributors and wait to hear back from them. You no longer know exactly what is going on, because you are not doing it. This can be a very stressful and unpleasant experience, especially if your manager is someone who is always asking for updates because she finds not knowing as unpleasant and stressful as do you.

Truth be told, the transition to management can be a very disorienting experience. Unlike a James Bond movie, if you don't manage your team well and there's a problem, your direct reports won't appreciate you coming into save the day. In fact, such an act would only make it harder for you to gain respect as a manager instead of as an individual contributor who happens to sign time cards.

What Is a Leader?

A question I get asked all the time is some variant of, "What is a leader?" The question may be, "How do I recognize a real leader?" or "What do true leaders look like?" or any of a dozen other versions of the question. I created a stretch of dead air on a radio show one time by responding, "Whatever we think a leader looks like." The host apparently didn't expect that!

We are biased toward seeing as a leader someone who fits our cultural image of a leader. Conversely, we build our model of leaders in the image of other leaders. As we discussed in Chap. 1, James Kirk was John Kennedy in outer space. This bias can get in our way, though, when it prevents us from recognizing the real leader or from giving people the opportunity to lead because they don't fit the image we're looking for. We'll look at some activities to identify real leaders when we discuss training in Chap. 8.

Conversely, how the leader sees her role is shaped and reinforced through television, movies, books, and other media. It is also shaped by the cultural assumptions each organization makes about what constitutes appropriate leader behavior. As a result, leaders act according to those assumptions often without ever questioning them. This can trap a leader into taking on a role that they are not comfortable in but feel obligated to play. This becomes a serious problem when it interferes with the ability of the leader to accept feedback or when followers become unwilling to provide feedback. Without feedback, error correction cannot occur: if the leader misses the "bridge out" sign, and no one is willing to speak up, the results can be more than a little embarrassing.

At root, though, being a leader really means only one thing: you have followers. A leader without followers is just some joker taking a walk.

Fortunately, there are many ways to convince people to follow you; unfortunately, there are many ways to convince people to follow you. People will follow the leader because that leader is the standard bearer for a cause they believe in, or for a reward, or because that leader exemplifies particular values or a vision, or because that leader is providing structure and certainty. People will also follow out of fear or greed or as a way of hurting someone else. There is no implied morality in being able to convince people to follow you. Fundamentally, people follow a leader for their own reasons, not the leader's. The art of leadership is, to a great extent, aligning other people's goals with the goals of the leader and the organization.

Much of leadership is based on a purely transactional relationship: you follow and support the leader, the leader rewards you. While this is the basis of almost all forms of leadership, if that is all the relationship consists of, it is very limited. The best leaders build on the transactional element to inspire their followers to greater efforts than can be obtained only through rewards. This is commonly known as "transformational leadership," which certainly sounds impressive. In a very real sense, the information in this book is really about to become that type of leader without getting trapped in definitions.

The other critical point of effective leadership is recognizing that being a leader is not a static enterprise. As the term implies, a leader must lead. Change initiatives fail when organizational leadership isn't out there in front showing the way. People stop following when the leader stops moving.

Part of how the leader moves forward is by changing and developing their own styles and techniques of leadership. As we discussed in the previous chapter, the needs of the team dictate the approach of the leader. A leader can no more treat a Stage 3 group like a Stage 1 group than a parent can treat a 15-year old like a 3-year old (despite, as many parents observe, certain behavioral similarities).

The key lesson here is that the external trappings of leadership are not leadership. Giving instructions, dividing up work, setting an agenda, taking questions, are all part of leadership, but they are not leadership. Those are tools which a leader might use to get a job done. Good leaders, like any master craftsman, learn to use their tools well.

Leaders Versus Managers

Before we go any further, it's worth addressing a question I hear quite frequently: what is the difference between a leader and a manager?

The most popular answers elevate leaders and disparage managers. Such a characterization is both unfair and inaccurate.

One person cannot single-handedly lead a large organization, particularly a geographically diverse one. That overall leader needs people who will act as her lieutenants, people who will convey the organizational narrative and shape it to fit the particular task, department, or location they are in. The job of the manager is to rally his team, develop their skills, and bring out the most in them. Good managers know that you cannot put into someone what is not there; rather, you build people by honing what is there. This is another aspect of leadership.

Ultimately, the biggest difference between management and leadership is scope: while the leader may set the overall vision and direction for the organization, the managers then bring it to life within their particular areas. People who truly cannot do that should not be managers.

What Is Power?

I once had the opportunity to work out with some very physically strong judo players. These people were strong enough to literally just pick me up and drop me on the ground. They were then subsequently tossed around by a skinny 75 year old man who didn't even work up a sweat in the process. Who was more powerful?

Power is a funny thing. Leadership is associated with power and power is associated with leadership. People appointed to a leadership position in an organization will often try to do things through the use of power: "I told you to do this. Now get it done or else!" Sometimes this works. Often, it produces some unexpected and unpleasant side effects. In one management training exercise I ran, one of the participants proudly boasted at the end that he got what he wanted by making it clear to others just what would happen to them if they didn't comply. He was subsequently shocked when he found he learned during the debriefing that his "team" was so angry that they had thoroughly undermined him. As one person summed it up, "You only got what you knew to ask about." It was the equivalent of proudly negotiating a $2500 bonus when you could have had $25,000 or even $250,000.

When you sweep away all the verbiage and confusion, power really comes down to a very few elements. Power originates from five sources or bases of power, and can be applied in three ways.

The bases of power are:

- Legitimate power
- Reward power
- Coercive power
- Expert power
- Referent power

The application of power boils down to:

- Power over
- Power from
- Power to

We'll look at each of these individually.

Legitimate Power

Legitimate power is the power someone is granted through their position or role in an organization. This can mean many things.

When someone is appointed to head a team or given a title, that is a form of legitimate power. A college professor, for example, holds legitimate power in his class. A manager holds legitimate power within her team.

Being chosen as the standard bearer for your particular cause provides a certain degree of legitimate power, at least within the community of people who believe in that cause. The presidential primary process in the United States is an example of that process in action: the winner of the primary is designated the candidate and gains a certain degree of power thereby. A common tactic, therefore, is for those competing in the primary to try to make it appear that their selection is inevitable or in some other way lay claim to the legitimate power they are seeking. Convincing enough people that you already have legitimate power is one way of gaining legitimate power.

To some degree, it almost doesn't matter how that legitimate power is obtained, provided it is gained through culturally acceptable practices that people agree bestow legitimacy. Founding a company is one way of gaining legitimate power, as is being appointed by a board of directors, being elected to office, being promoted, or even engineering a hostile takeover. The forms and rituals of how legitimacy is conferred are extremely important. Most organizations have some sort of small ceremony when someone is promoted into a role that confers legitimate power; part of this accreditation ritual usually involves showing people what the person being promoted did to earn their new legitimate power. This is part of the organizational narrative we discussed in Chap. 2. We will further at accreditation ceremonies in Chap. 8.

Because we have fairly universal cultural beliefs that persons who hold legitimate power, by whatever means obtained, should be listened to, legitimate power can produce obedience. It does not necessarily produce enthusiasm. Indeed, when someone who is widely disliked is granted legitimate power, it is not unusual to see some people leave while others take the attitude that the person must be obeyed because that's what we do.

Legitimate power can break down, though, when someone chooses to ignore it. Without some means of backing up the position of the person holding legitimate power, that position will cease to hold power. In one business, for example, the VP of Marketing decided to fire one of his employees. He terminated the person, at which point the CEO unterminated her. Exactly why the CEO waited so long to act was never clear; his method of handling the situation, however, completely destroyed any sense of legitimacy held by the VP of Marketing, who quit shortly thereafter. As we discussed in Chap. 3, when a team symbolically kills a leader, it becomes that much harder for someone else to take charge. We can now see that this is because the legitimacy of the leader's role is weakened. It is also the reason why, when a leader is removed from power by the organization, part of the process involves, or should involve, a degradation ritual in which the person is symbolically separated from their role: the act of separation, or demonstrating why the person is no longer holding legitimate power, preserves the power associated with the role.

Reward Power

Reward power is simply the ability to give rewards to those who follow you. As Bruce Bueno de Mesquita and Alastair Smith discuss in *The Dictator's Handbook*, this is the primary means that dictators use to gain loyalty. If you happen to be a dictator with effectively unlimited resources at your disposal, it's a great technique. However, most organizational leaders may find themselves a bit more limited.

Reward power is definitely a useful tool: the ability to give your followers awards such as higher salaries, bonuses, titles, recognition, vacation time, or other gifts is a powerful means of buying loyalty. The drawback, as we will discuss when we get to motivation, is that the loyalty is only as strong as the rewards. Moreover, as time passes, the same amount of reward buys less and less loyalty. When people are bound to you only through the rewards you give them, you are constantly risking losing them to someone who will give them more. However, small rewards tied to emotionally significant events, for instance recognizing an employee's birthday or anniversary with a small gift, can do wonders for building loyalty. This sort of non-job related reward helps demonstrate that you care about the employee as a person, and that is very powerful indeed!

Using reward power well is surprisingly tricky. When you make the reward the goal of the activity, you gradually shift people's goals away from the vision and goals of the company and focus them instead on obtaining the reward. That doesn't mean you can't reward exceptional performance or congratulate the team on hitting a milestone; it means that you make the celebration about the performance and the reward is merely the icing on the cake. Practically speaking, it's the difference between saying, "If you hit this milestone I'll take the team out to dinner," and saying after the fact, "I'm extremely impressed by how hard everyone worked to hit the milestone and to thank you for your efforts I'd like to take the team out to dinner."

Remember our discussion of feedback systems in the organizational narrative. Rewards work best when they are seen as feedback that you are helping realize the goals of the company. When the reward serves the purpose of telling people that they are on the right track and doing the right things, they work extremely well. People like having their efforts recognized.

The size of the reward also matters. Because large, lavish rewards are valuable in and of themselves, if the reward is too large it becomes the point of the effort. You want your rewards to be large enough to be meaningful, but not so large that people can convince themselves that they are only working for the reward. Make no mistake, this is a difficult balancing act.

Reward power often goes hand in hand with legitimate power, although not always. People holding legitimate power and not reward power are usually perceived as less effective leaders than those who hold both. In many organizations, a lack of reward power will undermine legitimate power.

Coercive Power

This is the power to punish or otherwise attempt to compel people to obey your wishes. Dictators, for example, usually couple their reward power with an army or a loyal police force in order to back up their desires. This can be a very effective combination, if you just happen to have an army at your disposal. Otherwise, it is useful to understand the strengths and limits of coercive power.

Coercive power in most organizations can include a sharp word, docking someone's pay, suspension, taking away vacation time, assigning less pleasant hours, assigning undesirable tasks, firing, etc. What any individual manager can do is determined by the rules and culture of the organization. Just because the rules say something is okay doesn't mean much if you happen to cross one of the unwritten cultural lines. While both managers and dictators generally have the power to terminate someone, dictators are better at making it stick.

Coercion is difficult to use because of the nature of the beast. The goal of power is generally to get someone to do what you want. Coercion, though, doesn't necessarily do that. It's very good at telling someone you didn't like what they did, but not what they should do. You also run into the problem that the harder you make it for someone to say no, the harder you make it for them to say yes. No one likes being compelled. When you apply coercive power, you force the other person to lose face if they give in to you; as we've already discussed, people do not like to lose face. Thus, coercion will often bring about resistance, grudging compliance, or a more subtle undermining of the team's goals. In many cases, when the coercion ceases, the behavior reverts, wearing the manager down over time.

Coercive power when used to remove someone from the organization can be very effective, if that person's presence is the problem. As we'll see in Chap. 7, organizational jerks need to be dealt with quickly and effectively. Coercive power is an effective way to address such situations.

The trick to using coercive power effectively is to use it sparingly and pay attention to when it doesn't work. If a few quiet words to an employee don't change the behavior, it's worth taking a second look at the situation. Quite often, the behavior is being rewarded in some fashion: a quintessential organizational error is criticizing someone for not being a good team player, and then evaluating everyone based on their individual performance. A very small amount of reward can offset a great deal of coercion.

In one rather dramatic example, at one company, a certain engineer would scream and pound on tables, essentially throwing a temper tantrum, when he didn't get his way. Although he was frequently criticized for his behavior, other people found the experience so unpleasant that they would give in, often preemptively, just to avoid the fight. His manager, sadly, took the view that so long as he was producing, the behavior wasn't enough of a problem to fire him. Anything short of that simply didn't counterbalance the benefit this person got from his behavior. The net result was that the behavior not only continued but grew worse over time. The damage done to the team was immense.

If you want coercion to work, first make sure the person isn't being accidentally, or intentionally, rewarded for the behavior you are trying to change.

Coercive power also tends to reduce feedback: people won't give you information if they think they might get punished. They might tell you what you want to hear, but real problems are hidden. This prevents the organization from taking effective measures to correct errors and improve performance. As fans of James Bond well know, many a Bond movie opens with the villainous Ernst Stavro Blofeld killing off one of his agents for failing SPECTRE. SPECTRE then goes on to make their usual set of mistakes and Bond defeats them. Blofeld is left to wonder why nothing ever changes.

Coercive power usually works best when coupled with reward power. Coercive power by itself, on the other hand, is more likely to be over used: in any situation, when we don't know what else to do, we do what we can do. If all we can do is apply coercive power, that's what we do.

Expert Power

Expert power is the power you gain through being recognized as an expert in some area. Within a specific martial art, a black belt is a marker of expert power. College degrees, titles, publications, are all markers of varying degrees of expertise. Being designated a Senior Engineer or Chief Scientist, for example, denotes a level of expertise with all the benefits that the bestowing organization or culture provides. Being a medical doctor or a psychologist represent different forms of expert power.

Expert power typically brings with it the ability to influence discussions and propel the group to adopt a particular decision. It adds weight and credibility to the actions of the group, to an endorsement, or recommendation. It is common to attach expert endorsements to all sorts of different claims. In the 1940s, one brand of cigarettes used to advertise that four out of five doctors who smoke preferred their brand.

Expert power relies on the belief that the expert knows more about their area of expertise than the rest of us, and hence following the advice of the expert is a good idea. Of course, paying careful attention to how the claim or advice is worded is often a good idea. In the cigarette commercial, for example, the claim is used to create an impression of experts backing smoking, but we have no data on how many doctors didn't smoke at all.

Organizationally, more senior experts are generally given more trust and are more likely to be assumed to be correct than less senior experts. This sort of seniority may be based on degrees, years of experience, project successes, or other metrics determined by the culture. At DEC, for instance, the ability to argue logically and well was often a key determinant of expertise rather than any particular degree.

Having expert power may also cause someone to be granted legitimate power, for example as the technical lead of a team or as an engineering manager. One of the problems with expert power is that it is often assumed that expertise in one area translates into expertise in a different area: for example, salesman and sales manager, engineer and engineering manager, etc. Unfortunately, a great deal is lost in translation. A manager needs to develop expert power as a manager, a leader expert power as a leader.

Under certain conditions expert power can also lead to reward or coercive power. A licensed psychologist can, in some circumstances, involuntarily commit someone.

Expert power can also cause someone to gain referent power.

Referent Power

Referent power is the power you gain because people admire you, believe in you, and want to be like you in some ways. There are many ways of gaining referent power.

Being a trustworthy person, living according to a set of values and not changing with the blowing of the wind is an important aspect of referent power.

Acting as a positive example of your organization's cultural values will usually enable someone to develop referent power. Having a reputation for honesty and fair dealing usually creates referent power—and it's wise to be wary in organizations where that is not the case! Simply being granted legitimate power in an organization can lead to referent power, as can taking the time to build positive relationships with your team; we'll discuss both of those later in this chapter.

People often gain referent power by doing things people admire or accomplishing something rare or difficult. Olympic athletes, for example, are popular spokespersons because their athletic success creates referent power: although we know that wearing Nikes won't actually make us jump like Michael Jordan, nonetheless the association is powerful.

Volunteers within an organization can also gain referent, and sometimes legitimate, power through their actions. Although they may not hold any formal position, by taking on certain roles, they gain respect and are viewed as having power sometimes beyond just the space in which they volunteer.

Both reward and coercive power are more readily accepted if the leader has also gained referent power. Rewards are seen as more genuine and punishments as more fair.

An expert with referent power is going to be more highly respected and listened to. An expert without referent power is more likely to be ignored or find that their opinions are not taken as seriously. Expert power and referent power support one another.

Although the act of awarding legitimate power will often grant some degree of referent power, unlike legitimate, reward, and coercive power, referent power is only partially granted by the organization: an organization cannot declare you admirable if you are not. Hence, it cannot be as easily taken away either. However, it is possible to lose referent power. This typically happens through either diminishing the accomplishment or demonstrating that the accomplishment was not attained in a fair or just fashion. In other words, someone can lose referent power if they cheated; whether they will or not depends on the situation. The efforts to argue that killing Osama bin Laden was purely a matter of luck, that Barack Obama just happened to be president when bin Laden was found, is an example of an attempt to destroy referent power by minimizing the accomplishment. The revelations about the Lance Armstrong doping conspiracy represent the second: Armstrong, who won seven consecutive Tour de France titles, was subsequently charged by the US Anti-Doping Agency with doping and running a doping conspiracy. In August 2012, USADA recommended he be stripped of his titles, and later presented a great deal of evidence supporting their claim. Whether these revelations will strip Armstrong of his referent power remains to be seen but the response does not bode well for him.

It is worth noting that some people are often able to maintain their referent power despite numerous revelations about dishonest methods, poor character, and failed projects. People who are that slick and charming are extremely dangerous. Their charm often masks a frightening degree of amorality and ruthlessness.

Once referent power is lost, particularly through the second method, it is very difficult to regain it. That profound a breech of trust is hard to repair.

Over time, running a team requires less and less technical expertise and more interpersonal expertise. Without referent power, the rest won't matter in the not so very long run.

From, Over, and To: Applying Power

Power over represents the sphere of influence of your legitimate, reward, and coercive powers. If you have power over someone, you can use your position to influence, reward, or punish them. You typically have power over the people in your team, but may not have power over the people in someone else's team. You typically have no power over someone in another organization. Power over also applies to expert and referent power, but the behavior is slightly different. Expert power can transcend your organizational boundaries: the greater your level of expertise, the more likely this is to happen. However, expert power is usually limited to fields in which that expertise is valued. Referent power also transcends boundaries, and may take you beyond the limits of expertise. People with a great deal of referent power are respected and emulated even by their competitors: consider top athletes, scientists, or famous business leaders.

Power from is the ability to resist someone else's application of power. Power of all kinds has its limits and costs. While you may nominally have power over the people in your department, someone with sufficiently high expert power may be able to ignore some or all of your attempts to use power. Someone with connections or influence may also be able to resist the application of power. At one company, one person who was the close friend of the CEO was able to get away with almost anything. He routinely blew off instructions and commitments, ignored bugs he was assigned to fix, and would frequently go off on his own tangents leaving the rest of the team in the lurch. However, nothing could be done because the CEO would defend him. This person had "power from" even though he had no power to actually do anything.

Power to is the ability to accomplish things. A software engineer has the power to write code. A manager with reward power may be able to give raises or bonuses to his employees, but not to other manager's employees. Someone who is good at sharing power has the "power to" influence others and enable them to get work done. "Power to" works best when you can use it to increase the power of others. Done well, this dramatically increases team performance. Granting power to others in this way requires trust and a tolerance for the inevitable mistakes that come with learning.

As you can see, power is somewhat fluid and the different bases of power interact with one another. When power is used unsuccessfully, the person using power is weakened. Depending on the nature of the situation, that person's ability to wield power in that environment can be temporarily or permanently reduced.

Communications

Communications get the blame for an awful lot of organizational problems. Sometimes it's even justified.

In order to function, members of any organization have to communicate with one another. If they don't, not a whole lot gets done. The trick is to recognize the patterns of communications and the nature of the message.

In many groups that believe they aren't communicating, they really are: just not with one another. If you're talking to the wrong person, it doesn't really matter how many good communications tricks you learn. Effective communications require a sender and a receiver. When you only have one of the two, it doesn't work so well.

Leaders easily and naturally become the center of communications in their group. Practically speaking, this means that no matter who is talking at the moment, the leader is the only one viewed as a valid sender or a valid receiver. People might address the group, but the message is really just for the leader; this is particularly true in Stage 1 where the leader is the one making the decisions. Similarly, no matter who is speaking, group members will often attempt to gauge the leader's response before expressing their own. If we were to draw the information flow, it would look like a wheel, or sometimes a letter Y or a chain, with the leader as the center. Once you know to look, it becomes comparatively easy to spot.

"But we send emails to everyone!" is a refrain I hear quite often. That may be true, but it doesn't change the basic wheel structure. When you are communicating in a wheel, many people will ignore the email until the leader responds or will rapidly recalibrate their responses. This does change as the group develops, as we will discuss shortly. The goal is to transform the pattern into a star or a circle where everyone talks, and listens, to everyone.

The level of urgency of the communications also matters. Some years ago I worked for one Silicon Valley company where my manager had a habit of walking into my office just before noon and asking for information that he needed "immediately." So much for lunch.

I quickly noticed that no matter how urgently he needed the information, he would not act on it for days. The urgency was really about satisfying his needs for control rather than any real business need. I learned to leave for lunch earlier.

When all communications are "urgent" or of "high importance" then pretty soon none of them are. People discount the urgency, which leads to an increase in "volume" from the sender. This triggers another round of scurrying about until people realize that this new level of urgency is also a chimera. Unfortunately, when you constantly amp up the urgency you have the side effect of reducing communications, not increasing it. In the end, all that really happens is that stress levels go up and information flow is blocked. Save the urgency for the things that really are. If you are convinced you always need an instant response, odds are something else is very wrong.

Emotions and Leadership

As *Star Trek*'s supposedly emotionless Mr. Spock so clearly demonstrates, emotions are a critical piece of leadership. While logic is fine to get people to think, emotion is what gets people to act. The trick is to understand which emotions really matter.

If your first thought is excitement and interest, you are on the right track. As we discussed in Chap. 2, people have to care about the goals of the company. The organizational story and vision is the beginning. However, we also need to support that interest and build the emotional structure to enable the team to be successful over long periods of time. In particular, we need to understand that the emotional needs and strengths of the team change as it develops from Stage 1 to Stage 4. To do that we need to look at trust, fear, autonomy, relatedness, and competence, after which we will discuss how leader behaviors need to change with the development of the group.

Trust

Effective communications comes from building trust, and trust comes from taking the time to build connections with employees and from, yes, communicating. The problem is that many people don't typically drop by to chat with the boss. If you only talk to the ones who do drop by, you end up with limited information and communications structure that's more like a game of telephone. There is also a very good chance that you'll split your team into an in group and an out group. If you really want to get people talking to you, you need to seek them out. IBM's founder, Tom Watson, was legendary for showing up unannounced at different IBM locations and just dropping into chat with different people. He was trusted as few CEOs have ever been: employees believed that he cared about them personally. The stories about him reflect that to this day.

Trust is not just about keeping your word. It's also about living up to the image of leadership in your organization and honoring the implicit promises in the organizational story and culture. If the story your organization tells is one of people being recognized for their work, you need to make sure that happens.

If something happens to cause a breech of trust, you need to acknowledge it, apologize, and explain what happened. Economic conditions or other surprises sometimes mean that promises can't be honored, be that a raise or sending someone to a conference they were looking forward to attending. When that happens, you need to be honest about the situation. Trying to deny it or fool people only compounds the problem whereas repairing trust makes it stronger.

In a very real sense, trust and safety go hand in hand: when we don't trust someone, we don't feel safe around them and, conversely, when we don't feel safe around someone we also don't trust them. We tend to be more on our guard and less willing to engage. Commitment, innovation, feedback, and intelligent risk taking are sharply reduced. Careless risk taking, on the other hand, tends to increase.

Trust, it must be remembered, is a two way street. As your employees learn to trust you, you also learn to trust them. That means developing an accurate picture of their strengths and weaknesses. If you force people to operate in their areas of weakness, they will be more likely to fail. This reduces your trust in them and causes them to view you as setting them up for failure. That, in turn, reduces trust in you.

Part of building trust is recognizing process. Every person in an organization tries to work in the ways they work best. Each person seeks to develop their own process. That process is, in a very real sense, a manifestation of who that person is in the organizational community. If you cannot trust someone's process, you will not be able to trust them; conversely, if you do not trust someone's process, they will not trust you: you are essentially telling them they cannot be who they are. When you trust someone's process, however, you build trust in them and enable them to trust you. This increases productivity, motivation and loyalty. Fundamentally, as psychologist Tony Putman observed, a person becomes what he is treated as being. How you treat the process is how you treat the person.

Recognize that trusting the process is not just about trusting that the results will be what you expect. That is important, but it's a surprisingly small piece of the puzzle. There is no such thing as a perfect process and no process will always execute without something going wrong. True trust comes when you know that people can be trusted to handle mistakes and unpredictable events. Trust in our own skills comes from learning that we can make a mistake and recover; without that, trust is brittle. Trust in a process comes from recognizing that the process may sometimes give us the wrong answer, but it also gives us the ability to recognize that fact and recover.

Finally, how you act in a crisis can make or break people's trust in you. A leader who panics in a crisis can undo months or years of team building and trust. On the flip side, being able to remain calm and focused in a crisis can increase trust as you become seen as someone who can be counted on when the chips are down. However, some trust must already exist for your behavior in a crisis to matter: in the Mann Gulch disaster, Wagner Dodge never built enough trust with his team for them to trust him when he figured out an innovative way to save their lives; as a result, most of them died. Conversely, after hurricane Sandy hit the east coast in October of 2012, President Obama won praise from some of his harshest critics for his calm, disciplined, organized response to the disaster.

Your response in a crisis is the model for how others will respond. If you remain calm and build safety, people will respond to that and trust you more than ever. If you panic, you will reduce perceptions of safety and trust will decline.

Fear

There are two aspects of fear that we need to look at: the leader's and the team's.

In the movie, "First Knight," Richard Gere's Lancelot explains to a young man the secrets of becoming a master swordsman: study your opponent, know how to recognize the moment of victory or defeat and wait for it, and not care whether you live or die. At the last, the young man stares at Lancelot in shock. In the modern sport of fencing, a master fencer will say almost the same thing: the secret to winning is to learn how, and when, to not care.

This is doubtless counterintuitive: the key to living is to not care if you live or die? The key to winning is to not care if you win or lose? Paradoxically, when an athlete cares too deeply about the outcome, they start to judge each action. In combat or competition, that judgment can lead to doubt or fear of failure. Doubt or fear lead to hesitation which leads to defeat. Only be developing his skill and confidence to the point that he believes the outcome is not in doubt can the swordsman successfully not care. However, the swordsman who never doubts himself will never develop that level of skill. When preparing, the swordsman must care deeply and passionately; once swords are drawn, it is time to not care. He must have the patience to create the moment of victory, recognize it when it comes, and then strike without fear or hesitation.

Oddly enough, a leader is in the same position as the master swordsman: the leader who cares too much chokes his team; the leader who cares too little does not prepare. Like the swordsman, to maximize his chances of success, the leader must learn how, and when, to not care whether they succeed or fail. This is no easy task. Teams regularly suffer from leaders who allow the fear of failure to guide their actions and who, therefore, never allow the team to operate at its highest levels. Recently, I heard a leader state that he would not provide his team with clear guidelines for a project, preferring that they check with him at each step, "to avoid problems." He couldn't understand why they were so "unmotivated." In fact, they were highly motivated: motivated to avoid the constant stream of criticism they received. And the leader? His primary motivation appeared to be fear of losing status if things weren't perfect.

Fear and trust go hand in hand: the leader who does not trust her team will always be worried about failure. The leader who does trust her team will have the confidence to move forward without hesitation. A leader who is scared of failure tends to pass that fear on to the team.

More generally, the team looks to the leader as the exemplar of how to behave or what to expect in different situations. When the leader is scared, the team becomes scared: after all, the leader supposedly knows more than the team. If the leader goes toward fear, the team follows. Thus, part of handling fear is learning to project confidence to the team without denying the presence of the real risks that may exist. When you deny the existence of a genuine risk, that only serves to tell people that it must be really bad if the leader won't talk about it.

Of course, this is only half the battle. Leaders also need to break themselves of the habit of using fear as a tool to increase performance. Fear can produce a short-term bump in performance, but at a very high cost in terms of team development. Just as a scared fencer is already defeated before the bout begins, a team scared of failure is far more likely to fail. What you focus on is what you get. We'll discuss more about this in Chaps. 5 and 11.

Autonomy

As we discussed in Chap. 2, autonomy is a natural and normal need. People want to develop their own processes and work in the ways that best fit who they are and how they approach solving problems. Effective team development is balancing this desire for individual autonomy against the needs of the team and the larger organization. At a basic level, autonomy stems from having an appropriate structure: too much structure stifles people, constraining behavior to the point where people spend the bulk of their energy just complying with the rules; too little structure creates chaos and uncertainty, forcing people to spend their energy just trying to figure out who is doing what.

The specifics of how organizational structures are set up will vary from organization to organization. The goal of structure is to enable team members to have some mechanism by which they can know what to expect and when to expect it. The mechanism must have some degree of flexibility, especially when aspects of the work may be ambiguous or novel. The openness or looseness of the structure is directly proportional to the degree of trust in the organization and the team. Lower stage teams have not yet developed much trust and hence need more structure: people need to see that everyone is involved. As members develop trust and confidence in one another, it becomes easier to increase autonomy.

Determining how much autonomy your team can handle is a process of testing and listening to the feedback you receive. Too little autonomy and you'll hear about it! People will be complaining that they feel tied in knots or can't sneeze without permission. Too much autonomy and you'll hear people complaining that they aren't sure what to do or that other people aren't around when they need to speak to them. When people are constantly insisting that they must be able to talk to someone else on the team Right This Minute, that's a sign that your structure isn't working. You might need to temporarily decrease overall autonomy, you may need to help people recognize that they don't need an answer right away, or you may need to help the team develop better problem solving techniques. No matter which it is, you'll need to modify the structure in some way.

Another benefit of autonomy is that it reduces team members goofing off, provided, of course, that you set it up correctly. Autonomy is the "I" in team. Without that "I," there is no personal connection to the results. When there is no personal connection, people are more likely to goof off. As we discussed in Chap. 2, one of the goals of the organizational narrative is to help people identify with the company by helping them see both how they contribute to the outcomes and why their contributions are important. When we lack that personal connection, when we lack autonomy, we get people goofing off. The more people feel their contribution is valuable, and the more they feel that they have the freedom to put their own personal stamp on how they work, the greater the connection and the harder they work. We'll look further at autonomy and control in Chaps. 10–12.

Relatedness

Relatedness operates on a number of levels: there is the relationship between the leader and the individual team members; there is the relationship each group member has with each other group member; there is the relationship between the individual and the team; and there is the relationship between the team and the larger organization. The organizational vision and narrative we discussed in Chap. 2 help build a member's relatedness to the organization. Also, the longer someone is part of the organization and the more deeply immersed they become in its culture also help build relatedness.

Within a group, though, it is initially the leader's ability to connect with each member of the group that determines relatedness: the biggest factor in people staying at or leaving a job is their relationship with their boss, followed closely by their relationship with their coworkers. The leader needs to set the example by building connections with each person, and encouraging group members to build connections with one another. Members of the team must become more than just the jobs they do: when we are too closely identified with the job, we become tools. When we speak to our tools at all, it is generally to yell at them for not performing as we wish.

Leaders create relatedness when they get to know their employees and appreciate them as people. It's fine to congratulate someone on a major out of work accomplishment: running a marathon, kid getting a part in a play, etc. When people feel appreciated, they work harder. When people learn to appreciate one another, they also develop trust and increase their ability to problem solve and innovate.

While it is not necessary that every member of the team be close friends with one another, team members do need a sufficient relationship to be able to agree on goals, debate methodology, and argue issues without it becoming personal. When it becomes personal, the game is over. The relationship must be strong enough to support the network of mutual helping.

Competence

This is not just about hiring competent people; indeed, that is possibly the least important element. The real key here is to focus on building an atmosphere of competence. Competence comes out of a belief that you can succeed and that the team can succeed. Leaders can build a mindset of competence through building trust and structure so that each team member knows that the others have his back. The more team members know that they can ask for help without losing face or being seen as incompetent and can offer help without it being seen as an insult, the stronger and more competent the team becomes.

Leaders also need to focus on successes: when you remind people of past success, they become more convinced of their ability to succeed in the future. On the other hand, when you remind people of past failures, they become more prone to failure. Comparing people favorably to non-existent others is a way of focusing people on success: "Of all the teams I've worked with, you are the best!" or "I've never seen a team make as progress in as short a time as you are making." Conversely, comparing people to one another creates friction and competition, reducing productivity.

When a team comes together, members have little sense of how competent they are as a group. The team does not yet know its capabilities. When you build a sense of competence, you are enabling the team to become competent: a person, or a group, takes itself to be as they are treated as being.

Part of building that atmosphere of competence is enabling team members to recognize that it's okay to accept and give help. Surgical teams, for example, that achieve this save far more lives than those that do not.

The Leader and the Team

Now that we've looked at power and emotion, we can look further at how the leader and the team interact. Knowing that the leader needs to adapt his style to the needs of the team is a good first step, but, as always, the devil is in the details. We'll touch on some of those details here, and others when we discuss motivation.

Stage 1

In a very real sense, Stage 1 is a wonderful time to be a leader. You are In Charge. Not only do you have legitimate power as the head of the group, being the head of the group gives you automatic, if limited, referent power. Everyone assumes you must be the expert in everything and the group will tolerate virtually any use of reward or coercive power. There is only one tiny fly in the proverbial ointment: group performance is sharply limited.

It's not that the group doesn't want to be helpful; they're just not very good at it. As the leader, you don't have a team so much as a group of henchmen. They'll do what you tell them, tolerate abuse, and hang on your every word. What they won't do is think for themselves, innovate, come up with creative solutions to problems, or take initiative. For the leader who enjoys personal power and dominance, this is a great place to be. The group members and the company pay a high price, but, hey, them's the breaks.

The leader whose goal is building the team, achieving high performance, and helping create a world class organization, however, has some work to do.

Rather than solve problems for your team or yell at people who don't accomplish tasks the way you want, it's time for you to use that referent power to set an example: guide the team through solving the problem. Help them reach a consensus even if you are making the final decision. It can be extremely frustrating to constantly ask for input and get nothing substantive in return, but that's the game at this stage. The objective here is to invite, invite, invite, and accept the fact that it may take a long time before people start to respond. If you attempt to force people to participate or single people out for not participating, you only make it harder for people to interact effectively. As the person in charge, this is your opportunity to set the standards through your actions and break down the barriers between people.

In a Forming group, members are reticent. They often fail to approach one another or refuse to push back on easy solutions. It's far more comfortable to come to a quick, if superficial, agreement and then dive into the work so that you don't have to talk to the other people. As the leader, your job is to start building the social structure of the team: talk to people, get their opinions, draw them out. Recognize that mistakes are inevitable at this stage, at least if you want performance to improve. Mistakes are simply feedback that problem solving and decision making are still not that good or the schedule is too aggressive, or simply that team members haven't yet figured out how to capitalize on one another's strengths. Focus your feedback on strengthening behaviors you want to see; directed, positive feedback is very powerful at this stage.

It's best to use legitimate and referent power in this stage. If you have expert power, try not to use it: that only cements you as the go-to person and discourages team members from solving the problems. You end up with a team that can't work effectively when you're not present. If you want to take a vacation someday, this may not be the best thing. Practice being a coach and mentor rather than the chief problem solver.

While you can use reward and coercive power, they are not without danger: you risk trapping your team in a motivational black hole of increasing rewards or convincing them to just keep their heads down and stay out of your way.

Stage 2

The point at which a group enters Storming can be a major shock to a leader, particularly one who has not read this book. One moment you're telling everyone what to do, the next moment they're pushing back. The cultural belief shared by many is this is where the leader must exercise his power to shut down the upstart! As we discussed in the previous chapter, that only serves to delay or even reverse team development. Pushback means that people are really starting to care deeply about the goals of the team and are becoming comfortable enough with one another and with you to argue about how to achieve them. This is all to the good!

Referent power and your hopefully growing expert power as a leader are your best tools here. Ask questions, lots of questions. You can apply the same principles we discussed in Chap. 1 about getting people on board for change to help sell your ideas. Moderate discussions, encourage debate, and help the team develop effective discipline around argument and decision making.

Recognize that at this point your group is likely to split in two. It will feel natural and comfortable to associate more with the in-group; after all, they are supporting you. You need to make a point of reaching out to the out-group. They already want to believe the worst about you, so let them see the best. Seek out their opinions and engage them in discussion. The example you set will be critical to your group moving forward or not.

The key point, as we discussed in the previous chapter, is to not get drawn into conflict with your team. If you lose, you lose. If you win, you lose. Pay attention to your own reactions. If you realize that you're getting caught up in conflict, call a break or announce one for the next day, whatever it takes to give you and the team some breathing room. If you can pull back from conflict, then the example you set will enable others to do so as well. If you allow the conflict to take on a life of its own, the group becomes stuck or retreats to Stage 1.

Stage 3

If you've made it this far, you're doing well. A lot of changes have occurred since the beginning of the group. Roles have shifted quite a bit, even yours. Although you're still in charge, many of the routine functions of leadership are being handled by the group. You are still an active participant in decision making, discussion, and organization but, at the same time, the group no longer needs your direct, daily intervention. This can be a very unsettling feeling. You may even start wondering what role you have left.

In fact, quite a big one.

As we discussed in the previous chapter, it's easy for Stage 3 to become a period of enchantment: everyone is feeling happy and comfortable with the new structure and no one wants to take risks. One of your tasks is to help the group continue to improve, to use its burgeoning skills in debate and decision making to take on more difficult tasks and confront problems head on. Part of your job now is helping the group recognize its progress and develop confidence in its skills. Encourage group members to take on more of the tools of leadership and organizing. Oddly enough, the more successful you are at this, the stronger, and more resilient, your referent power becomes. In Stage 1, you hold referent power because you are the person in charge; by Stage 3, your referent power is based more and more on who you are as a person and a leader.

Stage 4

Congratulations! Very few teams make it to this point. While, in many ways, you are still working with the team, you are also the respected consultant and coach.

Your biggest challenge at this point is maintaining your team. No matter how skilled the team, no matter how excited they are by the work, high performance is exhausting. Your job now is to monitor your team for signs that it's beginning to fray about the edges. You need to make sure they take breaks and shake up the routine occasionally. Do something fun to keep everyone fresh.

If you are adding members to the team, removing members, or causing other significant changes in the environment, you need to especially vigilant. If the team starts to unbake, you need to act quickly to stop the process before it spirals out of control.

Remember, the biggest challenge of a high performance team is keeping it there. Periodic status checks can help maintain performance.

Do Nice Guys Finish Last?

A question I get asked quite often is, "do nice guys finish last?"

The problem lies in the definition of nice.

Leaders should set high standards and then work like mad to help their team achieve those standards. That may require pushing people or telling them that they've screwed up.

There is a big difference between holding high standards, expecting people to meet those standards, and being an utter jerk. Jerks end up damaging the team and, given enough time, the company.

Similarly, leaders who refuse to tell you when you're doing something wrong or who refuse to provide negative feedback when that feedback would be beneficial are not helping the team either.

So, if you define nice as "not wanting to upset or offend anyone ever," then you probably will finish last. You'll deserve it.

The nicest thing you can do is treat people as the high performers you know they can become, constantly push people to develop their strengths, don't be afraid of difficult discussions, and don't be afraid to take the actions necessary to build your team. We'll look more at those actions in the next few chapters.

Questions to Consider

1. What types of power do you most often find yourself using? Why?
2. How can you tell if people on your team trust one another?
3. What emotions do you tend to evoke most often in your team?
4. How can you help your team best balance autonomy, relatedness, and competence?
5. In what ways is fear getting in the way?
6. What is the example you are setting?

Chapter 5
Motivation and Loyalty: Creating a Motivated Workforce

The situation was almost comical. Indeed, an independent observer might even be forgiven for thinking it was something out of an office sitcom.

Jack had a not very unique way of motivating the employees in his software engineering team to work the way he wanted: when someone displeased him, he assigned them to write the really annoying or unpleasant sections of code, or at least those sections that he viewed as annoying and unpleasant.

The problem was that the engineers did not always agree. In some cases, they found the work they were being assigned to be extremely interesting. The net result was that instead of realizing that Jack was angry about their performance, they thought they were being rewarded. Rather than changing their behavior, they engaged in more of it. Sure, Jack would sometimes talk about his displeasure, but his actions seemed to be saying they were on the right track. Jack got more and more frustrated while the engineers became ever more confused. Why was he acting so angry and then giving them such plum assignments?

In a very different organization, a similar scenario played itself out. In this case, it was a school. Norman, one of the teachers, had an extremely disruptive student named Sasha in his class. Norman decided that he was going to be strict with Sasha and lay down the law right from the start. If Sasha was disruptive, he would be sent out to sit in the hallway for five minutes. If it happened three times in a class period, Sasha would spend the entire class in the hall. Within a couple of weeks, Sasha's behavior degenerated to the point where he was spending the entire class in the hallway. Sasha didn't like being in class and saw being sent to sit in the hall as a reward in that it got him what he wanted. Rather than discouraging his acting up, Norman's approach only encouraged it. So much for Norman's brilliant plan.

On the more positive side, I've also seen managers hand out hundred dollar bills to employees who come into work weekends. It was quite the little show: Monday mornings, the head of the department would call everyone together and, if you were in over the weekend, you were handed a crisp new Ben Franklin. When the supply of hundreds ended, people also stopped showing up on weekends. What

S. R. Balzac, *Organizational Psychology for Managers*,
Management for Professionals, DOI: 10.1007/978-1-4614-8505-6_5,
© Springer Science+Business Media New York 2014

made this particularly noteworthy was that even the people who had been coming in on weekends before the hundred dollar awards were given out also stopped coming in on weekends. In other words, it wasn't just the people who only started coming in on weekends when they realized there was extra money involved who stopped doing it; everyone stopped. As it was, this particular attempt at motivation still worked better than many: it's not all that unusual for people to lose interest in the rewards or constantly expect more for the same performance.

This phenomenon is known as the Motivation Trap.

The Motivation Trap

Let's face it, motivating employees is frustrating. Most of the advice is full of disagreements and what seems easy and obvious often doesn't work, stops working with little warning, or produces results very different from what we intended. In one apocryphal story, *psychologist William James Hall was attempting to stop a bunch of kids from playing loudly under his bedroom window. No matter what he did to chase them away they came back again. Hall was heard to wonder aloud if they were part cat. Eventually, Hall decided that if threats of punishment, and, indeed, actual punishment, wasn't working, it was time to try something else. He told the kids he'd had a change of heart and decided he liked having them playing there. To thank them, he paid each of them $1. The kids were overjoyed.*

After a couple of weeks, Hall informed them that he could only afford $.85 that week. The kids grumbled a bit, but continued to play. Hall continued to drop the amount every week or two until he was down to $.25. He then told the kids that the next week all he could give them would be $.15. The kids stared at him for a moment, and then the oldest one said, "What sort of nonsense is that! We'll show you!"

The kids stormed off, never to return.

What Hall had successfully accomplished was taking the kids innate desire to play in a particular place and replace it with a desire to receive a particular reward. Once they were hooked on the reward, he decreased their motivation by decreasing, and eventually eliminating, the reward.

Fundamentally, the problem businesses have, and that Hall turned to his advantage, lies in viewing motivation as something external to the person. It is the pernicious belief that motivation is something we do to people, not something we do with people. As we discussed in preceding chapters, culture and organizational narrative are methods by which people are drawn into the organization and become part of it; they are not something done to people. As we saw with teams and leadership, the relationship between them is symbiotic: the leader and the team need each other. Similarly, organizations cannot exist without people and people need organizations in order to accomplish large tasks: people working together in a business or other organization can accomplish far more than can an individual, and a team of people who can work together well can accomplish far more than a group whose members just happen to be walking in the same direction. Motivation needs to be an integral part of the relationship between teams and leaders, members and the organization. When we push someone, they push back. It's instinctive. We want people who will charge forward so fast and hard that anyone who doesn't get out of the way will be trampled. What we often get are people who need to be begged, bribed, cajoled, or compelled.

To put things another way, motivation is almost universally done wrong.

What Are We Doing Wrong?

When motivation is focused around rewards and punishments, it is being done to people not with them. There are several problems with this approach.

First of all, as we touched on in the previous chapter, rewards need to be used carefully in order to motivate appropriately. The classical image of using rewards and punishments, as taught in many programs, is that you should always reward behavior you like and punish behavior you don't like. As we've already observed, different people have different ideas of what constitutes a reward and what constitutes a punishment. Even if we all agree that being fired is punishment, firing people does not motivate them, it only gets rid of them.

A more serious problem, as we've discussed, is that when people are taught to work for a reward, they do exactly that. When the reward stops, so do they. Even worse, though, is that rewards cannot remain static: the same reward will not provide the same level of motivation.

Consider a serious athlete. They compete in a tournament and, after a few years of trying, they win. They might do it again, but if they are good enough, it's not long before that tournament becomes too easy. It's just not worth the effort for one more identical trophy. They look for something harder, something more challenging, with greater prestige or rewards. If they are good enough, they might make it to the world stage, at which point there are no more higher level competitions to win. However, there is always the possibility of winning multiple Olympic gold medals, as swimmer Michael Phelps did, or winning multiple years in a row, as fencer Mariel Zagunis attempted in 2012. Phelps retired after the 2012 Olympics when he successfully became the most decorated Olympian of all time. Zagunis narrowly missed becoming the first woman to ever win three Olympic gold medals in fencing in a row.

Left to our own devices, we seek greater challenge. We also expect the benefits of overcoming those challenges to be ever greater. Conversely, doing the same thing becomes boring. The less interesting or inherently attractive the task is, the greater the reward required to keep us focused on it.

Another problem with the reward and punishment approach is that it works best in a metaphorically quiet environment. The famous behavioral psychologist B. F. Skinner once claimed that if he could completely control all inputs a person received, he could completely shape their behavior. In fact, it's not even clear that it would work as well as he thought even if he did have someone in a box where he had total control. It does sound good though.

The real world is a noisy place. People are receiving a constant stream of inputs and are reacting to a variety of different stimuli. Many of your messages are going to get lost or misinterpreted in the shuffle. A small, inadvertent reward can negate a great deal of punishment: a smile, a laugh, a nod taken to mean approval can be enough.

People also resist crude behavioral manipulation. The smarter and more capable a person is, the less willing they are to feel that their behavior is being manipulated: manipulation infringes on their feelings of autonomy and competence. For them, the reward becomes not responding. There's a big difference between having a coach push you and feeling that you are being forced into a behavior. Force triggers resistance. When deprived of control, we seek to reassert that control in some way.

I attended a jujitsu seminar in which the instructor, a skinny old man, effortlessly threw us around. When we tried the same technique on each other, we ended up sweating and gasping as we tried to force our partners to the ground. The instructor didn't even work up a sweat. There was no sense of power, no feeling of being grabbed, but we just flew through the air. When we did it, we applied force. The more force you apply, the more the other person fights back. The secret to defeating your opponent is to let them throw themselves to the ground and the instructor was a master of allowing us to do just that.

All that being said, there are situations where rewards are effective. Rewards are extremely motivating when structured as feedback that you are working toward a goal, rather than being the goal itself. Rewards are also effective, perhaps even most effective, when done in ways that build a relationship: as we've discussed, remembering to give employees gifts on their birthdays is powerful technique for building motivation and loyalty.

It's important to notice when your efforts at motivation are forcing you into a position where you have to apply more and more of your reward and coercive power. This is both exhausting on a personal level, and, if unsuccessful, it also reduces the effectiveness of that power. It's time to try something different.

What About Fear?

In Mel Brook's and Carl Reiner's classic comedy, *The 2000 Year Old Man*, the title character is asked about the primary means of motivation thousands of years ago. He replies, "Fear."

When the lion shows up, you are motivated to run the other way.

Fear can be a very powerful tool for getting people to move, except when it causes them to freeze. Even when people do move, they do not move in a coherent, logical way. In jujitsu, pain compliance techniques work because they cause fear of injury or death. That fear can cause someone to move very rapidly into the nearest wall. The effects are dramatic.

A team running on fear also has a distinct tendency to hit the wall. While the results generally don't' involve blood and broken bones, it is no less destructive. The damage to morale, cooperation, and trust is considerable. Scared people are less inventive, less able to take initiative, and less able to do high quality work. As we'll see in Chap. 11, high levels of fear degrade performance in both the short and long term and block the ability of a team to develop a highly optimistic, success oriented mindset.

Would You Work Without a Paycheck?

Sooner or later, someone always argues that of course rewards and fear work, after all we wouldn't work without a paycheck. The paycheck is a reward and people obey because they fear losing it.

This is an argument that demonstrates a profound failure to understand motivation.

At one level, a paycheck is the quintessential feedback that you are working toward a goal. Receiving that check is the organization's way of telling you that you are helping to advance the goals of the organization. People who are motivated only by the receipt of the check tend not to be particularly loyal.

At another level, the paycheck is what makes motivation possible.

Before we can look at how to motivate effectively, we have to recognize something: when someone is blocked from doing a task, or perceived that they will be blocked, it becomes very hard indeed to motivate them. No matter how many rewards I offer you, if the power is out and you can't turn on the computer, you won't do the work.

If your chair is uncomfortable and your back always hurts, it'll be very hard to motivate you.

At one company, the women's room was unheated and against an outside wall of the building. This company had trouble keeping female employees. It didn't matter if they got a paycheck; in fact, the company literally couldn't pay them enough to do the job. The women felt disrespected and unimportant.

When people feel hungry, or afraid, or that their work doesn't matter, they are very hard to motivate.

Think about the organizational narrative. The point of that narrative is to show people why they matter to the organization, and why the organization matters to them. Part of why the organization matters is that it helps make it possible for people to fulfill their own dreams and goals.

A job means a great many things: it is the source of food and shelter, as well as a means to accomplishing goals and fulfilling dreams. The paycheck is merely the vehicle by which job performance is translated into all those things. Take the paycheck out of the equation and you also take away present safety and future dreams. It's hard to create a bigger block to motivation than that!

Remember, the world is full of people who accept smaller paychecks to pursue their passions.

Escaping the Motivation Trap

So how do we escape from the motivation trap?

I've frequently walked into an organization and been told, "The problem is Phil. He's unmotivated."

When I chat with Phil, I quickly find out that he's a marathon runner, or a black belt in Tae Kwon Do, or volunteers in a homeless shelter, or one of dozens of other activities that require a great deal of consistent, focused, effort. In other words, motivation.

Phil isn't unmotivated. He's just not motivated to do the thing his manager wants him to do at that moment.

The first step to escaping the motivation trap is simply the realization that people are always motivated to do something. We want to make it easy for them to channel that motivation into their jobs.

When it comes right down to brass tacks, an organization is a community of people with a purpose. It doesn't matter whether we're looking at a corporation, a non-profit, a school, a hospital, or a cycling club. Every organization has a purpose, expressed through its culture and conveyed in its vision and organizational narrative.

People who join the organization are going to be at least open to the organization's vision. At best, they are already excited and eager to be part of it. If either of these points is not true, you have a serious problem in your organizational culture and narrative, the ability of your people to convey the purpose, or your hiring process—we'll discuss that last point in the next chapter.

The next point is that it is the rare person indeed who comes to work wanting to do a bad job. However, if we just get wrapped up in our use of rewards and punishment, it is possible to turn enthusiastic people into people who no longer care or are happy to do a bad job. Unfortunately, we have some cultural beliefs that tell us that people don't want to work and are lazy, uninterested, and take no pride in their work. The myth that workers don't want to be there and have to be forced to work is a cultural value dating back to a time during the industrial revolution when horrible working conditions did, indeed, destroy motivation. As is often the case, cultural values have not yet caught up with reality.

People who are part of a community seek to gain status in the community. Thus, given the opportunity, members of an organization will act in ways which increase their status in the organization, provided they believe their actions matter and can see a path from where they are to a place of higher status. That status will typically translate into greater referent, legitimate, or expert power as well. We can take this a step further and observe that people always choose actions that they believe will increase their status in some way: we need to feel we are making progress in the activities to which we devote our time and energies.

The other side of the equation is that any large project is going to be draining at times. There will be moments of frustration and points where people are so tired, angry, or upset that they feel like just throwing in the towel and storming off. This is not something to just ignore or say that "professionals keep going" and other trite phrases. Professional athletes have people cheering them on and helping them through the long down periods.

Thus, motivation really comes down to unleashing people's natural desires to do well, increasing their competence and status, and supporting them during difficult periods. It's about using referent power to build those individual relationships we discussed in the previous chapter, and being there for people.

In this case, a necessary component of referent power boils down to how do you present yourself and what sort of example are you setting?

Are you genuinely interested in your team members as people, or is your interest in them only to further your own career? As Google found out, employees respect and trust managers who have the employee's interests at heart. Similarly, if you want people to respect and trust you, you have to respect and trust them first. Motivation comes from working with someone who respects you and cares about your career: that is what makes it possible to trust the feedback that you are making progress.

Do you have strongly held beliefs and values? In other words, are you committed to something other than yourself? When someone is only committed to themselves, it's very hard to trust them; you never know which way they'll jump. However, people who are committed to a clear set of values can be trusted to hold those values even when it's inconvenient.

Along the lines of strongly held values, do you demonstrate integrity? Remember that all leadership is at least partially transactional. While transactional leadership is quite limited on its own, it is the basis for anything deeper and more powerful. Without integrity, that transactional foundation will be unstable. Without the transactional foundation, inspiring others becomes impossible, and you're back to using force: inspiring promises won't work particularly well if no one believes you. At one company I worked with, a certain manager always found a reason to not follow through on promises he'd made; it wasn't long before he had a department full of people who spent most of their time sitting around grumbling and doing the minimum amount of work necessary to keep getting a paycheck. The most bizarre part of the experience was that he seemed genuinely bewildered by their reactions, which brings us to the next point.

Can you make an emotional connection to other people on the team and in the organization? Logic is all well and good, but when it comes to deciding whom to trust and whom to listen to, emotion drives the train. If your team can't make an emotional connection with you, they'll never really trust you and will abandon you when a better opportunity comes along. Sometimes, they won't even wait that long. That was, in the end, what happened to the manager I just mentioned. His personal brand became toxic; no one would stay in his department. He went back to being an individual contributor, where he was much happier.

So, with these points in mind, how then do we actually enable motivation?

Before answering that, let's recognize something very important: there are no magical motivational techniques. Although the techniques we will look at are ones that can be easily done with people rather than to them, it's still possible to turn each "with" into a "to." It depends on your presentation.

Start with Your Own Example

The higher your position in the organization, the more you are an example of the organization's culture, values, and future. Your own enthusiasm and motivation are a key element in inspiring the same feelings in others. If you seem disinterested, so will everyone else. If you act like a jerk, so will everyone else. If you are excited about the job, everyone else will be excited. You matter.

It's easy to fall into the trap that showing your excitement and dedication means working long hours and burning yourself out. Not so! As you look at each of the techniques that follow, think about how you can implement them for yourself. You might not do everything on the list, but you should be doing at least some of them. It will be difficult at first, but it will also become easier as you get better at it and as your organization develops.

Leaders lead, it really is that simple.

Make the Vision Personal

Most people are connected to a great many communities: their work, congregation, clubs, social groups, etc. That means that people have a great many personal goals and desires, at least some of which are connected to those other communities. Part of the goal of the organization is to enable people to see how their personal goals and the organizational goals are connected: helping the organization is helping themselves. If there is no visible connection between personal and organizational goals, motivation becomes very difficult; you are back to using force.

The organizational narrative is the first step to building the bridge between personal desires and the organizational needs. The narrative is hooking into certain basic desires that are held by most people. Remember that part of the goal of your organizational narrative is to attract the people who find it exciting; in other words, you are selecting for those people who are predisposed to find being part of your organization interesting and motivating.

Once you have those people, you need to connect the dots. You need to help them develop a personal vision of their future with the organization. This is not always easy as not everyone starts out thinking in those terms. Drawing it out of them can take time, and if you don't have the skills to do that you either need to learn them or get help from someone who does have those skills.

It can help to encourage people to daydream or to ask questions along the lines of, "Imagine it is five years from now and the company is doing well, in no small part due to your efforts. What would you have done to make that happen?" When you take a future retrospective, you are better able to spark people's imaginations and dreams.

It's important to avoid the "no one gets rich here, but you'll always have a paycheck" mentality. Fundamentally, that view kills dreams and invites mediocrity. I remember hearing that when I first worked for IBM after college, and it was like being hit by a jet of cold water. You may as well say, "Don't bother trying to excel, no one will notice," which is what it amounts to.

Your objective is to enable people to develop their own, personal, narrative in which they are the central figure and their success goes hand in hand with organizational success. They need to see how the organization doing well helps them do well, and how their work matters to the organization's success.

Once you have the basic narrative, you need to keep updating it, keep expanding and embellishing the story as time passes. Completed projects become part of the narrative, and help launch the next project. It's the ongoing story that keeps us interested and excited: the perception of progress is critical. Use the vision and the story to help formulate specific goals. We'll talk more about the mechanics of goal setting in Chap. 9.

At the risk of belaboring the point, if your team members don't trust you or don't see you as genuine, they will not believe in the vision you help them create. As they come to trust you, though, they will become steadily more enthusiastic partners in the process.

Coaching

One thing that every professional athlete and every top athletic team has in common is that they all have coaches. In fact, it's impossible to develop the skill level to compete on the world stage if you don't have a coach. These top athletes and teams are all composed of highly dedicated, extremely talented people. They have also all learned that dedication and talent only get you so far.

Presumably, every person on your team is dedicated and talented. If you're hiring people who don't have the skills necessary to do the job, or, better yet, the capability of learning those skills, you have some serious problems. That dedication and talent must now be focused, honed, and supported. How that is done depends to some degree upon the stage of team development.

Early stage teams, and newer members of existing teams, will need more direct, skill-based coaching. They need to learn to work with one another, develop a sense of community and relationship with one another, and develop the sense of trust that permits them to work as part of the group. This means:

- Focus on past successes in order to build the confidence to tackle current projects. Nothing succeeds quite like the expectation of success and for a team to succeed, it has to believe that it can succeed. When you remind people of their previous successes, both in and out of the workplace, you increase their belief that they can succeed again. On the other hand, when you focus on failure and the consequences of failure, you only reduce people's confidence.
- Help members define short-term and long-term goals. Don't leave it to chance; it takes an outside perspective to enable people to set appropriately challenging goals.

- Build status. As we've discussed, people choose actions that increase their status. Find ways for each person on the team to build their own status, display their knowledge and expertise. Assigning some people low status leads to infighting and destructive competition. When status increases, people are more excited, more dedicated, and more highly motivated.
- Build a sense of community or connection amongst all group members. No man is an island and no one is the center of the universe.
- Guide the team through the process of problem solving and decision making. It will be tempting to just make the decision; that's easy and fast. Resist! Instead, invite input, get opinions, encourage discussion, and help team members engage with one another. Remember that it takes time to become comfortable with other people.

As the team develops, you will need to spend less and less time on each of these components of team building. Just as a coach with a beginning athlete focuses on skill development, as the athlete progresses the coach's role becomes more focused on long-term goal development, encouragement, and strategy. You will do the same. As we discussed in the previous two chapters, your stage four team will have mastered problem solving and decision making; they will have strong relationships, high status, and confidence. It is through the process of scaffolding their skills, that is, supporting them as they learn the skills and then slowly withdrawing your support as they achieve proficiency, that enables the team to develop.

Keep in mind that the occasional failures along the way are merely a form of feedback: it tells you where the team needs to build its strengths or it tells you that you're moving too fast. Failures give the team the opportunity to learn that they can screw up and bounce back again. Just as sports teams develop resilience by battling back from behind, so do organizational and business teams develop resilience by rebounding from errors. If failures continue to occur, that can tell you that you are pushing the team too fast; slow down and figure out what's wrong. It does no good to hit the ground running if you keep twisting an ankle.

In many cases, managers will be able to effectively coach their teams. Similar to sports, though, the odds are extremely high that you'll be considerably more successful if you have someone coaching both the leader and the team together. When leaders and teams train and practice together, they achieve much higher levels of performance. For instance, Schein observes that surgical teams where the chief surgeon trains with her team master more complex surgical procedures and achieve more successful outcomes than teams where that is not the case.

It is critical, however, that leaders who coach their teams not be perceived as being in competition with the team. A leader who is little more than a glorified individual contributor is often going to have trouble building the necessary levels of trust to coach effectively. When there is a perception that advice is more for the benefit of the giver than the receiver, that advice is ignored or resisted.

When you work together to improve your ability to work as a team, the organizational environment becomes a more exciting, compelling place to be.

Involve the Team

It may seem like the leader has a lot to do. To a certain extent, that's the case, particularly in a stage one group. However, it cannot and should not remain that way, particularly if the group is to evolve.

By a rather funny coincidence, it is the job of each group member to do exactly the same things as the leader: each member must act like a leader! When each member contributes to the building of the group structure, the group becomes stronger. Group members cannot sit back and let the leader do all the thinking, all the organizing, all the talking, or all the status building. The best way to build your own status is to build the status of those around you. The best way to get people to listen to your ideas is to listen to their ideas. The best way to get people to care about you is to care about them. The people who seek be islands or the center of the universe may be physically present but are not really connecting to the team.

When the leader involves the members, people feel more connected, more personally invested in the organization. They feel that their actions matter, which increases competence and relatedness. Contributing to group structure strengthens the team and also increases trust, both of which have the side-effect of increasing autonomy. All of these factors, in turn, help build strong, sustainable motivation.

Continuous Learning

Providing people with opportunities to learn new skills is a win for the organization and the person. Continuous learning helps people become more competent and raises their status in the organization. In addition to being a motivating experience, increasing individual competencies also improves team performance and organizational loyalty. Learning can include classes taken online or at local colleges, hobbies, or various trainings the organization might conduct (we'll discuss training in detail in Chap. 8).

The trick is to handle learning opportunities correctly.

Continuous learning must be as much a part of the job as meeting with clients or hitting deadlines. If the organization views learning as an afterthought, something to be done in people's spare time, it will be less likely to occur and be less motivating. Consider that if people are already working forty or more hours per week, adding to that is going to leave them exhausted.

Do not restrict the opportunities available. Some companies will only pay for classes taken in specific areas relating to the employee's job description. Unfortunately, this is extremely limiting for both the employee and the company. First of all, they are already knowledgeable in their areas of expertise, so more of the same may not be interesting. Second, part of the goal of learning is to develop new skills as well as hone existing skills. Third, creative and innovative ideas come from unusual and unexpected sources. Steve Jobs combined widely diverse areas of knowledge to produce his creative breakthroughs. When you encourage employees to pursue their passions, you end up with more passionate, skilled, and creative employees.

Celebrate progress just as you would with any other project. Employees who are seeking new degrees or advanced degrees should be congratulated as they hit major milestones on their journey. Not only does this provide encouragement to the employee, it also helps shape your organizational culture and narrative, demonstrating that your values are taken seriously.

Make sure you help employees find opportunities to apply their newly developed skills within the organization. Part of what makes learning motivating is that it makes the employee more valuable to the organization; if the employee does not perceive that value, they won't stick around. This is where updating the employee's personal vision and good coaching can be extremely important; it's useful to review the organizational narrative and brainstorm with the employee new paths and new directions for them to continue to advance.

Remember also that enthusiasm can take time to develop. You, or the team's coach, need to keep offering and encouraging until they start responding. The trick is to find that balance between making the offer and nagging. If you nag, it doesn't work.

What about the person who shows no interest in learning or in improving their skills? Well, what are they doing in your organization? If they are contributing to the organization, buy into the vision and narrative, and are an asset to the team, this may not be a problem; their performance will tell you if their skills are actually increasing or not. If, on the other hand, you find yourself in a position where you are constantly balancing their specific contribution in some area against a generalized negative influence on the team, that is often a clue that that person may not belong in that position or even in the organization.

Focus on Experiences, Not Things

I've spent a lot of time talking about the perils of rewards, and now I'm going to talk about using rewards. Bear with me. As we discussed earlier, rewards can be very useful when they are a form of feedback. It's when they become the goal that they become problematic. The nature of the reward also matters: some rewards force us into the motivation trap, while others are easily amenable to becoming something we do with people.

It turns out that the most common rewards, cash bonuses or items, easily slip us into the motivation trap. Cash or items, be they t-shirts, fleeces, laptop bags, tech toys, all produce much the same results: a short-term blip followed by, at best, nothing, at worst long-term dissatisfaction. While some people use cash to buy something they'd like, most of the time the extra cash goes to paying bills or toward a rainy day fund. Cash also creates an expectation of an even larger cash reward the next time around.

Giving people tech toys or other things seems like a nice idea, but actually doesn't work. First, the reward feels impersonal: look, everyone in the department got a new phone. Of course, that can get tricky, since some people like Android and others iOS.

A more serious problem, particularly with technology, is that the gift loses its appeal very quickly. All it takes is a newer, fancier tech toy to hit the market and suddenly that old gadget is no longer cool: Now it makes you look behind the times. In early 2012, Apple announced the iPad HD, popularly referred to as the iPad 3. It was definitely an amazing gadget. In October, they announced the iPad Retina, an even more amazing gadget. As several newspapers reported at the time, Apple fans were furious. Suddenly their new iPad HDs were obsolete. One analyst commented that he didn't understand the fuss: if the HD was a good device on Monday, before the iPad Retina was announced, why wasn't it a good device on Wednesday? He was, of course, missing the point: the excitement wasn't in having just any gadget, it was in having the newest gadget. In the end, things lose their motivational power very quickly: getting a new iPhone is fun for a week or two, but after that it's just another item that I stick in my pocket along with my wallet and keys.

Rather than things, lasting happiness and motivation are produced through experiences. It is the opportunity to go off and do something that we enjoy that really builds long-lasting motivation. There are several reasons why this works.

First, in order to give someone an experience, you have to have taken the time to get to know them and know a little bit about what they'd like. If you have an employee who loves watching the Olympics, giving her tickets to attend the games would be extremely effective. However, if you gave her tickets to the opera, maybe not so much. As we learned as kids, it's the thought that counts. While that is not an absolute truth, as anyone who has ever received a particularly ugly sweater can attest, knowing that someone cared enough about you as a person to arrange for you to do something you deeply care about is a very powerful motivating force. Again, treating someone as a person as opposed to a generic tool on the team is extremely important.

The other thing about experiences, though, is that they never lose their value. Our memories of the fun times we've had remain positive memories. They don't stop being positive just because we might do something else. Graduating from high school can still evoke memories of pride and accomplishment even in someone who went on to gather advanced degrees from a top college. If you enjoyed learning to wind surf while on a vacation, the memory of that enjoyment will always be with you even if you never wind surf again.

The things we do become part of who we are; they shape us as people in a way that gadgets cannot. Sure, it might be nice to receive a new camera right before a major vacation, but the camera isn't what makes the vacation fun. It may help us remember our trip and it may enable us to share some of our enjoyment with others, but rarely is it the point of the trip.

Experiences do not have to mean vacations, although that is important. We'll discuss that further later in this chapter. Experiences can be work related. For example, continuous learning is a form of experience provided by the organization to those who desire it.

Providing people with the opportunities to do things they value builds their relationship to the organization: by providing the opportunity, you become their virtual partner or supporter.

Experiences can be used on a group level as well. While having organized, group activities is certainly a good thing, it should not be the only thing. Low level teams try to do everything together to build team unity. This is silly and counter-productive. In one case, a certain organization sent members of a group to a state fair. The manager insisted that everyone stay together and attend the same events, whether everyone was interested or not. Rather than building unity, it only created division.

Physical objects are ephemeral. Experiences never grow old, never get stale, and don't become obsolete when someone announces a new model.

Get Out of the House

As we've discussed, all organizations have a purpose. That purpose, or vision, is a central part of how you motivate members of the organization. There is a danger, though, that the vision can get lost in the pressure of day-to-day work. Part of how you avoid that and reenergize members of the organization is by getting out of the house. In other words, attend professional and industry conferences. Having people network with their peers is a great way for them to keep tabs on their fields, helping promote continuous learning. Attending events with clients helps make the organizational purpose come alive: rather than a purpose that involves serving some faceless other or a semi-mythical "customer," meeting people face to face makes them real. It's exciting to hear from the people who are benefiting from your work. All too often, all that ever filters back are the complaints. A steady diet of discouraging words is not motivating!

Visiting customers has the added benefit of helping people better understand the work they are doing and become better able to do it. It provides a fresh perspective, one that may be lost if you spend all your time in the office staring at a computer screen. The customers also appreciate it, leading to better relations with the organization, also increasing motivation: happy employees lead to happy clients, and happy clients help maintain happy, motivated employees. Conversely, of course, unhappy employees lead to unhappy clients; you get to choose whether the cycle is virtuous or vicious.

Getting out of the house is also a form of experience. While not everyone will want to take advantage of this particular experience, having it available for those who are interested can dramatically increase motivation and commitment to the organization.

Social networking, despite its popularity, will not provide the same level of connection and experience. Face to face has much higher resolution. In other words, we need to actually experience the connection with others, not just read about it.

Contain Unpleasant Tasks

No matter how much we might enjoy what we do, there are always parts that simply are not much fun. That may be documenting code or calling clients or preparing reports for the boss, or something completely different. There are always tasks that we don't want to do. Left to themselves, those tasks either expand to fill the day or pile up and turn into a crisis. Neither of these options is particularly motivating. At best, they leave us drained and feeling like we haven't accomplished anything; at worst, we feel frustrated, exhausted, and overwhelmed.

Fortunately, there is a better way.

The trick here is to put boundaries around your unpleasant tasks: work on them for a specific, pre-determined amount of time. At the end of that time, you should feel free to stop or you might continue until you hit a logical stopping point. Said logical stopping point might be going home at the end of the day.

This technique is very powerful: if you stop at the end of the time you've allotted, you know you've done what you promised yourself and hence you gain a sense of accomplishment. If you continue to some other logical stopping point, you can feel virtuous that you worked on the unpleasant task longer than you planned, and you got something done. Because you are doing "bonus" work, you also can stop at any time.

It's when you leave the time open-ended that the problems come in: without a pre-defined endpoint, the unpleasant task just keeps expanding until you can't possibly get it all done. Failure, of course, reduces motivation. But when you promise yourself that you'll work on something for "an hour," not only will you likely spend more time, you'll accomplish more, and you'll feel better about it. That launches you into your next task, or the next day, with positive momentum.

To maximize the benefits you get from this technique, you need to honestly look at how much unpleasant work you have to do, allocate your time accordingly, and actually do the work during the time you've allocated. The important things are to not allow the unpleasant tasks to build up until they become a crisis and to never let the parts of the job you don't like dominate the parts that you do like. If that happens, burnout is not far away.

Take Breaks

As counter-intuitive as it may sound, taking breaks is one of the best ways to increase productivity and motivation. There are several reasons for this.

Our brains are extremely good at focusing on a problem for relatively long periods of time. How long "relatively long" actually is depends a great deal on the person; it's probably longer for a chess master than for many of the rest of us. However, no matter who we are, staring at a problem for too long causes us to get stuck. We start to run through the same solutions or approaches over and over; the more we do that, the harder it becomes to see other possibilities. Taking a break forces us to metaphorically sever our train of thought, opening us up to new possibilities. Anyone who has experienced the phenomenon of staring for hours at a problem before going home in disgust and then having the solution pop into their head first thing the next morning is familiar with the importance of taking that break. More generally, taking breaks after we've pounded on a problem for a while also increases our odds of finding creative, unusual solutions.

It's also important to remember that most activities are marathons, not sprints. Short breaks allow us to physically and mentally catch our breath. Periodic breaks keep us from getting mentally fatigued, which otherwise leads to increased distractibility and errors. It's working when we're drained that reduces productivity, undermines our enjoyment of the job, and, over time, burns us out.

We've long known that we sleep in roughly 90 min cycles from light sleep to deep sleep and back. During the day, our alertness follows a similar pattern: our "wake" cycles are about 90 min long. In other words, on a day-to-day basis, we need to take a break roughly every 90 min to recharge our batteries. If we don't, we are draining our reserves and reducing productivity. We also can't spend too much of the day working without productivity suffering. It pays to listen to our bodies and not override our signals of physical or mental fatigue! This is why it is so important to get away from hours on the job and look at goals, topics we'll discuss in Chaps. 9 and 10.

In addition to short breaks, longer breaks, sometimes known as vacations, are also important. Our brains are built to focus on novelty, so after a while we start to tune out the same old same old. As important as routine is, too much of it is counter-productive. Eventually, we have to spend more and more effort forcing our brains to stay focused. Taking a vacation allows us to reset our sense of what is routine. It enables us to return to work refreshed and with a new perspective. According to one article in the NY Times, Ernst & Young found that every 10 h of vacation a person took increased their performance by 8 % compared to those who did not take vacation. Companies that offer 4 weeks or more vacation from the start have more productive, engaged, committed, and loyal employees than those that offer less vacation.

It is important, however, to not take work along on vacation. If you spend all your time on the beach working, it won't do you much good. Bringing your phone along and staying in touch with the office the entire time is the psychological equivalent of inviting your coworkers to come with you on your trip. Maybe that works for you, but probably not. If the office truly can't along without you, odds are there's something more serious wrong.

People who take vacations experience less burnout. Vacations are, of course, a specific type of experience. For all the reasons we've already discussed, actually having the experience is critical to maintaining motivation, loyalty, and productivity.

Take Hobbies Seriously

You could view this as a combination of valuing experiences and taking breaks. You'd be only partially correct. It is that and more besides.

People who take the rest of their lives seriously are generally more productive than those who don't. Someone who leaves work at 6 pm to get to soccer practice on time or take her kid to softball practice is going to use their time more effectively in order to make that happen. The self-discipline required to focus your efforts so you can leave on time carries over into other parts of the job as well: doing quality work, dealing respectfully with others, working with difficult clients, etc.

People who take the rest of their lives seriously are also constantly reminding themselves how their connection to the organization makes their other activities possible. That experience helps tie their personal vision to the organizational vision, further increasing motivation.

When you recognize that employees have a life outside the office and respect that boundary, you are further building trust. When I was a manager, I would chase my direct reports out of the office if I found them working because they thought they needed to maintain appearances. As a result, whenever a real need arose, they put in the extra time. They knew I would never ask them to stay late or come in on weekends unless it was really important. Most of the time, I didn't even have to ask.

Respect and Encourage Efficiency

Remember that culture often contains assumptions that we are so accustomed to that we just don't question them. One such assumption, dating back to the industrial age, is that hours present equals hard work and dedication, while someone who gets the job done quickly and goes home is lazy.

If you take your car to the mechanic, would you rather a mechanic who demonstrates hard work and dedication by taking days to do the job, or the "lazy" guy who gets it done quickly?

I worked with one manager who said, "You did an amazing job. Since you made it look easy, I'm not giving you a raise." I can't make this stuff up!

When the focus is on hours in the office, often known as "face time," you discourage people from working efficiently and effectively. You are, in fact, rewarding people for wasting time, which actually reduces their enjoyment of the job. Being disciplined and focused and, as a result, getting the job done is deeply enjoyable. That discipline and focus enables people to enter a state of flow.

Flow, identified by psychologist Mihaly Czikszhentmihalyi, is a state of deep concentration, in which we lose track of time and focus completely on the task at hand. It is incredibly enjoyable and enables people to work at extremely high levels of productivity. In fact, productivity is generally many times higher in flow than it is working in a non-flow state, particularly one where people are feeling that they will be punished for efficiency.

When you force people to waste time, you are also undermining several of the motivational techniques we've already discussed and forcing yourself into the power game. Instead, reward getting things done and help your teams develop the flexibility and structure that enables people to use their time well.

While teams do need a certain amount of time together in order to develop, as we discussed in Chap. 3, forcing people to move in lockstep is counter-productive. If you use time in a fashion which reduces motivation, you also slow team development.

We will look at this further when we discuss productivity in Chap. 9.

Pictures Motivate No Matter How Many Words They're Worth

Many people find it motivating to put a picture of a spouse, kids, or someone else important to them on their desk. Having that picture is a constant reminder of why they're doing their job. The presence of the picture encourages people to work harder and more persistently toward their goals. This doesn't work for everyone, so don't force it.

Celebrate Progress

One of the most important things you can do as a team is periodically celebrating progress. It is always more motivating to look at how far you've come rather than how far you have yet to go. Indeed, it's more motivating to say, "we're half done," than to say, "There's still half left to do." The two statements may be mathematically equivalent, and IBM's Watson, the Jeopardy playing computer, would probably find them identical. If you happen to be employing Watson, then it may not matter what you say. However, if you happen to be employing people, it matters.

In jujitsu practice, the students who always focus on how far off the black belt is tend to not finish the journey. Those who focus on how far they've come are the ones who keep coming back.

You don't need to highlight individuals every time you do this; in fact, you shouldn't. The goal is not to make anyone feel bad for not getting as much done as someone else; rather, it's simply about sharing success. Feeling that the team is making progress helps boost everyone's morale, increases team cohesion, and helps build trust.

Depending on your organizational culture, you can occasionally highlight individual accomplishments in much the way that some sports teams will highlight most valuable players. It's important, though, to pay close attention to how people work and what they expect. At Atari, a new CEO tried to transform the highly collaborative, team-based culture into a more individual, competitive culture. He focused heavily on "engineer of the week," and other such awards. However, engineers at Atari viewed game development as a collaborative process, where everyone worked together to produce a quality product. The focus on individual performance shattered the team structure, turning high performance teams back into struggling level one groups. Atari never recovered.

When you celebrate team successes, you build relationships, strengthen competence, and provide the trust necessary for greater levels of autonomy. Success builds on success just as failure feeds on failure. What you focus on is what you get.

A Final Thought on Motivation

Effective motivation is not something you can do as a checklist. Each of the techniques discussed above have to be adapted to the people in front of you. Different people will be more responsive to some techniques than they are to others. That's not just okay, it's normal! Unless you're hiring the clone army from *Star Wars*, you shouldn't expect people to be the same.

Motivation also becomes easier as the team develops. The higher the level of the team, the more exciting it is to be part of it.

The trick to making motivation work is to keep reminding yourself that it is something you do with your team, not to them. Be willing to experiment and ask people if what you are doing is helping them focus and enjoy their work. Listen to what they say and be open to feedback.

Finally, remember the immortal words of the late Zig Ziglar: "People say that motivation doesn't last. Neither does bathing. That's why we recommend doing it every day."

Questions to Consider

1. What motivates you?
2. What motivates your employees? How do you know?
3. Where is the motivation trap playing out in your organization?
4. What are you doing to coach your employees and build their sense of success?
5. How are you involving your team?
6. What experiences do you enable people to have?
7. What does your organizational culture tell you about continuous learning?
8. How often do you take breaks?
9. When you do take breaks, what benefits do you personally gain? If you haven't been taking breaks, try it for a while and then answer this question.

Chapter 6
Recruiting with Confidence: Developing Effective Strategies and Having the Confidence to Use Them

Near the end of the award winning movie, *Lord of the Rings: The Return of the King*, Aragon leads his pitifully small army to the Black Gate of Mordor, realm of Sauron the Dark Lord. Sauron's forces outnumber Aragorn's by easily a hundred to one. On the surface, there appears to be little chance of success. Indeed, during the planning of the assault, Gimli utters the famous line: "Certainty of death, small chance of success... What are we waiting for?"

As those familiar with the story know, the attack is diversion. Its goal is to draw the attention of Sauron so that Frodo can destroy the Ring of Power. Aragorn, however, cannot let on that the attack is anything but an all-out assault on Sauron's fortress. To fool Sauron, indeed, even to convince his soldiers to follow him, he must act and speak as though he has complete confidence that his badly outnumbered army can win. Aragon must not just be confident, he must be so confident that people will be inspired to follow him to almost certain death. That act of confidence is what makes it possible for Frodo to succeed and for Sauron to be defeated.

Small chance of success indeed, but a small chance is better than no chance at all. No chance at all is exactly what they had if they did nothing. It took immense confidence to seize that opportunity, but it worked in the end.

Okay, *The Return of the King* is fiction. What about reality? Whether in sports or business, confidence is key. Confident teams are more likely to win. Confident entrepreneurs are much more likely to get funding. Confident salesmen are more likely to sell. Confident engineers successfully solve more difficult problems than their less confident brethren. Confident CEOs are much more likely to build a successful business. To hire effectively requires confidence.

Why do People Lack Confidence in the System?

I heard a hiring manager comment that she would "Prefer not to hire anyone at all."

Her company is growing, they are actively looking for people. At the same time, this manager who has been tasked with building up her team is openly telling

S. R. Balzac, *Organizational Psychology for Managers*,
Management for Professionals, DOI: 10.1007/978-1-4614-8505-6_6,
© Springer Science+Business Media New York 2014

candidates that if she has her way, not one of them will be hired. Indeed, given the choice, it's hard to imagine candidates accepting an offer if they did get one, compared, say, to an offer from an enthusiastic and confident employer.

While making the observation that this woman lacked confidence might be something of an understatement, it is only a start. Confidence begets confidence, just as lack of confidence begets lack of confidence. This manager was demonstrating a lack of confidence in herself, her company, their hiring process, and in the candidates. That, in turn, makes it extremely difficult to attract top people: if the hiring manager doesn't seem confident, what does that tell the candidate about the company? Those who can get other offers will go elsewhere, leaving this manager to choose less qualified people, further confirming her lack of confidence! Therefore, it is important, and far more useful, to understand why she lacked confidence. Only then is it possible to do something to increase her confidence and make it possible for her to hire effectively.

Indeed, this manager cited one major reason for her unwillingness to hire. No surprise, it was the economy. Despite what she'd been told to do by her boss, she fundamentally did not want to hire anyone because she was terrified that the economic recovery would fail and the company would go under. Listening to the news of that day, it's easy to understand why she felt that way: The fact is, it is hard to listen to the news without feeling discouraged. It's even worse in a world where the news is always on, as close as our computer or cell phone. When we hear the same five dire forecasts over and over, it reinforces the message of doom and gloom, even when it's the same news story being repeated five times! Being tough and bucking up only works for so long. Eventually, even the toughest will get tired: a steady diet of discouraging words can undermine anyone's confidence in a variety of subtle or not-so-subtle ways.

In the end, though, while this woman's lack of confidence may have been made obvious by the economy of the time, further investigation revealed the economy wasn't the actual cause. The actual cause was both more immediate and less obvious: she fundamentally didn't trust the hiring process her company used. If you don't trust the process, it's hard to have confidence in it, and the more vulnerable you are to surrounding influences such as the news. In a strong economy, her lack of trust could easily go unnoticed simply because the positive news flow would allay her fears; without the positive backdrop, however, her fear and her lack of confidence in the system were fully exposed. Sadly, this lack of confidence appears to be the case in a great many different companies.

Now, lest I give the wrong impression here, this lack of confidence is not necessarily unjustified. In fact, when people don't have confidence in the system, there is often a reason. Let's take a look now at those reasons and what can be done to build confidence so that you can find the best people and convince them to come to work at your company. Believing that they'll come to you because they're desperate is not a good strategy! In the best case, you get a lot of desperate people who will likely have second thoughts as soon as they don't feel quite so desperate any more. If you don't mind being a way-station for those seeking better jobs, that's fine. But if you'd like to be a destination for the best, that requires having confidence your system.

At root, any system for recruiting and hiring candidates needs to do four basic things:

1. It should attract the right people, the people that the company wants to employ, and convince them to apply.
2. Of those who apply, it should identify the people who are well-qualified to do the job.
3. It should provide the tools to convince those people to accept offers.
4. It should have a feedback mechanism to correct the inevitable mistakes.

I have yet to work with a company that didn't claim that their recruitment process did exactly that, yet I see company after company where the people tasked with hiring lack confidence in the system. Even though I am often told that "our system does all those things," the statement is made much more in the mode of someone whistling past a graveyard than someone who actually believes in what they're saying. So what is missing? Why this shocking lack of confidence? There are several reasons.

Attracting the Right People

First, the hiring managers may not believe that they are attracting the right people. In a poor economy, if the company announces a job opening anyone with a pulse applies, and maybe some things without a pulse as well! In a good economy, there's a fear that the best people are going somewhere else and you have to grab the people you can even if you're not sure they're qualified. Let's face it, although every company claims to only hire the best, that's a bit like Garrison Keillor telling us that all the children in Lake Woebegone are "above average." You've already set yourself up for failure.

The key here is to return to your organization's narrative and make sure you can apply that narrative to your specific division, department, or team. A big part of attracting the right people is telling the story that will appeal to those people. Don't spend your time trying to convince people who aren't interested in the organizational narrative: if the purpose of the organization does not excite them, it doesn't matter how skilled they may be. When someone isn't interested enough to be engaged, that forces motivation into the "doing it to them" mode. As we already know, that is exhausting and counter-productive for all concerned.

How do you know who those people will be? You don't. Rather than trying to attract a specific person, you are turning yourself into a talent magnet. Your goal now is to attract those people who fit your organization. If you have not created a compelling organizational narrative, as we discussed in Chap. 2, you are starting with a tremendous handicap: you will have no coherent framework for judging whether someone's interest in the company is motivated by more than just a paycheck.

Who is Qualified?

This brings us to the next problem: it can be extremely difficult to determine who is and who is not qualified. Hiring is difficult, which is one reason why I hear about HR people hanging out on Facebook trying to weed people out. It's a lazy approach. Similarly, I hear about recruiters rejecting resumes because of a "single typo or grammatical error." Seriously? Sadly, yes. As one recruiter put it, "My reputation is on the line; I won't pass along a resume with a typo because I know the hiring manager would reject it." Actually, my observation is that most hiring managers don't notice minor typos or grammatical errors. It's a false tell. If you find out that's what's going on, get a new recruiter: they clearly are not capable of actually understanding what you are looking for!

Answering the "who is qualified" question is a problem on multiple levels. At the most basic, you have to decide what "qualified" or "the best" really mean for your organization. Too often, businesses focus on a narrow skill set as a way of determining qualification. Skills are certainly important, but they are also something of a false tell. You are not just after people with certain skills: you are after the people with certain skills who can and will use them effectively in your organization. This is where your corporate culture plays a major role: if your culture is one of aggressive individualism, then team players are less likely to thrive; conversely, if you're working to build high performance teams, then someone who has never cooperated with their team in the past isn't likely to change just for you. Identifying the intersection between top performers and your cultural values takes more than listing buzzwords on a job ad and then hoping for the best. It requires taking an honest look at your company and how you're doing business; it requires paying attention to the things that you normally take for granted: those are the elements that a new person is most likely to notice and react to.

In other words, that top person may not be the world's best Java programmer or the world's best marketing expert, if that world's best expert can't fit in with your organization. Indeed, it is almost a cliché now when some manager tells me how they went to great effort to hire that person with the great skill set, how they gave that person everything they asked for, and how that person quit a few months later.

In order to determine if someone fits, an effective system asks candidates about their prior experiences not their future intentions. We'll discuss how to make that work later in this chapter. At the moment, though, we have a different issue that gets in the way of identifying qualified candidates: the paradox of perfection.

The Paradox of Perfection

The trap of looking for the perfect candidate manifests in a few different ways.

The first manifestation is something I refer to as the Godot Effect, based on Estragon's line in *Waiting for Godot:* "Personally, I wouldn't even know him if I saw him."

All too often, a prospective hire becomes the repository of every hope and every need of the hiring organization. The fact that the person does not yet exist in the organization only makes this worse. I've seen this particular phenomenon happen in front of me more than once. In particular, I was sitting in a product design meeting while the team discussed the next few hires it needed to make.

They started by observing that they needed someone who could handle some specific piece of technology. So far, so good. Then things went downhill.

We don't have anyone on the team who can handle [...technology...] either.

That'll be the next hire.

Wasn't the next hire supposed to be [...original problem...]?

We'll need someone who can do both.

From someone who could do "both," it quickly morphed into someone who could do three things, then four. After a while, it did become clear that things were getting just a bit ridiculous, but that didn't help. There still wasn't a serious return to reality; by the time the people in the room were finished, the only person who could have met their needs was Doctor Who. In other words, they were looking for a fictional, centuries old, omni-competent Time Lord. Alternately, if he wasn't available, they could have tried to hire the professor who teaches the most courses in a typical college catalog: a scholar known as Staff. Unfortunately, Professor Staff isn't usually available either. The net result is that they were so busy looking for someone with a highly improbable set of skills that they couldn't recognize a qualified person when they walked in the door.

Closely related to the Godot Effect is the idea that, to misquote the X-Files, the perfect person is Out There and is always the person who is Not Here.

In one training exercise I ran, participants were presented with a problem and were given the names of other people who might or might not be able to help them. The trick was that not everyone was present: some of the people listed weren't available. While some of the participants made do with the contacts that were available, many of them fixated on the people who weren't there. Just as Clint Eastwood, at the 2012 Republican Convention, imbued an empty chair with all the characteristics he disliked about President Barack Obama, participants in the exercise imbued the people who weren't there with all the characteristics of the person they were looking for, including the belief that this person would be eager to help them. This idealized mythical individual prevented them from recognizing the imperfect, but physically present, individuals who could have actually helped them!

The next form of the perfection paradox is a little more subtle. Ask any hiring manager if they'd hire someone who never takes decisive action, refuses to consider alternatives, and has never challenged themselves, and the usual answer is, "Of course not!" Despite the vehemence of their response, however, that's exactly what they are doing.

Naturally, it doesn't look that way.

It looks like they are hiring people with strong track records and consistent employment: People who have a history of successes, not failures, and who have never been responsible for something going wrong. The problem, though, is that they rarely take the time to understand why those people have those perfect records. At best, I've seen managers attempt to break down someone's record, in order to see if it was airbrushed.

While there is value to verifying that someone is being truthful on a resume, those managers are missing the point. The real problem is that the resume really is as perfect as it looks.

Basketball great Michael Jordan famously said, "I've missed more than 9,000 shots in my career; I've lost almost 300 games; 26 times I've been trusted to take the game-winning shot— and missed. I've failed over and over and over again in my life. And that is why I succeed."

Michael Jordan is so good exactly because of his willingness to take chances, to push himself, and to act without a guarantee of success. All too often, that perfect resume is really showing you someone who carefully burnished his image or selectively chose projects which would not risk that beautiful façade. When you focus on perfect resumes, you are quite often weeding out the people who are willing to seek out challenges and push the envelope. In other words, you are screening out the people who are most likely to be out of the box thinkers. Far more important than someone who has never failed is the person who can fail and get back up again: as one of my jujitsu instructors once said, "The fight's not over until you can't get up." The ability to fail and recover is a sign of optimism and resilience, critical attributes of developing a success driven mindset. Those attributes should be part of your definition of a qualified person.

The final aspect of the perfection paradox relates to the stages of team development that we discussed in Chap. 3.

Recall that teams in early developmental stages are very focused around conformity and appearances. There is a strong tendency toward a mentality of "what you see is what you get," or, in this case, "what you see is what you look for." A WYSIWYLF (pronounced wizzee wolf) may sound more dangerous than a WYSIWYG, and it is. Simply put, our image of the right person to hire is shaped by the people around us. We look for people who look like us or like our coworkers. A poor manager is unlikely to hire a good manager in large part because she doesn't know what a good manager looks like! This part of the interplay between organizational culture and recruiting; we'll go into that in more depth later in this chapter. Suffice it for the moment to say that even advanced teams can be trapped by what our organizational culture tells us is the image of the "right" person.

The net result of all these factors is a lack of faith that the hiring process will get the results we want.

Faith Matters

That lack of faith translates into lack of confidence, which shows when managers and other interviewers are talking to candidates. Even if an offer is made, a candidate is less likely to accept it if the manager or the other employees appear to lack confidence in company. Step three, which seems like the one most likely to work, is also failing!

Feedback

No system will work perfectly in all situations and with all people. Thus, feedback is key. Legendary stock trader Jesse Livermore made a fortune listening to the feedback he got from the market. Even though he lost money on over half his trades, he made hundreds of millions of dollars. Recognizing that he would make mistakes and using feedback to make sure that the damage from those mistakes was minimized enabled him to succeed. Livermore's confidence came from understanding his system and knowing that he had a way of recognizing, containing, and correcting mistakes. Michael Jordan's failures were feedback that told him how he needed to improve his game and that he could bounce back from a screw up.

The lack of confidence most people have in their company's recruitment and hiring mechanisms traces most often to a weakness in step four. In the case of our hiring manager, part of her fear was the belief that if she hired the wrong person, she would be blamed and would lose her job. If she hired no one at all, she took no immediate, personal risk. While not hiring might be risky for the company, or deprive the company of manpower at a critical moment, that was an abstract concern next to the very real personal danger she felt.

Solving the problem, therefore, needs to happen at multiple levels in the company. Each step of the process must be examined to make sure it's doing what it's supposed to be doing and the mechanism for handling errors must be identified and verified. If there is no error correction, there will be *limited* confidence in the system. If people are afraid of being punished for errors, there will be *no* confidence and no willingness to use the system. We will look more at feedback systems later in this chapter.

Confidence doesn't come from pretending that errors will never occur: athletes who assume that the tournament will go perfectly are easily beaten once something unexpected happens. Confidence comes from knowing how to use the system and knowing that the system provides you with the tools to minimize errors, contain any damage that might result from those errors, recover from errors, and learn from those errors so that they can be avoided in the future. To put it another way, while no battle plan survives encounter with the enemy, having a good battle plan is what enables you to make each encounter steadily more successful. Making the system work better and better builds confidence for all those who need to use it, and the more confidence they have in the system, the better it works.

Culture and Hiring

In Chap. 1, we discussed organizational culture and, briefly, the interaction between culture and hiring. The effects are considerably stronger than our brief example in Chap. 1 might imply.

On a broad level, how an organization approaches the recruiting process and treats candidates during that process says a great deal about the culture and, in turn, reinforces the culture.

For example, how a company treats candidates during the recruiting process teaches those candidates a great deal about how to succeed in that company. In the early 1990s, a certain company, which we'll call Asteroid Systems, was infamous for its recruiting process: candidates were called back for interview after interview. This process could take weeks and attempts to call and get information on the process were ignored. Those who were eventually hired had learned the lesson that decisions should be made slowly, that everyone needs to have input, and that it was better to take an arbitrarily long time to make decisions than to make a mistake. This was reflected in how the company did business. While their market was hot, it wasn't a serious problem, but when competitors moved in, their inability to make rapid decisions or risk mistakes lead to major problems. The candidates who got tired of waiting and went elsewhere were sufficiently invisible to the employees that they did not provide disconfirming evidence for the success of their policy.

Meanwhile, the Wasabi Corporation had a slightly different approach to recruiting. In their case, the people who called constantly and generally made pests of themselves were the ones who were called into for interviews. If you were passive, they didn't want you. Employees at Wasabi learned from day one that if you wanted to get things done, you needed to take action and that taking action was rewarded. For the most part, this worked out pretty well for Wasabi. They did have some problems with employees being so pushy that it was difficult to get them to work together, but they were able to solve that.

A brief caution here: do not assume that the best way to hire is therefore to ignore passive candidates and just call in the people who keep making noise. Wasabi's method worked for them in that time and place and because it connected to the appropriate elements of their culture. If you attempted to just graft that approach on to another company, the results would probably not be so pretty. A common mistake is to take a mechanism from one company and graft it to another. That can work well when the two companies have similar underlying values and beliefs, the *why* of culture, but can be disastrous when those underlying values and beliefs do not match.

So how do you avoid inadvertently reinforcing the wrong aspects of your culture or allowing some parts of your culture to become too strong at the expense of other aspects of the culture? It's not easy, and the more enmeshed you are in the culture of the organization for which you recruit, the harder it will be (Fish do not discover water) and people who spend their days within a culture tend to take it for granted. This can make it difficult to recognize the subtle and indirect effects of your recruiting approach. However, there are ways to design your recruiting process that will allow you to become more cognizant of how your culture is shaping the process, and enable you to focus on the elements that really matter.

What are Your Values?

Start by reviewing your values. A large white board will help with this step!

Write down what you believe to be the values of the company. Have the other interviewers independently do the same. Once everyone has their values written down, put them all up on the white board. How much overlap is there? How much difference? Hopefully, your team largely shares a common set of values!

Now, compare those values to those portrayed in your organizational narrative. Obviously, if the company lacks an organizational narrative, this will be difficult. Without that larger organizational framework, it's harder to be consistent in your message, and hence harder to hire people who are going to fit well into your organization.

Assuming there is an organizational narrative, how do the values expressed there match with the values held by your group? While differences are not necessarily a problem, as they might just reflect local conditions or decisions on doing business, they are important to look at. If nothing else, you need to make sure that the person you hire into your group is compatible with your values and the organizational values. Someone who cares about the latter and not the former is not going to fit into your group.

It is also helpful to look at places where your listed values contradict larger organizational values or contradict how people are actually working. Such contradictions alert you to a potential reef waiting to sink your metaphorical ship. New hires brought into an ambiguous environment are going to be less comfortable, less motivated, less productive, and more likely to feel they just don't fit in. The exception is if your office is part of an established counter-culture within the organization, similar to IBM's Watson Research Center discussed in Chap. 1. Even then, however, there is still agreement with the basic vision and narrative.

Calling Doctor Staff!

Take the time to write down the characteristics of the perfect hire. What does that person look like? Have you just described Dr. Staff? Or have you just described someone already on your team? If the latter, you are at least working with someone real.

Next, take the time to note down why you described your perfect hire the way you did. Are those characteristics reasonable, realistic, or even possible? One company I worked with in the early 2000s advertised for an employee with "at least 15 years of Java experience." At that time, the Java programming language had been around for considerably fewer years than the fifteen they were looking for! Unless they found a time traveler, odds were poor that they'd satisfy their criteria!

Remember that we tend to look for people who are similar to the people we already know or to those our culture teaches us are good to have around. This may mean people currently on your team or people you've worked with in the past. Does the person you've described fit either of those categories? If similarity guides your hiring too strongly, you'll find yourself with a team that is extremely homogenous, exactly the problem that we discussed with Robotic Chromosomes in Chap. 1. Teams where the members are all similar may feel easier to work with, but are considerably less productive and less able to handle divergent thinking than teams with a more diverse membership.

Is your perfect hire all about hard skills or do you have soft skills in there as well? If you don't include ability to work on a team or engage in productive argument, you won't look for them!

Which areas of your description are objective and which are subjective? You need to pay particular attention to the subjective characteristics as those help identify hidden values and beliefs of the organization and will be most influenced by cultural values of your organization.

The Crystal Ball is Cloudy…

Once you've honed your description to the point where you can now say that you know who you're looking for, you still have a couple of questions left to answer.

First, how will you measure the criteria you've selected? Some may be hard to measure during an application process, for example the ability to design large-scale software projects or execute a months' long marketing campaign. Thus, you'll need to identify metrics that you can use to predict success in your criteria. How you choose to do this will be heavily influenced by your organizational culture, and hence should be subject to careful review. As we discussed in Chap. 1, many software companies like to use logic puzzles as a way of identifying good software engineers. This doesn't work, but that doesn't stop people from trying. To demonstrate this point, I took a logic puzzle one software company was using and gave it to a number of people not at that company. The people to whom I presented the puzzle included a number of top software engineers. None of them got it, at least not for several days. The only person who solved it immediately was a psychologist who had never programmed a computer!

Logic puzzles as predictors are a cultural myth of the software industry. Most industries have their own myths about what will predict a good employee. Although it's popular to claim that every legend has a germ of truth, that's not a good thing to count on. Rather than being trapped in mythology, you need to take the time to identify the real factors that predict the criteria you value. Otherwise, you will end up looking for the wrong person.

How common and powerful are cultural myths in organizations? Very. For some examples, consider the following statements heard in many companies:

1. Happy workers are productive workers.
2. All individuals are most productive when their boss is friendly, trusting, and approachable.
3. Everyone wants a challenging job.
4. You have to scare people a little to get them to do their jobs.
5. Everyone is motivated by money.
6. Most people are much more concerned with the size of their own salaries than with others'.
7. The most effective work groups are devoid of conflict.

If these statements are true, that would tell us that we are looking for people who are fundamentally happy, amiable, seek challenge, motivated by money, are not concerned with fairness, and are not argumentative. As we've already discussed, high performance teams are full of brief, productive conflict and money is not a strong motivator over the long term, so we know that at least two of these statements are false. To spare you the suspense, I'll reveal now that the others are as well. Companies where they are believed, however, find themselves looking for the wrong people and then cannot understand why their new hires don't work out. Even worse, when someone does work out, the company doesn't really know why.

At the beginning of this section, I wrote that you had two questions left to answer. The second question is this: now that you know what your perfect employee looks like and how to identify him or her, how much imperfection is still good enough? For each characteristic you've identified, ask yourself if you could remove that and still have someone worth hiring. Repeat this process until you feel you cannot remove any more characteristics. This is your least perfect employee. You are not going to hire anyone who does not meet at least that minimum standard. Over time, this process will become part of your culture, which will help reinforce effective recruiting methodologies.

Hire for Loyalty, Not Disloyalty

This point probably seems like a no-brainer. Yet, companies routinely hire for disloyalty and are amazed when they get it.

Fundamentally, a person can be most easily dislodged from a company when they don't feel appreciated, when they don't feel their work matters, when the environment they are in makes them feel incompetent, when they don't get along with their boss, or when they don't feel connected to the team. So, if you're looking for someone who is basically unhappy in their job, then poaching from another company might make sense. It's certainly true that there are some good people who can be found that way.

But we also have to ask, "Why? Why does this person feel unappreciated? Why do they not feel their work matters? Why do they feel incompetent at their company? Why don't they feel connected to the team?"

Is it the person or is it the company? And how will you know? I've found that a surprising number of very talented and skilled people will remain loyal to a company even when conditions are poor, management is weak, and they are not really all that happy.

Now, let me be clear: if we're looking at recruiting people from a company that's in trouble and in danger of going under, that's a very different situation. In that case, the forces that hold someone in the company are rapidly disintegrating. It's when we're trying to pull people away from a reasonably stable environment that loyalty really comes into play.

Consider how often people take the job with lower pay or a more annoying commute in order to pursue a dream or work for a company they believe in. When you try to lure someone away from a company with promises of higher pay or any of the usual prizes and bonuses, are you giving them something to believe in? Or are you just hiring mercenaries? Basically, you are falling into the motivation trap of rewards and punishments. In the end, the people you are most likely to get are those who are most loosely attached to their current job, or who can be lured away by those things that your competitors can use to lure them away from you: in other words, you're looking at the least loyal and, quite often, the ones whom you will find it hardest to work with.

Again, there is an exception: if you can attract someone with your organizational narrative, then money or other perks can provide added incentive to make the jump. However, you should be very very certain that it's the vision of the organization driving that particular train. Companies such as Google or Apple, that created powerful, exceptionally vibrant organizational narratives, will pull people toward them.

Study the Process

Correctly identifying the people you are looking for is only half the process. You also need to look at your hiring process. As we saw with Wasabi and Asteroid, the process has a major effect on shaping the culture of the organization. The hiring process is also a reflection of your organizational culture, so if you see something not working in one place, you can bet you'll find plenty of other examples of that throughout the organization!

Again, it can help to find a room with a large whiteboard. Write out the flow-chart of your hiring process. Identify the decision points. How are those decisions made? How easy is it? What criteria are being used? Are you using the ones you just developed in the previous section, or do you find that other criteria are sneaking in?

Once you have the process you believe you have written out, put that to one side. Over the next few hires, document the process as it goes. If you have a match, that's a good start. You may still need to fix faulty decision making or you may discover that, like Asteroid Systems, no one is willing to make a decision. At least, though, you've correctly identified the key points. Now you can focus on connecting the process to the rest of your organization. If something isn't working, you can tell whether it's peculiar to your hiring process or a reflection of your organizational culture. The latter will be harder to change.

On the other hand, you may find that you don't actually have the system you think you have. In that case, you need to understand the discrepancies. Odds are, you are running up against wishful thinking, cultural reefs, or both. Either way, you've just identified points where your process is likely to be shaping your culture in wrong, or at least unpredictable, ways.

Recognizing and Understanding Feedback

As we discussed earlier in the chapter, feedback is critical to designing a system that people can trust and use with confidence. Feedback includes measuring both short-term success and long-term results. In other words, you have to recognize several success and failure cases:

- The person who appeared to be a good hire is, in fact, a good hire. Hooray! Something is working right.
- Your hiring process led you to conclude that a particular person was not a good choice. That's fine. However, do you have any way of following up on that? Are they really unqualified? This is a very hard question to answer. Sometimes you can find out how they do somewhere else, and that will give you useful information. Often, though, you'll never know if the person you didn't hire should have been.
- You hired someone who looked good, but now they aren't working out. Why not?
- You hire people who initially work out well, but then become less productive or motivated, or simply quit. What went wrong?

The last two cases are far and away the most interesting. That's where feedback is the most valuable because it is pointing to weaknesses in the process. If you hire an apparently qualified person and they don't work out, this could be an error in how you are attracting people or in your criteria for determining who is qualified. It could also mean that you've hit one of those cultural reefs we've mentioned before: now that the person is actually working for you, they simply aren't happy or comfortable in the organization. If you feel the person really is qualified, you may well want to spend some time working with them to turn them into a productive member of your organization. How much time and effort should you spend? Well, that requires us to recognize a number of feedback systems. Culture figures in here as well, as we tend to selectively focus on the feedback that fits our cultural biases. We must also consider the assumptions we are starting with, and whether our feedback is meaningful. While it is not possible to examine every permutation of culture and feedback, as an example we will deconstruct one of the more common intersections between culture and feedback: the question of do you hire slow and fire fast, or do you hire slow and fire slower?

How often have you heard someone say, "We hire slow and fire fast?"

I've heard this line so often that it sounds sort of a like a mantra or one of those wise sayings that are taken for granted but are generally wrong: "I invest for the long term," or "There is no room for emotions in the work place," or "The Red Sox will never win."

This is not to say that it's always wrong to "hire slow." However, it's important to understand the different ways that a company can hire slow. Some of them make more sense than others. What, fundamentally, does it mean to hire slow? For that matter, what does it mean to "fire fast?"

Remember our old friend, Asteroid Systems. As we discussed, Asteroid had a hiring process that was not so much slow as glacial: candidates were called back for round after round of interviews with more and more people. Some of them did, apparently, get hired. Many others found different jobs long before Asteroid could make up its collective mind. Did Asteroid hire slow? Yes. Was that particularly useful? Not so clear.

A company can hire slow for two major reasons: because they know exactly who they're looking for and are willing to wait for the right people to apply, or because they don't know who they're looking for and believe they'll know when the right person applies.

The first is more useful. If you've done your homework and figured out the characteristics of the employees you're looking for, and if you've trained your interviewers to recognize those people, then by all means hire slow. Take your time and wait for the right people or, better yet, go out and attract them to the company.

Asteroid Systems, though, wasn't doing that. They didn't really know what they were looking for. Some interviewers were looking for top performers; others were looking for someone who would be "fun to work with" and "not threatening." Still others were searching for people who "wouldn't damage the culture." Sadly, Asteroid Systems is hardly unique; I've observed the same behaviors over and over. Let's take a moment, therefore, to understand what they mean.

Seeking Top Performers

This is a worthy goal, no question about it. As we've discussed, it's not easy, but at this point you should have at least some idea of how to go about doing it. We'll discuss some additional approaches later.

Fun to Work with

I am frequently told that the goal of the interviewing process is to find people who are fun to work with. In one case, the same person who told me that they had a great system that enabled the company hire people who were fun to work with later told me that it was successful one time in three. In other words, it was failing twice as often as it was succeeding!

Fun to work with is a not a particularly good metric. Not only does it get you the wrong people, it can easily get you the wrong people who are the best at masquerading as the right people. More broadly, gut instinct, positive or negative, is easily fooled. It takes a lot of training to develop a smart gut, and, even then, it'll be wrong more often than we like to admit.

Not Threatening

This is an odd statement. What does it mean to be looking for someone who is "not threatening?" After all, as long as the candidate didn't show up for the interview armed to the teeth, one might assume that they are "not threatening."

When I've asked people what they meant, the answers were as varied as the people asked: "won't disrupt the way we work," "good team player," "respects others," "isn't a know-it-all," "will be loyal," and so forth. A common element, though, was a key element of the corporate culture: employees at organizations with highly competitive "fire fast" cultures were more likely to view strong candidates as "threatening" than employees at organizations where people were not pitted against one another. Quite simply, if the company takes the attitude that the poorest performers will be fired, then many people will instinctively respond by making sure not to hire anyone more qualified than they are! While I've had managers tell me that such an attitude is highly unprofessional, it's also highly intelligent self-preservation. I've observed that most people would rather feel smart and unprofessional than stupid and professional, especially if the former lets them keep their job and the latter does not!

Not threatening also comes into play in organizations that have a culture that does not tolerate mistakes. The less tolerance there is for mistakes, the less willing people are to make decisions. At RC Systems, a manager made one hiring mistake, bringing in a candidate who turned out not to be qualified (despite all the appropriate reference checks!). This error was brought up at his reviews over and over again! It takes little imagination to guess how likely this particular person was to take a chance on even the most perfect appearing hire after that!

Wouldn't Damage the Culture

Another popular explanation for hiring slowly is to "not damage the corporate culture." This might be a real concern... if the company is extremely small, as in tiny, or if you're hiring someone into a very senior leadership position. Organizational culture is one of the most powerful, most immovable forces in any business. As we've discussed, culture is extremely resilient and does not change easily. Now, if you're hiring a new CEO, then a cultural fit is very important. If you have a cultural mismatch between a CEO and the organization, then one or both are going to be extremely unhappy: a culture mismatch produces a culture immune response as we discussed in Chap. 1. Apple under John Scully is a good example of an organization suffering from a culture immune response: morale disintegrated, motivation collapsed, innovation suffered, and so forth. In the end, the culture won: Scully was driven out.

If you are hiring for less lofty positions, though, there are couple of things to recognize: first, if someone really doesn't mesh with the culture, they probably won't stay; and second, even when you've done your homework it's still going to be hard to tell in advance. Not impossible, but difficult. Remember that if you focus only on the surface trappings of organizational culture, it's easy to be misled by cultural artifacts. As we've discussed, it does take a fair bit of effort and training to identify the "why's" of culture that underlie the "what we do around here."

Now, it is certainly possible to hire people faster than the organization can assimilate them. Surprising as it may seem, that won't damage the culture. It may damage team cohesion though, and bring out weak points in the culture:

Digital Equipment Corporation had a very aggressive culture, where ideas were constantly debated and challenged. This worked in large part because DEC had developed a very tightly knit team structure, in which a strong sense of trust and connection between employees kept the debate focused and manageable. When DEC grew too rapidly, the team structure couldn't keep up and trust was lost: the teams regressed to earlier stages of development. The culture didn't change; however, the mechanisms of the culture were no longer functional in the new environment. This was not a problem with hiring people who "damaged the culture," though so much as it was a problem with hiring a lot of people faster than the necessary socialization could take place.

Finally, let's take a look at "fire fast" and what that says about your hiring process.

First, and just to get this out of the way, if someone is committing corporate malfeasance, breaking the law, harassing others, and so forth, you should already have policies in place to deal with that. If you don't, you have bigger problems than anything we will address.

There are times when it becomes painfully obvious that someone just isn't working out well in a job. In that case, it really is worthwhile having a frank discussion with them to find out what's going on. It may be that the kindest thing you can do is fire them: they really aren't going to thrive in your company. Take that as an opportunity to look back at your hiring process and see if you can figure out where the process was flawed: not where a person screwed up, but where the process didn't work. If you focus on the former, you'll get nowhere. If you focus on the process, you can change things. Some mistakes really are part of the business, so get used to it! By the way, if you do have to fire the person, do what several top companies do: give them a generous severance package. After all, they just helped you discover a problem with your system. Besides, it's a cheap price to pay to have someone singing your praises after they've left.

What about someone who seemed really good in the hiring process but just isn't living up to expectations? If you're quick to fire, that says more than anything else that you don't have a lot of faith in your hiring process, an issue we discussed earlier in this chapter.

Assuming you have faith in your hiring process, though, and you really believe you have someone good, it's more worthwhile to invest some time to understand why they aren't performing. Focus on their strengths: if your hiring process is well-designed, you should have a good idea of what those strengths are! It is not unusual that once a candidate is immersed in the culture of your company some weakness will emerge that they might not have even known they had! If you value their strengths, don't spend a lot of time fixing the weakness; rather, find a way of working around it. When a weakness prevents someone from using the very strengths your hiring process was designed to identify, the key is to remove the obstacle. Legendary martial artist Bruce Lee used to say that if you built your strengths, they would eventually overcome your weaknesses. The same is true in business.

A hiring process that lets you correctly identify the right people most of the time may not always be quick, but the slowest part should be getting the right people to apply. If you really know how to recognize them, the process should be clear and transparent to the applicant. And if you have invested the time and resources to build that process, firing slow gives you time to take advantage of the talents it's bringing you. But you can only fire slow if you know how to hire right.

At Asteroid Systems, the process was slow because no one was willing to make a decision, an issue we touched on in Chaps. 3 and 4. It wasn't about finding the right people, it was about an inability to recognize them and a fear of making mistakes. Don't be an Asteroid.

Designing the Process

At this point, it is hopefully clear that your hiring process is a reflection of your organization. As we've discussed, any issues present in your organization are likely to manifest in your hiring process. This is particularly true with organizational dysfunctions. Unless you are extremely careful, you will find yourself hiring the people who prolong and increase the dysfunction, rather than those who help alleviate it: remember that the system selects for those who fit the system. Even if you avoid that trap, if the system is already stressed, adding more people to it only increases the pressure.

Lest it seem like I'm trying to make things sound impossible or like huge disaster is right around the corner, I'm not. Most advice on designing a hiring process focuses on what to do, but not on where the system is likely to break down. That oversight makes it difficult, at best, to debug the process when the inevitable problems crop up. And yes, I promise that we will discuss interviewing technique.

The first step to recruiting is to figure out who you want. We've already discussed how to identify your perfect employee and how to determine just how far from that ideal is still acceptable.

The next step is to clearly articulate the goals you expect your new hires will accomplish for the company. While we will go into goal setting in depth in Chap. 9, the important thing at this point is to consider both the short-term and long-term outcomes that you are looking for. Remember that strategy is the art of looking forward to your desired outcome and then reasoning back to figure out how you'll get there from here. Your hiring process needs to fit into that larger strategy.

Look at your organizational narrative for clues: which elements do you want to focus on? That will shape the population you attract: depending on your short-term and long-term goals, you might find yourself emphasizing particular tasks, more or less autonomy, and so on. Your strategy and organizational narrative need to be in sync or your strategy will be pulled off the rails.

Regarding skills, you need to look at hard skills and soft skills (also known as harder skills). Sometimes skills are very difficult to learn on the job: for example, you don't hire a talented amateur into your medical practice hoping he'll learn open-heart surgery on the job. Conversely, knowing a particular programming language such as Java is not a hard skill; it is a manifestation of the broader hard skill known as "programming." While you might expect a skilled programmer to pick up any computer language, you might not expect someone without programming skills to be able to do so.

Soft skills are that entire spectrum of skills having to do with being organized, working with other people, and generally being a responsible human being. You can hire the best engineer or the best salesman in the world, but if they can't work with other people, your organization will suffer. Sure, they might do just great individually, but the damage to the team and the organization will be considerable. Soft skills are very much the difference between just getting something done, and getting something done well.

In terms of assessing skills, there are numerous assessment vehicles available. Unfortunately, in today's fast moving world, generic assessments are not always all that useful. Some organizations may wish to design their own assessments. This is a fine thing to do, provided you take the time to test them out: if your organization is reasonably large, you can have current employees take the assessment and then you can compare how people did on it to how well they are doing in their jobs. If your top performers don't do well on the assessment, something is wrong with your assessment! You want to see a high correlation between people who do well on the assessment and your existing top performers. If your organization is small, you may have to look outside to get enough samples to have meaningful data. If you don't bother verifying that your assessments screen for the right people, you won't be able to trust the results, and you're back to the problem of not having confidence in the system.

However, rather than look solely at skills, it's much more effective to look at past behaviors and results. First, when we focus on skills and hypothetical situations, everyone is a genius. This isn't because people are being dishonest; it's because we always imagine ourselves doing the right thing in the future. Second, we are trying to gain a clear picture of how someone will behave in a variety of circumstances, which means we need to look at a variety of behaviors and circumstances. That is one of the best ways of figuring out if someone will fit in your organization.

The better you have defined what your ideal employee looks like, the easier the decision making process will be. Remember that the stage of group development influences how decisions are made. Early stage groups have a particularly hard time making decisions, so the more clearly you can define the criteria, the easier it will be. It also helps to make your hiring decisions early in the day or right after lunch, rather than late in the day when people are tired. Hiring someone always feels more risky than not hiring, and tired people tend to be more risk averse.

The Interview

Despite their popularity, unstructured interviews are not a particularly reliable method of finding the right people.

The problem is something that I jokingly dubbed the "hydrangea effect," after the Russian spies arrested in New Jersey by the FBI. The neighbor of one of the spies was quoted as saying something to the effect that, "She couldn't be a spy. Look what she did with the hydrangeas!"

Planting hydrangeas is so far outside the image of a spy that this simple act created a very powerful illusion. After all, who would imagine James Bond planting hydrangeas? This, of course, is exactly why he would plant them—and, being Bond, probably knows detailed information about seven different cultivars!

By the same token, many interviewees learn early on how to conduct themselves in an interview. In fact, most candidates probably have more experience being interviewed and more knowledge about how to evoke the hydrangea effect than the interviewers have about how to interview: job hunters conduct mock interviews all the time. The worst prima donnas are generally extremely charming and friendly. It's only when you've worked with them for a while that the problems emerge. Perhaps even more disturbing is that some of the least competent leaders are often particularly charismatic, are generally skilled communicators, and are extremely good at masquerading as effective leaders: they've learned how to fool others; it's the only way they can survive in the workplace.

Given the degree to which people are aware of how interviews work and the prevalence of interview coaches and workshops, unstructured interviews are only going to become less reliable.

The key to making structured interviews work for you is to recognize that the best predictor of the future is the past: I call this the "Chinese food principle." That is, if we go out to dinner at a Chinese restaurant once, I can't draw much information from what you order; however, if we go to dinner multiple times and you routinely order one of a small set of dishes, I can observe that pattern and make a pretty good guess that you'll order one of those dishes the next time (assuming you haven't been tipped off that I'm keeping track).

While we can't sit and observe someone for months or years before we hire them, we can still get at that information. The key is to ask open-ended questions about the past:

> When there was a conflict on your team, how did you handle it?

> When you held a strong opinion and the rest of the team disagreed, what did you do?

> When everything was running behind and everyone was stressed out, what was your approach?

By asking about the past, we get information about what they actually did. Sure, someone could lie, but it's difficult to fabricate an entire history on the fly. Mostly, what happens is that people naturally put the best possible face on what they really did. That's fine: use multiple interviewers.

The real art form here is not in the questions, but in piecing the answers together into a coherent picture of the person. It takes some practice, and a bit of training can't hurt, but someone skilled in interviewing can draw out a good deal of useful information; conversely, if the interviewee refuses to open up, that's also information. Why not? What does that tell you about how they'll communicate if you hire them? Having several people interview a candidate and then working as a group to assemble the pieces is a very powerful way of understanding how qualified a candidate is and how well she will fit your organization. Remember to first agree on the picture, then evaluate the person against the metrics you've already defined. If you try to do both at once, you'll find that you'll change the picture as you go.

It can also help to hold interviews in locations other than the office. According to an article in the NY Times a few years ago, Teresa Taylor, at the time the chief operating officer at Qwest, commented that she liked to take candidates out to dinner. The change in venue gave her the opportunity to see how they behaved in a relatively unstructured situation: were they polite to the wait staff and other diners? How did they handle a noisy environment? Did they drink too much? Did they maintain appropriate boundaries?

Don't forget that part of the interview process is to attract the candidate to the organization. Sharing a meal with someone has the added benefit that it's a way to build rapport. That can make the difference between the candidate accepting your offer instead of one from your competitor.

You can also use some of the organizational change principles from Chap. 1 to help convince a candidate to accept an offer. In other words, rather than push them to accept, let them persuade themselves.

For example, you could ask, "On a scale of 1–10, where 10 is perfect, how do you see this job?"

When they answer "seven," or whatever they pick, ask them why it's not a three. That's not an error: if you ask then why they aren't a ten, they'll tell you what's wrong with the job. If you ask them why not a three, they'll tell you what's right. Respect their autonomy: let them talk themselves into accepting the offer.

If you want interviews to be effective, the interviewers must be trained and must practice! Otherwise, you will never have the confidence in the process that you need to make it work. Also, although it might seem an obvious point, the interviewer must take the interview seriously. At one company, the interviewer sat down at the desk across from the candidate and started reading her email. When the candidate said something, the interviewer said, "We multitask here."

Would you hire someone who spent the interview texting on their smartphone?

The candidate got up and walked out.

Hiring is a tricky process. If you don't take it just as seriously as any other part of the business, you aren't going to get the results you want. However, you just might get the results you deserve.

Questions to Consider

1. What does your hiring process say about your organizational culture?
2. How will you know when you've found the right person?
3. What is your story? How did you get where you are today?
4. If you've never hired the wrong people, why not?
5. What questions might you ask someone to get them excited about your firm?

Chapter 7
Justice and Fairness in Organizations

Once upon a time there was a technology startup company. They recruited a team of highly skilled, extremely enthusiastic engineers. For reasons which remain shrouded in mystery, they insisted on assigning titles to the engineers as they were hired, such that some were designated senior engineers, some junior engineers, and some just engineers. This was initially seen as highly amusing by the engineers, who saw little significance in the titles since they were all doing the same work.

One day, one of the senior engineers, we'll call him Sidney, dropped his pay stub and it was found by one of the other engineers. It turned out that the Sidney was being paid double what many of the rest of the team were being paid, even though he was not doing double the work. He was, in fact, not doing anything different so far as anyone else could discern. Some of the other engineers complained to management that this vast salary gap seemed rather unreasonable given the distribution of labor and expertise. The VP of engineering replied that this man was the senior person on the team, and simply deserved more money. This, as one might imagine, did not go over well. A couple of the engineers quit, and most of the rest found excuses to not work so hard. Even amongst the other senior engineers, there was great unhappiness. More and more problems were dumped in Sidney's lap and there was an open attitude that if was going to be paid that much more than the rest, he could bloody well earn it.

At a different company, a similar scenario was playing out. In the second company, one of the senior people, we'll call him Charlie, discovered just how much more he was being paid than the rest of the people on the team. As shocking as this may sound to some people, he complained to management that the pay gap was unfair. After all, they were a team and were all doing equivalent work. The head of his department carefully explained to him that he really did deserve more than everyone else. Over time, though, Charlie found himself becoming increasingly uncomfortable in his job. Rather than delegate tasks, as he used to do, he started doing more and more of the work himself; he said later that he felt he had to do more to deserve the salary he was getting. The other members of the team, meanwhile, became increasingly frustrated at what they saw as Charlie taking the

S. R. Balzac, *Organizational Psychology for Managers*,
Management for Professionals, DOI: 10.1007/978-1-4614-8505-6_7,
© Springer Science+Business Media New York 2014

plum projects for himself and not giving them a chance to show how hard they could work. Eventually, Charlie resigned and went to another company.

At company number three, this rather odd tale took a very unusual turn. The new CEO came into find a shocking lack of organization and structure. No titles, no hierarchy, and, worst of all, no one seemed to care. Clearly, this state of affairs was absolutely intolerable. The CEO immediately imposed structure. He assigned titles. He instituted Employee of the Month awards. He watched in shock as, one after another, his best and brightest employees left the company.

In each of these cases, the common element was a simple one, one which children know and adults too often forget: people felt that the situation was fundamentally unfair. In the first case, why should Sidney be paid twice as much for what appeared to be the same work? If that really were the case, it's not all that surprising that the rest of the engineers were upset. If there were other factors, such as a specific expertise or education or something, then the CEO should have made that clear. Once the news was out, the perception of unfairness was devastating to the team.

The second case was much like the first, except that Charlie was the one who felt he was benefitting unfairly. His efforts to rectify the situation only made it worse. Whatever reasons were given for the apparent inequity, they failed to satisfy Charlie's innate sense of fairness.

In the third case, the employees all felt that they were engaged in a cooperative, team effort. They felt they were all making valuable contributions and deeply resented being singled out and rewarded individually for the efforts of the team. The more the CEO tried to impose hierarchy and rankings, the more he unraveled the structure of the team until it dissolved completely.

The first step in achieving a sense of justice and fairness in your organization is to build structural equity. In other words, it's not that everyone should be treated the same way or be paid the same amount; rather the structure of your organization should provide a framework for understanding differences and for understanding how to change them. Thus, while two employees might start at different salary levels due to education, this should not be a permanent condition. Assuming they are doing the same quality and significance of work, they should rapidly converge on the same salary. Differences must always be based on elements that the person can control, not things that she cannot: part of motivation is having a sense of control of your life. Thus, in addition to being illegal, gender-based, and other forms of discrimination also reduce motivation and productivity and can increase burnout.

At a very basic level, highly effective teams have a strong sense of justice and fairness. When people perceive an inequity in how they are being treated based on performance and contribution, they will act to reduce that inequity. They might not work as hard, as in the first case, overwork and burnout, as in the second, or quit, as in the third. No one likes being taken advantage of, and most people dislike feeling that they are taking advantage of others. Although in each example you can make logical arguments to justify the situation, the best logic will do is get people thinking. Emotion is what gets them to act. Thus, you must have the structures in place so that people will trust the system: maybe Bob is getting paid more because he has a doctorate while Jim does not. If that is set as an expectation, and employees who pursue advanced degrees are given raises when they complete those degrees, it can work quite well.

However, it's not enough to simply have a fair and just system. Of course, you do need to address the obvious points: fairness with respect to information flow, rewards, and procedures. However, having these pieces doesn't guarantee that your organization will be, or will be perceived to be, fair or just. They are important foundational elements, but are all too easily undermined.

There are a number of additional factors at play that affect how just and fair an organization is perceived to be. If we don't get those pieces right, the rest really doesn't matter. Some of the factors are perceptual: the way we think or the types of conclusions we tend to draw; some are cultural, such as whether the organization apportions blame versus solving systemic problems; some have to do with how the organization deals with jerks, bullies, and bad apples; and some have to do with how we provide and solicit feedback and enable growth. We will look at each of these in turn.

Don't Reach for the Ground!

My first jujitsu sensei would constantly yell at us to not reach for the ground when being thrown. His point was that if someone is throwing you and you yield to your natural reactions, you will try to catch yourself with an arm or a leg. In jujitsu, this is good way to end up with a broken arm or leg. What makes learning to fall difficult is that our tendency is reach out is so natural, so deeply ingrained, that we do it without thinking. Students sometimes don't believe they are doing it until they see themselves on video. Reaching out like that is a very simple, reflexive way of protecting our heads when we fall: it's better to break your arm than your head. For very young children, it's great since it takes no training, their bodies are light, and bones are still flexible. However, for adults, it's not so pleasant and is a serious problem in a great many situations where an untrained reaction is not appropriate or safe: knowing how to fall is why I didn't get badly hurt the time a car ran a stop sign and helped me dive over the handlebars of my bicycle.

By the same token, we have cognitive shortcuts or biases that are decent default behaviors in many situations, but are of limited value to us in the workplace or other modern organizational settings. Like reaching for the ground, they are simple and easy to use: we are built to use as little energy as possible whenever possible. Particularly when we are tired or distracted, we tend to fall back on these cognitive shortcuts. However, like that untrained jujitsu student's reflexive reaching for the ground, they are just setting us up for organizational injury. Just as the jujitsu student is being thrown with too much force to reach without serious injury, organizational issues are almost always too complex for us to get away with cheap answers.

Fundamental Attribution Error

"There's a guy in your office named Joe. Joe's not getting his work done, he's missing deadlines. How come?"

I will often pose this question when I conduct management training or when I speak on leadership. It's always interesting how people answer. Most of the time, people tell me what's wrong with Joe: he's not dedicated, he's goofing off, he doesn't care, he's incompetent. Eventually, someone will say, "Wait a minute. You didn't give us any information about Joe." Sometimes this takes ten minutes! It might take longer, but I always stop it by then.

What's happening here is that we automatically attribute problems or poor performance to the person, not to situational factors. This makes sense when we are all experiencing the same environment and doing essentially identical tasks: for example, people living in a small community or working on an assembly line. If most factors are identical, one person's poor performance is probably due to the person. This can cause trouble in our modern society: When our dinner date doesn't show up, we assume it means she doesn't actually want to spend time with us rather than assuming her car broke down or she was caught in traffic. Did that client not return my call because he didn't want to talk with me, or was it because his office is in Manhattan and he lost power after Hurricane Sandy? In the actual, real-life situation from which I drew the story of Joe, the reason Joe was missing deadlines was that the vendor who was supposed to provide the material he needed was always late and Joe didn't have the option of changing vendors.

We will often apply the fundamental attribution error to ourselves retrospectively: how could I have ever made such a stupid decision? We forget that the decision may have made complete sense with the information we had available at the time or that other situational factors might have contributed.

When we know someone well, however, the fundamental attribution error will often reverse itself: I know Bob. Bob is a hard worker. Something must be wrong. If you've arranged to meet your wife at a restaurant after work and she doesn't arrive in time, odds are you'll start worrying that she might have been in a car accident or something, rather than assuming she doesn't want to spend time with you.

One of the biggest problems stemming from the fundamental attribution error is that it can trap us into playing the blame game instead of understanding why a system isn't working. We'll look at that in more depth shortly.

Self-Serving Bias

This is the time-honored tradition of taking credit for success and sharing the credit for failure. This particular cognitive slip can be both a blessing and a curse. As psychologist Martin Seligman observes, optimists view success as due to their efforts and failure as due to external factors that are unlikely to be repeated. Pessimists, on the other hand, view success as due to chance, and failure as a result of their fundamental flaws. This is why optimists are more likely keep trying until they succeed while pessimists are more likely to give up.

However, too much of a self-serving bias can blind us to our own mistakes, making improvement difficult. A self-serving bias on the part of a manager or other organizational leader—that is, one who takes credit for the success of the group, but blames others for failure—can permanently block motivation and cause a team to stop progressing or even regress to an earlier stage of development.

A less obvious manifestation of self-serving bias is that people often see themselves as contributing more to the team than they really did. If you ask each person privately to tell you their percentage contribution, you'll find the total in excess of 100 %. This is one of the reasons why it is so important to be able to deliver effective feedback and conduct meaningful and accurate performance reviews. Otherwise, people will always perceive themselves as not being rewarded commensurate with their contributions.

For an organization to be successful, you do need a bit of self-serving bias. Teams need to believe that their actions lead to success and that failure is unlikely and not due to some inherent flaw in the team. The important points are to not let it get out of control and to make sure people are given appropriate credit for their accomplishments.

Halo

Many years ago, I left IBM to find a software job in Silicon Valley. Naturally, I wore a suit to the interviews. I interviewed for weeks with a great many companies with absolutely no success. Eventually, an engineer took me to one side and said, "Lose the suit. Around here, people in suits are salesmen, not engineers."

I lost the suit and had a job a week later. In the Silicon Valley high tech boom of that time, if you showed up in a suit then, as a friend of mine later put it, "we try not to hold it against you."

At that same time period, to get a job in Boston or New York you had better have been wearing a suit! As a different friend put it, "Dressing up shows you care."

In each of these examples what we're seeing is a generalized example of the hydrangea effect I referred to in the previous chapter: the Halo Effect. Halo is when one particular aspect of person shapes our entire judgment of them. Thus, a person who wears a suit to a job interview is usually perceived as more sincere, more skillful, and more committed, than someone who does not. There are, of course, exceptions! However, there is a good reason why politicians, salesmen, and confidence artists are well-dressed: their appearance shapes your perceptions of the value of the promises they are making, the product they are selling, or the great deal they are offering.

Halo is not restricted to clothing. Any behavior or mannerism can cast a halo. As we saw with the two different responses to wear a suit, that halo can be positive or negative. Halos can be true, as when positive performance in one area really does predict strong performance everywhere else. Halo can be false, as when employees who stay late in the office are perceived as being more productive than those who leave earlier, even when the former are actually playing World of Warcraft! In one software company, the guy who spent all night at the office fixing the problems that he routinely caused was heralded as a hero, while the people who wrote higher quality code and never stayed late were seen as slackers.

Halo can often cause us to believe that because someone does well in one position, they will do well in any other position to which they are assigned. Thus, the guy with amazing design sense was promoted into management even though he routinely infuriated the rest of the team with his abrasive interpersonal style. Becoming a manager didn't help.

Halo, by the way, does not just apply to people. In one amusing episode of a cooking show, wine experts tasted wines poured from beautiful, fancy bottles with expensive labels and wine from bottles with cheap, peeling labels. They rated the former as tasting much better than the latter, not realizing that it was the same wine.

Appropriate training scenarios can help determine whether the halo is true or false.

Selective Perception

Ever notice how an unexpected problem will cause each department to argue that if they just had more resources, they would have prevented the problem? Marketing says that if they had more money, they could have done a better job. Sales says, no, if they had more money, they could have prevented the problem. Product design says, well, you get the idea. Alternately, if you believe that Fred screws up all the time, then when something goes wrong you have no trouble seeing that all the clues point to Fred. It's simply obvious. It may be wrong, but it is obvious.

This is selective perception: the tendency to see in a situation only those aspects that reinforce our own beliefs, values, and needs.

Confirmation Bias

Ever notice that after you buy a new car, you see that model car on the road all the time? In fact, if you asked someone during the first week after buying a car what is the most common car on the road, they'd probably tell you the car they have.

Similar to selective perception, with confirmation bias we tend to look only at those pieces of data that support the decision we've made and ignore those that contradict it. Having bought a car, many people want to reassure themselves that they made the right choice. As a result, they pay attention to all the other people driving the same car, and ignore those who are driving different cars. In the stock market, investors will buy a stock and then focus only on the evidence that says it should go up, ignoring the fact that it is actually doing just the opposite. The example, cited earlier in this book, of the GM executive pointing to the parking lot full of GM cars and proclaiming that to be evidence that everything was going well is yet another example of confirmation bias.

Similarity Bias

You're sitting across the desk from a prospective candidate and you find yourself being favorably impressed. Eventually, you realize that this person reminds you of someone very important: you, or at least your younger self. Naturally, you want to help them.

Salesmen always try to find points of similarity with their prospects. Job hunters will seek to bring up points of similarity with their interviewers: college background, sports, etc. Team members will often attempt to share activities with the boss, essentially visibly demonstrating that they enjoy the same things. Each of these cases is evoking the similarity bias, in which our evaluation of someone is shaped by how well they remind us of ourselves. The stronger the similarity, the more favorable our impression of the other person. Thus, a manager who is proud of his aggressive manner will tend to highly rate more aggressive subordinates, often independent of actual accomplishment. In one case, the aggressive manager told an employee that he was too passive, not standing up for his ideas. That manager left, and the new manager, who prided himself on his ability to build consensus, told the same person that he was a strong team player for being willing to put his ego to one side for the good of the team.

Conversely, subordinates who are careful observers will often seek to mimic characteristics of the boss in order to win favor. If the boss falls for it, the best actor wins; perhaps not an Oscar, but at least money, promotions, and other perks.

Similarity isn't all bad though. That favorable response to similarity is part of how groups learn to work together and progress past the Forming stage of development. The trick here is to be intentional about the process and to build similarity around what really matters.

Projection

People work at their jobs for their reasons, not for your reasons. You might be aggressively pursuing position and power in the organization, while someone else might be more interested in solving complex technical problems or closing the most difficult customers. Projection is where you forget this point and assume that other people want the same things that you want. Remember that effective motivation requires leaders to understand their followers well enough to know what those followers value; when you get caught up in projection, you may well be offering the things that would motivate you, but not the things that would motivate them. I've seen this happen many times, leaving managers angry and frustrated that the office outing they arranged or the gifts they gave were greeted with such a resounding lack of enthusiasm. Projection leads us to evaluate people according to the wrong metrics and forces us into the motivation trap.

Contrast

When I tested for my second degree black belt in jujitsu, the person testing before did a competent, but very slow exam. I was more energetic to begin with, and coming after the person who went so slowly, I looked even better. Had the order been reversed, he might well have failed. This is a contrast effect: we tend to rate someone better or worse than they really are based on a recent experience with someone similar. Salesmen use this trick all the time to manipulate buyers by showing an overpriced piece of junk first, so that the actual highly priced product both looks incredibly good and like a real bargain.

First Impressions and Recency

With some people, you never get a second chance to make a first impression. For other people, though, every impression is a first impression. In other words, some people form an initial judgment on first meeting someone and change that initial judgment slowly, if at all. Others base their judgment of someone on their most recent interaction, good or bad. Most recent project was a success? You get a great review, no matter how bad the rest of the year was. Most recent project didn't go so well? Terrible review, again no matter how good the year was. It's easy to see how this approach would lead your team to feel that the organization was basically unfair, or at least blind, to quality and performance!

Self-Fulfilling Prophecy

In this case, it's not so much What You See Is What You Get as What You See Is What You Expect. Remember that it takes time for a team to develop an accurate assessment of its own capabilities. Even extremely competent individuals need feedback in order to perform at high levels. Your attitudes and your behavior are the feedback: you are the reflection of your team, whether you like it or not. What they see in you determines how they view themselves.

The manager who views an employee as someone who will "steal time" from the company, will treat that person in one way. The manager who views an employee as a potential star will treat that same person very differently. People respond to how they are treated and people become what they are treated as being. Therefore, it pays to expect high performance and treat people in the ways that will enable it to happen!

As we get to know people, the more likely our relationships with them will influence how we perceive them and how we evaluate their performance. The more comfortable we feel with people, the more likely our perceptions of them will be favorable and the more likely we are to excuse poor performance; conversely, the less comfortable we are with them, or the less strong the relationship, the more likely our perceptions will be unfavorable: we will focus on those aspects that confirm the relationship we already have. That, in turn, will shape the relationship going forward: confirmation bias and self-fulfilling prophecy play well, or poorly, together depending your point of view!

Fortunately, these cognitive shortcuts are not fate. Becoming aware of them is the first step to not being caught by them.

Blame and the Vortex

When there's a problem, perhaps a critical deadline was missed or you lost an important client, what could be more fair and just than finding and punishing the person responsible? Surely fixing blame is the best way to make sure such problems don't happen again! Blame is, after all, a natural response when something goes wrong. It's what we do in our larger societal culture: after all, if you get a speeding ticket, it's clearly your fault, right? You did something wrong. You were to blame for going too fast. Or maybe the real blame lies with the unfair and ridiculously low speed limit, or the cop who just happened to pick you even though other people were obviously going much faster. In any case, though, you've learned an important lesson: pay more attention to whether there's a police car on the road and maybe invest in a good radar detector. What about the speeding? Well, that behavior may change for a short time, but rarely does the occasional ticket produce permanent, lasting change.

This is the problem with blame: it may fix responsibility, but it does not fix the problem. While it can be very satisfying to identify the perpetrator of the disaster that lost the sale or crashed the server, actually solving the problem that led to the lost sale or crashed server is considerably more useful. This requires returning to the concepts we introduced in chapter one, looking at the organization as a system, and understanding how the system is failing. Failure is feedback. If you listen to that feedback and learn to understand what it is telling you, you will identify a weak point in your organizational systems.

At Koloth (once again, the names have been changed), an internet startup, website malfunctions were a regular event. Each time a problem occurred, the person responsible for making the mistake was identified and punished. The problems didn't go away. Even firing repeat offenders failed to stop the website problems.

What was really going on? Upon investigation, it turned out that several factors were contributing to the problem. First, the company had a very aggressive, eight week development cycle. The aggressiveness of the cycle meant that serious design decisions were constantly put off in favor of short-term, "temporary," solutions.

Next, the database engineers were chronically overworked, so developers were instructed to not bother them unless it was really important. As a result, developers would roll their own database code, usually copying it from somewhere else. This created numerous subtle problems which the database engineers had to spend their time tracking down, further reducing their availability.

Finally, a particular senior engineering manager was infamous for his last minute demands on his team. It was not unusual for him to walk into someone's office as they were leaving for lunch, or at 7 pm as they were getting ready to go home, and announce that "this component must be completed right now!" When the component failed or was not completed on time, said manager was quick to blame the team member to whom he'd assigned it. Of course, obvious a problem as this may be, it didn't come out until we investigated to see why there were so many failures. Once we got past the blame, and saw the outlines of the system it became possible to address the actual problems and change the outcome. Along the way, it turned out that the manager in question was secretly running a web-design business out of his office at Koloth: his clever use of blame prevented anyone from noticing for quite some time.

Now, one might argue that Koloth involved actual dishonesty, and that blame is an effective tool when dishonesty is not present. Unfortunately, when people are given an incentive to be dishonest, dishonesty emerges: this is our self-fulfilling prophecy at work. At Double Coil Systems, a bioinformatics company, when someone was found responsible for costing the company a major client, that person was disciplined or fired outright. As shocking as this may sound, it wasn't long before no one was ever responsible for anything. Each person involved in any problem had some explanation for why it wasn't their fault. The problem was always due to some other event. When someone did end up taking the blame, it was usually some hapless member of the IT staff. Apparently, the most junior member of the IT department at Double Coil ran the whole business and had complete control of every laptop at all times. Employees at Double Coil had mastered the art of CYA, and so the actual problems were never addressed. Even worse, when employees did notice a problem, they concealed the information lest they be blamed for it (particularly if they had made the mistake!).

The difference between Double Coil and a world class organization is that at the latter they take the time to understand all the components of why they are losing sales, identify the real bottlenecks, and fix them. Blame isn't the goal; solving the problem is the goal.

In the end, affixing blame only encourages people to conceal problems or pass the buck. No one wants to be the one to take the hit, so they try to avoid it altogether. When the problem finally does come out, it's far bigger and much uglier than it would have been had it been addressed early. Even worse, your employees are going to be too busy trying to dodge the blame to really concentrate on fixing things.

If you actually want to solve your problems, focus on the organizational system and understand how it may be inadvertently contributing to the problems you are observing. You may want to use a room with a large whiteboard! Take the time to identify the flow of information and see where things could get confused. Find out the different perspectives on what happened: when you get rid of blame, it's amazing how helpful, energetic, and creative your employees will be in helping you solve the problem. Build up a picture of the interactions on your team and understand how inadvertent actions could cause miscommunication or misunderstanding. When Fred promised the deliverable by Wednesday, he might well have assumed that meant end of day since that's been the standard for all his projects, while Bob might have assumed first thing in the morning because that's what he's used to.

It can be tricky to map out people's assumptions and beliefs about what they expected and why. It can be even trickier and considerably more difficult to resist the urge to judge before you have all the information. Your goal, though, is not just to deal with the immediate problem, but to help your team develop better processes and methods of working so that they can continue to develop to higher stages of performance.

Focusing on the interactions helps you identify the ways in which your group of strong performers is not taking full advantage of one another's strengths. Those who recall the first Olympic Basketball Dream Team might remember how disappointing they were: sure, they played good basketball; that many greats in one place could hardly do otherwise. But they never achieved the level of performance that people expected: they were all members of separate teams and hadn't really learned to work together.

You will recall from chapter three that team development takes time. This is one of the reasons why. Failing to navigate this step is where many teams get stuck.

But what about the person who really is a bad actor? I'm glad you asked.

Jerks, Bullies, and Bad Apples

Jerks and bullies are basically interchangeable. How your organization handles jerks will shape how members of your organization view the organization and whether or not policies and procedures are fair and just. A caution before we begin, though: everyone has bad days and can be irritable when stressed. With jerks, we're looking at a constant level of bad behavior that leaves others angry, depressed, uncertain, or afraid.

The following vignettes may sound quite familiar.

For a routine team meeting, the tension in the room was palpable. A careful observer might have noticed the quick, side-long glances the first two speakers directed at Jim. Jim just sat there, though, quietly, apparently barely paying attention. Then, Rob, the new guy, started to speak. Older team members exchanged worried glances.

It's not clear what Rob said that set Jim off, but set Jim off he did. Jim laced into Rob in no uncertain terms. Afterward, one of the older team members explained to Rob that, "Jim's a top player, so we cut him some slack. We try to avoid issues that he feels strongly about."

At another company, members of the engineering team carefully avoided any discussion on coding styles or standards lest they set off Jason. Jason wasn't nasty in the same way that Jim was, but when coding styles came up, Jason wouldn't shut up. He would continue to argue his point until everyone gave in. Eventually, they learned to just not go there unless they wanted meetings to drag on for hours. Jason, like Jim, was viewed as a top performer. At one point, the VP of Engineering commented that, "I know he's hard to get on with, but he's really skilled."

In both cases, their performance came at a high price: other employees were afraid to disagree with them, limiting the spread of ideas and preventing effective error correction. Even worse, as employees observed the behaviors that were being rewarded, more and more of them adopted similar techniques. The offices rapidly became extremely unpleasant places to work. Senior management, however, did not want to fire either Jim or Jason because they were perceived as high performers, despite being "bad apples." In fact, they achieved their apparent high performance by bringing everyone else down: think about how a jerk can undermine team development. Real top performers bring everyone up.

At one firm, the top salesman was also a serious bad apple. No one at the company approached his level of sales. Eventually, though, his behavior became so egregious that he was fired. Rather than seeing sales decline with the loss of their top salesman, overall sales shot up over twenty percent.

The biggest problem with bad apples is not just that they create an environment in which others cannot perform well. The real issue is that their bad behavior is contagious. Nastiness, subtle insults, and other inappropriate social interactions, if not halted, may then be imitated by others. Sometimes this is because, as mentioned above, the behaviors come to be seen as the path to success in the office. Other times, employees adopt the inappropriate behaviors as a form of self-defense: if she knows I'll bite back, then maybe she'll pick on someone else. In some cases, engaging in the bad behavior is seen as preferable to the feelings of helplessness and lack of confidence that come of being picked on. If nothing else, constantly dealing with a bad apple leaves people edgy and irritable, more likely to engage in inappropriate behavior, and less able to focus on actual work. Whatever the reason, the spread of bad behavior means that instead of one jerk in the office, you have an office full of jerks. Let it go far enough and your organizational culture will be infected: eventually the bad apple spoils the barrel. This destroys morale, productivity, and trust.

While in some cases it can be hard to identify the initial jerk once conditions spiral out of control, in most of the cases I've dealt with finding the jerk was easy. Pretty much everyone knew.

The real question, though, is why jerks are allowed to thrive despite the damage they can do. Why do so many managers refuse to take action?

The first reason is the belief that it's okay for a top performer to be "just difficult to get on with." After all, these are adults. Can't they take a little obnoxiousness or whatever? Yes, they are adults; as adults, they probably have little interest in working in an environment with all the ambiance of middle school. No one likes being insulted, and allowing it only guarantees poor performance all around.

A related issue is that managers often feel that their job isn't playing traffic cop or referee. People should be able to just work it out. Unfortunately, that's exactly what the bully counts on. You can't "just work it out" with a jerk. They count on management passivity, the stress and rush of business, and managers being irritated by "whiners" to help mask their bad behavior.

Remember, while almost anyone has their moments when they are difficult to get along with, bullies are that way most of the time. They are also the first ones to point fingers at other people and complain that those others are the ones who are being difficult. In fact, a bully will seize on a single slip on someone else's part to justify their own continual bad behavior or may attempt to make other people angry or defensive so that they can appear reasonable. They make such a big deal of the other person's behavior that managers don't always realize that they are looking at an occasional mistake versus constant inappropriate behavior: the jerk plays the contrast effect extremely well. It's very important to push for details when you find yourself in the position of having to deal with a jerk or bully: the details are what enable you to determine whether they are constantly talking about the same incident or a variety of incidents.

For example, in one situation the argumentative and offensive behavior of the resident jerk regularly caused product delays that were blamed on other members of the team. Whenever anyone tried to raise the problem with management, the conversation between Bob the manager, Fred the person raising the issue, and Jerry the Jerk would go something like this:

Fred: Jerry, I'm concerned that every time we have a big deadline coming up, you argue until we either do things your way or we have to scramble to not blow our schedule.
Jerry: Whoa! You're saying I'm solely responsible for us being late all the time?
Fred: No, I'm saying that...
Jerry: Well, it sure sounds like you're claiming that the only reason we don't have a killer product on the market is because of me.
Fred: I'm saying that when you continue to argue even after the team makes a decision...
Jerry: So you think we should be shipping crap? That none of us should bring up problems?
Bob: Of course we want to hear about problems. Fred, don't you think you're being oversensitive here?
Fred: I am not oversensitive.

And so it goes. Note Jerry's use of exaggeration to make his actual behavior seem insignificant by contrast. Also note how Jerry never really answers the points Fred raises, but constantly responds by highlighting his own implied virtuous behavior. Before long, Jerry has Fred sounding defensive and Bob is ready to wash his hands of the discussion. If Bob is a little more alert to the potential problems, Jerry might eventually concede that maybe his enthusiasm for the product and his concern for the customer led him "to be a little short the other day." This apparent concession is, of course, only designed to make him appear reasonable and force Fred to either concede his point in return, or appear to be the unreasonable one.

Reason number two that it's hard to get rid of a jerk is the belief that the jerk is simply such a top performer that the company simply cannot afford to get rid of them. As we saw with the salesman example, jerks are top performers mainly because they drag everyone else down: at minimum, jerks make team development slow to a crawl, stop altogether, or even go into reverse. They make others unwilling to volunteer, which enables the jerk to take his pick of the tasks, and then constantly complain that no one else is doing their part. They will often play hero by jumping into other people's projects, all the while complaining that, "I don't have the time to deal with this, but you've made it necessary." The more they convince others to disengage, the better they look. And, of course, their aggressive "volunteering" often triggers the Halo Effect: because they appear to be doing something good in one area, they create the image that they must be an asset overall. If you do it right, when you remove the jerk team performance will skyrocket.

In some cases, managers don't get rid of the jerk because they are uncomfortable with confrontation, or are afraid of an argument. As we discussed just above, managers might be afraid the person will leave, not realizing the high price the team is paying for their performance.

Finally, managers, or even other employees, are unwilling to get rid of the jerk because they feel guilty. Refrains I often hear include, "Oh, but he's done so much for the company," or "She's so dedicated, we need to figure out a way to keep her," or "That would be such an awful way to reward someone who sacrifices so much for the business," or "I'm sure he'll change eventually," etc.

Successful jerks are very good at playing on the feelings of those around them. If they weren't so good at it, they wouldn't have lasted so long in the job: they are extremely effective mimics, appearing reasonable just enough to trigger our friendship and sympathy. They don't change because, quite simply, they keep being rewarded for their bad behavior. Their occasional moments of niceness are calculated to keep hope alive that they'll change eventually. It makes you feel that maybe they aren't so bad after all or that other people are exaggerating when they complain about the jerk. Since most of us don't like to think badly of other people, they are counting on our confirmation bias to cause us to pay more attention to the moments of good behavior instead of the days of bad behavior. It works quite often, particularly when we are not aware of the trick.

The temptation is often to put jerks on a behavior plan or hire a coach for them. Behavior plans are effective only when you are dealing with someone both willing and able to change. Before you implement a behavior plan ask yourself if this person has ever made a lasting change in response to feedback—indeed, have they ever received feedback or is no one willing to give it? Too often with jerks, you are just delaying the inevitable. As far as coaching, focus your coaching on the people who really are your strong performers. Otherwise, you're just paying for a short-term improvement that will swiftly disappear once the coach is gone.

One instance where I helped an organization get rid of a bully on its senior management team was fascinating. The bully would lace into other team members, sometimes embarrassing them publically. But, she would also apologize profusely afterward, and seemed so contrite that people would feel guilty that they had made her lose her temper! For the other team members, it was the psychological and moral equivalent of the wife apologizing for making her husband so angry that he beat her, with the bully in the role of the apparently contrite abuser. I eventually presented the rest of the management team with a history of incidents going back several years before they were all convinced. One person commented afterward that he hadn't realized how often he'd been the target of her wrath, but looking at the history made him realize how thoroughly he'd been played: he kept thinking he should be professional and let his personal feelings of being offended slide. A few months after we got rid of the jerk, that same person commented that team interactions had become considerably more relaxed, friendly, and productive.

Getting rid of a jerk can feel awful, right up to the point when they are gone. At that point, suddenly the atmosphere, and your team's performance, improves to such an extent that you are left wondering what took you so long.

Feedback Systems

Feedback takes many forms. Equity, blame versus problem solving, and dealing with jerks provide feedback that tell people how the organization works and handles difficulties. In addition, there are the explicit feedback systems:

There is the feedback that people get that tells them how, and whether, the organization views them as people. This is feedback about the nature of the relationship between members and the organization as a whole.

There is feedback that goes up the organizational hierarchy, informing those higher up about conditions, the market, problems in the organization, and successes. This system often fails.

There is feedback in the form of performance reviews. Done properly, which rarely happens, performance reviews are very powerful and valuable to the organization: they provide a route by which members of the organization can grow, develop their skills, and build their status. They provide an important connection to the organizational narrative.

Relational Feedback

Psychologist Robert Cialdini observes that every culture has a social rule around favors: when someone does something for you, helps you, or gives you a gift of some sort, you are expected to reciprocate in some way. People who do not reciprocate, that is, those who take but do not give, are viewed as greedy moochers, and are often shunned by the rest of the society. Similarly, as Schein observes, those who give help but never accept it, are often viewed with suspicion or resentment.

In an organizational setting, people want to understand what sort of relationship they have with their coworkers, their boss, and with the more nebulous construct that is the "organization." Reciprocity is one of the ways people explore that relationship. How the team and the organization handle reciprocity thus becomes a proxy for the relationship.

In early stage teams, people might refuse to accept help in order to avoid a feeling of indebtedness or incompetence, or might attempt to help another in the hopes of receiving help later or building status. In fact, for the team to be considered just and fair, there needs to be that mutual exchange of helping behavior in the early stages. Eventually, as the team develops, the mutual exchange of favors turns into a more abstract helping network in which team members automatically give and receive help as necessary to the accomplishment of the task at hand. It's no longer about the individual ledger; rather, it's the confidence that we will all engage in helping behaviors for the good of all of us. The trust that enables that to happen comes from demonstrating reciprocity in the early stages of team development.

Similarly, when members of an organization put forth an extra effort or engage in pro-organizational behavior outside the normal expectations, they expect that the organization will, in some way, acknowledge and repay their contribution. When the organization refuses to do that, or, even worse, treats the exceptional effort as "just part of the job," this creates the image of someone who takes and takes but gives only grudgingly, if at all. For example, when employees work long hours or weekends in order to meet a deadline, they are sacrificing their personal time for the good of the organization. This is not, or at least should not be, a routine event. If it is, you have some serious problems!

How the organization responds to that sacrifice provides feedback on the relationship: reciprocity of some sort says that you are a valuable person; failure to provide reciprocity says that you are a tool or a slave, that the boss is selfish, that the organization does not value its members, or all of the above.

I've met many people who tell me that long hours are part of the job, and ask why they should thank or reward people for doing their jobs. The reason is simple: reciprocity is a proxy for the relationship, and the relationship determines trust. Without trust, motivation, team development, and leadership all start to break down.

Soliciting Feedback

The human body is an amazing thing: our brains enable our bodies to act, and the sensations we get through our actions and senses tell our brains what is happening in the world. Take a away that feedback, deprive us of one or more of our senses, and we are in trouble. Our ability to navigate our environment decreases and difficulties increase.

Organizations are much the same: information needs to flow both ways. An organization inevitably runs into trouble if it stops receiving feedback from its environment. Consider what would happen if, for example, you lost the ability to feel pain: you could put your hand on a hot burner and not notice until you smelled the roasting meat. Unfortunately, organizations put themselves in this position over and over by blocking or shutting themselves off from feedback from the people actually doing the work. As a result, the information that finally reaches the top levels of the organization is often distorted or wrong.

As we discussed earlier, IBM's Tom Watson was famous for showing up unannounced at different IBM locations and dropping into speak with employees at all levels of the organization. He stationed representatives on site at major customers in order that they have someone on hand to help them, and so that he would get rapid feedback if there was a problem. Although Tom Watson, Jr., continued his father's policies, future CEOs did not. When Lou Gerstner took over IBM in 1992, he made his vice presidents go out and visit customers again, and then had them send their direct reports to customer sites as well. Gerstner, like Watson before him, well knew the value of feedback!

The major reasons organizations have trouble getting feedback boils down to safety and trust. Telling the boss you think he's screwing up or you see a problem with the way things are run is often a good way to lose your job. Getting useable and useful feedback requires creating a safe place for that feedback to occur. Schein observes that in Japan, it is customary for workers to go out drinking with their bosses after work. Under the cover of being "drunk" they can tell their boss things that they would never say in the office. In Japanese culture, according to Schein, you are not held responsible for the "alcohol talking," and, on the other side of the equation, the boss does not lose face by being criticized by a subordinate. The next day, nothing is said, but the boss can now act on the information brought to his attention. While this specific approach would not work in America due to our different cultural attitudes and beliefs around alcohol, it does work in Japan to create a safe space for feedback.

Specific mechanisms for creating a safe space for feedback will vary from one organization to the next. Fundamentally, though, if trust and safety do not exist in a general sense, nothing you do will make people trust you or feel safe giving you honest feedback.

Keep in mind that the level of team development will affect how accurate feedback will be. A Forming team is going to have a great deal of trouble providing negative feedback to the leader. If team members do provide such feedback, the odds are very good that it will be about trivial issues. Forming teams tend to view the leader in such a positive light that it's hard for them identify the flaws, much less speak about them. What Forming team members will sometimes do, however, is complain about anyone who isn't conforming to the arbitrary standards the complainer thinks are important, or even the arbitrary standards some members of the team consider valuable. This is a form of feedback, and it's important to hear them out without getting caught up in their point of view. You are finding out about the level of cohesion and development of your team, and that information will guide you toward helping your team advance.

This is another situation where it can sometimes help to appoint someone to hold the role of Devil's Advocate. They are tasked with raising concerns if no one else does. You might also want to meet privately with that person on a regular basis to get their feedback. It can be much easier for the leader and the team for the leader to hear problems privately, particularly if the problem is about the leader's leadership style.

Doing a "Tom Watson" and meeting regularly with people under you is another good approach. It may take a while to establish trust and the sort of relationship where you will get honest feedback, but it's worth the effort. Taking people to lunch or something, asking them about their work, and then actually listening can go a long way. Speak to enough people this way and you start to get a pretty good picture of what is really going on.

It can also help to bring in an outsider. Provided the person you bring in is open about what they are doing and why, people are often more comfortable talking to a stranger than someone they know. In this situation, the person you bring in should be tasked with giving you a gestalt picture rather than detailed individual reports on individual people. The one exception to that is if anything is uncovered that is illegal or could materially damage the company: in that case, confidentiality can be waived. Again, though, it helps to be upfront about that as well.

Ultimately, the key points here are that you can't compel honest feedback, and you must take pains to demonstrate that the messenger won't be shot. This latter point is not easy, since we do have a tendency to blame the bearer of bad news: weathermen, for example, are often blamed for bad weather. However, if you've shown yourself to be trustworthy and consistent in your behavior, worked to build strong relationships with your teams, and developed an atmosphere of trust, you are well on the way to having a team that will provide you real feedback.

Giving Feedback and the Art of the Performance Review

Performance reviews are one of those annual rituals that get lots of press. Every year I am interviewed on the topic at least once, sometimes multiple times. I've even been interviewed on performance reviews by the New York Times! Apparently, this is a matter of national attention. Or perhaps what makes it newsworthy is that they are so often done badly: if performance reviews were handled well, no one would comment on it.

Performance reviews are, or at least should be, a means of directly connecting an employee's performance to their overall goals and to the organization's narrative and goals. Done well, this reinforces an employee's connection to the organization and strengthens their motivation. Done badly and the opposite happens.

When Should I Give Feedback?

Let's explode one myth before we go any further: feedback, whether in the form of performance reviews or less formal structures needs to be more frequent than once a year or even every six months. Feedback is a continuous, ongoing process. While one might view the performance review as the climax of the process, unlike a mystery novel there should be no surprises in the performance review. It is an opportunity to sum up a period of accomplishment, identify strengths, and move forward. It cannot be the only feedback someone receives.

If you've done a good job building strong, positive relationships with your team and coworkers, giving and receiving feedback will be much easier!

Why are Performance Reviews Difficult?

Why are performance reviews so hard? It seems like they should be so simple: you sit down with someone and tell them how they've done and how they can improve. It just doesn't seem like it should be so complicated! Yet, not only do people dread receiving performance reviews, many managers dread giving them. All too often they are punctuated with argument or received with passive acceptance, and rarely does either option lead to lasting change. Rather than accepting feedback, people frequently are left with a sour feeling in their mouths and a deep sense that the organization is fundamentally unfair or looking for excuses to not give raises.

At root, the performance review is a very unusual ritual: how often do we sit down with someone and tell them what we think of their work? Parents do it with kids, teachers with students, the master with the apprentice, but rarely does it happen between equals. The closest you might come is doctoral students with their advisors, skilled athletes with their coaches, or someone in a mentor/mentee relationship. In fact, it is very difficult to give feedback or to convince someone to give us honest feedback, particularly when we may have learned that what appears to be a request for feedback really isn't: "Does this make me look fat?" Thus, the review process is often uncomfortable for both parties.

It is also common to confuse the tool with the job. The job is providing people with the feedback they need to grow, identifying the supports that will enable and facilitate growth, and creating an environment in which the person receiving feedback will be receptive. Tools such as 360-degree feedback and the like are just that: tools. They are useful if they help you do the job. Otherwise, forget about them.

In an organization, particularly one with highly expert members, feedback is tricky. The superior/inferior relationship doesn't really work: the power dynamics, as we discussed in chapter four, are more complex than that. Recall as well our discussion on leadership: leaders need to foster key emotions of competency and autonomy, while still building the connections to the group. Part of how a leader does this is by focusing on the coaching aspects of the role. A performance review thus needs to shift from being in the mode of a master talking to an apprentice to that of the mentor or coach working with the elite performer.

How do we make that happen?

Honor Autonomy

Start by honoring the autonomy of the person being reviewed. Rather than tell them when the review will be, let them choose. Give them some options as necessary for scheduling purposes, but as much as possible let them pick the time. As simple as that may sound, it immediately sends a message that this is a meeting between peers working together toward a common goal. That alone increases cooperation dramatically and makes possible constructive feedback that can produce lasting improvements for both the individual and the organization.

Look at the Goals

Next, make sure you are familiar with the goals of the person being reviewed and that the two of you are on the same page. You do have goals, right? Going into a performance review without having defined measurable goals ahead of time is rather like racing in the Indianapolis 500 in a car with no engine: It's a nonstarter. Goals can be built around objectives, strategy, or learning, but they need to be there. Otherwise, the performance review is little more than an argument about differing perceptions of the work and those conflicts end badly: no matter who wins, everyone loses. We will look at defining goals in Chap. 9.

Be Specific

Stay away from mind-reading or making judgments about someone's personality or thoughts.

It's easy to get caught up in telling people, "I know that you were thinking…" or "You must have wanted this project to fail…" or "You clearly have a difficult personality and…"

The problem is that such statements accomplish little other than to convince the person listening that your feedback is a waste of time. Even if you've made a fortune performing a mind-reading act in Las Vegas, anyone gullible enough to believe you can actually read their mind probably isn't worth having around anyway. No one starts out wanting their project to fail, although many organizations do convince members to want other people's projects to fail. Complaining about someone's personality is commenting on something pretty much unchangeable and what you are reacting to may be a manifestation of the fundamental attribution error. If they really do have a difficult personality, well, so what? If it's so bad no one can work with them, then maybe they shouldn't be in the organization. Otherwise, it's not relevant.

Instead, you need to focus on specific behaviors for both positive and negative feedback. It does no good to say, "You are too passive," or "You are too aggressive." As we discussed earlier, in one situation, an employee was told by one manager that he was too passive because he wouldn't fight for his ideas and, by another, a good team player because he was willing to put his ego to one side and work to build consensus. You need to provide examples of the behaviors you are talking about so that people know what to change: it's all about what they can control and what they can't. Consider the differences between:

> *Jim, you were really on the ball at the sales meeting,* and *Jim, I really liked the way you handled that sales meeting. You were able to address every concern the client raised. You had a chart for everything he was worried about. I can tell that you had done your homework.*

> *Bob, you are much too aggressive. I'm not sure you have what it takes to succeed here,* versus *Bob, I'm worried about how the interdepartmental meeting went last week. Every time someone asked a question you got red in the face and shouted them down. It seemed to me that you were treating every question a personal attack. Heck, I almost felt afraid to ask you anything and I've known you for years. This really leaves me wondering how I can possibly give you more responsibility.*

Not only does the process of providing specific feedback help the person improve, it also helps you avoid being caught up on any of those cognitive shortcuts that we are so often prone to. Your gut feeling is almost always shaped by the most recent or the most intense events; when you are taking notes throughout the year and then reviewing specifics, it's not unusual to find that the data tells you something far different. When you focus on specifics and leave the door open for discussion, you also have the opportunity to engage in constructive dialog about what the employee was thinking or why they made the choices they made, making it easier for them to accept your feedback.

Remember that the goal of feedback is growth and change. Change is hard when you try to force it: the harder you make it for someone to disagree with you, the harder you make it for them to agree. Change is much easier when you make it easy for the other person to agree with you: you've recruited them as a willing ally.

Avoid the Remediation Trap: Focus on Strengths

Our strengths are the things that we enjoy doing. The reason our strengths are strong is because we feel good when we succeed and so we do more. Weaknesses, on the other hand, are often things that do not provide any internal reward no matter how well we do them.

It is very easy to focus people on remediating weaknesses. Unfortunately, this produces neither effective growth nor motivation. There is nothing particularly satisfying about doing something that you never enjoy no matter how hard you work at it or how proficient you might become.

It makes much more sense to focus people on building their strengths. Legendary martial artist Bruce Lee used to say that if you built your strengths they would overcome your weaknesses. Bruce was quite correct: he became a formidable martial artist despite being nearly blind without thick glasses and having one leg so much shorter than the other that he needed special shoes to stand normally. Instead of bogging down in weaknesses, he focused on his strengths.

Focusing on strengths increases motivation and enjoyment. As people become better and better at what they do, you and they will find ways to negate or work around their weaknesses. Along the way, you are increasing their sense of competence, enabling them to take more autonomy, and building the relationship by showing that you care about their growth and development.

It's worth noting that the Harvard Medical School special health report, "Positive Psychology: Harnessing the power of happiness, mindfulness, and inner strength," found that focusing on strengths and what people are doing right **increased** performance by 36 % on average. Conversely, focusing on weaknesses **decreased** performance by 27 %. That's what is known as a Dramatic Difference.

Finally, don't worry that everyone isn't good at everything. This is normal. We are not clones.

End with Goals

At the end of the review, it's time to start building out goals going forward. You probably can't plan the year out in detail; that's okay. Goals need to be specific, but they also need to be flexible. Part of your goals will be to meet periodically to review progress and continue the process of goal definition.

Some Final Thoughts on Justice and Fairness

It's not enough to have a just and fair organization: you must also have an organization that is perceived to be just and fair. Being aware of the natural ways in which we instinctively "reach for the ground," understanding how to look at contribution instead of blame, dealing effectively with jerks, and having effective feedback systems are all key to making that happen.

Questions to Consider

1. What are you doing to make sure you have equity in your organization?
2. What is the fundamental attribution error? Where have you seen it happening?
3. Consider the last three times something non-trivial went wrong or didn't go as expected. How did you handle it? What underlying causes or contributing factors were in play?
4. How will you recognize a jerk or a bully?
5. What feedback are people receiving about the nature of their relationship to your organization?
6. How are you getting accurate feedback from members of your team or department?

Chapter 8
Organizational Learning

Fans of James Bond movies might recall a scene that goes something like this:

We are looking at an unidentified room. Two people we've never seen before are standing in front of a desk. We might be able to see the back of the head of the man who sits behind that desk. A voice rings out:

"You have failed SPECTRE. Number 3, why did you not kill 007 as ordered?"

Number 3 stammers out some response and the voice turns its attention on the other person.

"Number 5, you have also failed SPECTRE..."

Eventually, Number 3 is told everything is forgiven and he can leave. Of course, this is SPECTRE. As soon as he walks out of the room he's dropped into a tank of piranhas, or the bottom of the elevator turns out to be a trap door and Number 3 learns that Maxwell Elevators really are good to the last drop, or he dies in some other Rube Goldberg-esque manner.

SPECTRE, as all Bond fans know, is the villainous organization headed by Ernst Stavro Blofeld, the evil genius who spends most of his time trying unsuccessfully to kill 007. Given his track record, as evil geniuses go, he frequently seems more like Wile E. Coyote.

Blofeld's problem, of course, is that every time one of his agents makes a mistake that agent dies. Those whom James Bond doesn't kill are terminated by Blofeld himself. This makes it extremely difficult to conduct any form of on-the-job learning. When every mistake is fatal, the lessons tend to come a little too late to do much good. As learning organizations go, SPECTRE has issues.

Although the consequences are generally not so flashy, businesses do face some similar problems. Granted, most business mistakes don't make for a good action movie, and dropping people in piranha tanks is generally frowned upon. However, there is still the very real problem of figuring out how to enable people to learn from their mistakes without those mistakes harming the business. James Bond, after all, at least gets a script.

Part of the challenge is that even when leaders are well-trained and highly skilled, there is a big difference between what one learns in most management

S. R. Balzac, *Organizational Psychology for Managers*,
Management for Professionals, DOI: 10.1007/978-1-4614-8505-6_8,
© Springer Science+Business Media New York 2014

training classes and the actual experience of leading a team, department, division, or company. That doesn't mean that the training is useless, but it does mean that the training needs to be appropriate.

In sports, for example, athletes drill constantly: they practice the fundamental skills of their sport until they can execute those skills without thought. Doing that, however, is not enough to make an athlete a successful competitor. Such training is necessary, but it's not sufficient.

As a soccer-playing friend once commented to me, there's a big difference between the drill and the game. The drill is controlled and predictable; the game is not. The game is confusing and chaotic, and in the moment of truth all those carefully drilled skills simply vanish away. The problem is that chaos is overwhelming: it takes getting used to in order to navigate it. The Japanese term, "randori," used to describe Judo competition, means "seizing chaos."

Athletes practice getting used to chaos by moving past drills and practicing in various free play scenarios: mock games, spring training, practice randori, etc. These experiences enable the athlete to experience the chaos in small doses and hence become increasingly comfortable with it. They learn which skills to execute when. The day of the actual tournament, they are ready. When they do make mistakes, they have something to fall back on to help them recover quickly, as opposed to something to fall into and get eaten.

Businesses are in a fundamentally similar position: while there are some obvious differences in the details between learning the skills of a sport and learning sales or management or computer programming, the fundamental process is the same. Since organizational performance is ongoing instead of being organized into discrete chunks such as tournaments, organizational learning needs to be ongoing as well. Optimally, organizational learning should also be an enjoyable experience, not just because that makes people happy but because people learn best when they are enjoying themselves. The methods and approaches to organizational learning should also serve to simplify other issues, such as orientation, accreditation, and organizational change. The lessons of sports and games will serve us well in understanding how to make organizational learning effective.

To begin with, though, we need to understand what learning is and how it works.

What is Learning?

It is very easy to find long and detailed discussions of what learning is and what it means to learn. Most of these definitions, while interesting, are of little practical use. Of considerably more practical use, however, is this:

Learning is the (hopefully!) permanent change in behavior resulting from practice and experience.

Sounds simple. Unfortunately, it's not quite so easy. We have only to look at the number of failed learning initiatives and the frustration so many people feel around learning to see just how often learning is not handled well. Part of the problem is that learning is treated too often as an event, not as a process: a single class rather than an ongoing practice of skill development. To understand how this works, consider the process of learning a skill.

As I often tell students in my jujitsu class, learning a move is easy. Performing the move when you want to is what's difficult. For example, it takes only a few seconds to demonstrate how to block a punch. Most people, upon seeing that demonstration, are then capable of moving their hand in the correct manner. They are not, however, blocking the punch yet; they are only moving their hand. In other words, they are repeating an action but they have not yet internalized the action. Under carefully controlled conditions, they can block the punch: it's slow, it's clearly telegraphed, and their partner doesn't really want to hit them. If their partner does something unexpected, the student freezes, panics, gets hit, or all of the above. Similarly, a sales trainee might learn a script to use or a set of phrases and actions designed to make the prospect sign on the dotted line. So long as the prospect behaves exactly according to the script, the trainee is fine. Should that prospect deviate in any way, the trainee is lost: their brain is full of the script and there is no room for anything else, such as improvisation.

Eventually, after enough practice, the block improves, right up until there is some pressure: a belt test, a more aggressive partner, or anything else which suddenly raises the stakes of getting it right. At that point, many students instead of blocking with their hands block with their nose. It takes a great deal more practice before the skill works reliably under pressure. Similarly, a trainee might do well on practice exercises, but fold when tested or put in front of a real client.

This process of continual practice is known as automatizing the skill. Because we are not actually that good at thinking about multiple things at once, if we have to think about how to use the skill, we can't pay attention to what's actually going on. We have to learn something so well that we no longer need to think about it. At that point, the skill is becoming reflexive and we only need to recognize the need to use it for it to happen. This frees a tremendous amount of brain power, enabling us to take in more information and respond more effectively to our environment: the beginning basketball player is so busy concentrating on dribbling the ball that an experienced player can walk right up and take the ball away. The beginner will often report that, "I didn't even see him coming!" As dribbling becomes automatic, the basketball player becomes more able to pay attention to the other players and evade the person trying to steal the ball. The beginning salesman is so focused on her script that she misses the warning signs that the sales call is about to go off the rails. The experienced salesman notices the subtle shifts in the prospect's behavior, and is able to adjust his strategy accordingly. The rote action is transformed into a framework for activity.

Of course, there is a catch. As I alluded to a moment ago, we have to recognize the need to use a skill in order to use it. It doesn't matter how much we've automatized the skill if we don't realize that we need it. Thus, part of skill learning is situational: like an actor, we need to know our cues. The more time spent looking for our cues, the slower our response will be. Just like a scene in a movie seems artificial and unbelievable when actors don't realize it's time for their lines, so too do behaviors ranging from leadership to engineering to sales seem artificial, and hence unbelievable or not trustable, when we don't recognize our cues in those settings. The leader who is not aware of the signs, or cues, that indicate a group is entering storming is thus more likely to respond inappropriately or too slowly to the changing team dynamic. In the worst case, like the jujitsu student who misses the warning signs that it's time to block, he may be gob smacked.

As a result, proper training includes coupling the behavior and the appropriate cues for the behavior. This pairing must also be automatized, although not necessarily at the same level of reflexivity as the base behavior. Sometimes we want to be able to choose between several trained choices. The important thing is that the appropriate cues bring the appropriate options to mind, and that we have the cognitive resources available to evaluate the situation and choose. Training conducted in an artificial environment which divorces situation from action reduces the value of the training; similarly, management training that does not include the rest of the team lacks appropriate cues from the team, and often teaches the manager behaviors that the team doesn't know how to respond to. As we discussed in earlier chapters, training the leader and the team separately is not all that effective: this is one of the big reasons why.

Another important point of how learning works is that people have to be able to get it wrong. Learning is not just absorbing, memorizing, and rehearsing behaviors. It is also experimentation and exploration. Making mistakes is a critical part of skill mastery: being able to execute a skill reflexively is great, but you still need to be able to adjust when something unexpected happens. When people learn without the opportunity to make mistakes, the skill is brittle. Failure becomes a catastrophe, and fear of making a mistake can paralyze performance under pressure. That jujitsu student learning to block will get hit many times along the road to mastery: under training conditions, the student might end up with a bloody nose or black eye, but otherwise will be unharmed. Along the way, they learn how to make their own movements more effective. More to the point, they learn that getting hit isn't the end of the world: it isn't fun, but you can keep going. This enables them to relax under pressure. Paradoxically, the less afraid you are of getting hit, the less likely you will get hit. The less afraid the salesman is of screwing up, the less likely she is to screw up. The leader who is confident that he and his team can recover from mistakes is more open to trying new and innovative ideas. That confidence and that lack of fear come from making mistakes. Note that there are limits to this: I have been told that the best way to avoid being stung by a bee is to be unafraid of the bee. I can state from personal experience that the bee does not know this.

Unfortunately, too many learning situations are focused around fear of failure, a lesson we all learned in school, when failure meant bad grades and quite possibly Not Getting Into the College of Your Choice. These learned habits often interfere with ongoing learning in organizational settings. Typically, when we learn something new in a class or training exercise, we will only have time to get down the rote memorization piece of it: the process of then mastering the skill, that exploration and experimentation piece, needs to happen on the job. If you can't handle making mistakes, you just wasted roughly 90 % of the training.

Is this all there is to learning? Of course not! If it were, we'd have a lot more experts out there! A key part of making learning successful is understanding what your goals really mean and understanding the context in which learning is occurring.

What are You Doing by Doing That?

Psychologist Peter Ossorio liked to pose the question, "What are you doing by doing that?" For example, imagine watching a fencer thrusting his sword at a golf ball hanging from the ceiling.

"What are you doing?" you might ask.
"Hitting this ball."
"What are you doing by doing that?"
"Practicing my lunge."
"What are you doing by doing that?"
"If I lunge well enough, I can score against my opponent."

And so it goes. We can keep asking the question, eventually tying the observed behavior back to the overall goal of winning the match and the tournament. Each step along the way illuminates an aspect of the learning process. Why is this so important?

At one company, someone in upper management decided the reason that sales were low was because salesmen suffered from call reluctance (a discomfort in making phone calls to strangers). He decreed that all salesmen must take classes on being more effective on the phone. People spent hours practicing appropriate phone technique, to no avail. Sales did not improve. Had they gone through the process of asking, "What are you doing by doing that?" they could have identified each step in the process and discovered that even the best salesmen suffer from call reluctance: it's the satisfaction of victory at the end that makes all the difference to them, not hours of training on how to make phone calls. Asking "What are you doing by doing that?" would have led them to understand that they were heading down the metaphorical rabbit hole, and given them valuable information on where to allocate their training resources.

As we will see when we discuss goal setting in the next chapter, a key part of goal accomplishment is connecting the beginning with the end. Learning is really a type of goal. A key part of learning, therefore, is making sure that the beginning connects to the end: the falling exercises beginning jujitsu students learn are critical to achieving black belt rank and, as fans of the *Karate Kid* will remember, even the apparently senseless "wax on, wax off," turns out to be important. Unlike in a movie, however, students in a real jujitsu class get to see the higher ranking students using the skills the beginners are just learning.

What is the Learning Context?

The learning context is both the situational contextual cues which we've already touched on, and the broader organizational environment and principles of learning. That second piece is what will focus on now.

How Does the Organization Influence Learning?

Organizations develop attitudes around learning: when is it necessary? Who gets trained? Why are people trained? How are mistakes viewed? etc. These attitudes shape how learning is viewed and, to a very great extent, how successful learning is.

Many years ago, I was participating in a training exercise. As a part of that exercise, I was assigned to play a manager who had been recommended for coaching. Having been a serious competitive fencer for many years, I knew that the only people who were recommended for coaching were the best athletes. One of the other participants in the exercise was stunned at my happy response to the role and said, "How can you be so happy? You're playing someone who was recommended for coaching!" Her experience with coaching was that it was the last step before you were fired.

Similarly, it matters how the organization views training: is this something done to build people up or "fix those who are broken?" Is it developing strengths or remediating weakness? Is training something fun or something to be endured and forgotten? Will you have the opportunity to exercise your new skills or not? How the culture views training is critical to the success of training. If the organizational narrative is one that teaches us that training is for losers or that Real Experts don't need training, it's going to be very hard to make training work. That, in turn, will reduce engagement with the material and, hence, make it difficult for organizational members to grow in their roles. On the other hand, if training is viewed as an opportunity to increase competencies and status in the organization, and those who engage in training are given opportunities to exercise their new skills, training can have dramatically outsized benefits compared to the investment.

All too often, training is viewed as an afterthought, something to do when nothing important is going on. There is frequently a strong attitude of, "Sure, take classes, but don't let it interfere with the real work."

If you want training to be effective, it needs to be taken as seriously as any other part of the job. The products you build today are built with the skills you learned yesterday. The products you build tomorrow will be built with the skills you learn today. View training as an afterthought and it will be treated as one. Demand that people already working long hours add more time for training and it will be resented. Either of these factors will dramatically reduce the benefits of even the best classes or training exercises. This may not matter for classes which are done for legal protection more than anything else; it will matter for training that it intended to achieve that goal of a permanent change in behavior.

When training is intended to alter the way people in an organization do their jobs, such as learning new technology or systems, deadlines must be adjusted for that learning to occur. If people are expected to maintain the same levels of productivity during the learning and adoption period as before they started to learn something new, the new technology or systems will not be learned: people will naturally and reasonably opt to meet their deadlines by doing things the old way, rather than investing the time in learning something new. There is almost always a dip in performance in the early stages of adopting new systems and technology: people need time to get used to the new ways of working. This is perhaps the most difficult part of learning as no one likes feeling incompetent. Performance improvements only come once people have become sufficiently comfortable with those new ways of working that they can work faster than they can in the old way: remember, even if the old way is less effective or less efficient, it is very well practiced. That practice enables a great deal of speed and efficiency, which will not initially be present in the new system. Recall our recent discussion of automatized skills and cueing: the old skills are automatized; the new ones still need to be.

What are Principles of Learning?

There are some facts about how our brains work that we can take advantage of to increase the speed, ease, and enjoyment of learning. The more the training process incorporates these different factors, the greater the effectiveness.

A big part of learning is making as much of the learning process mimic actual performance whenever possible. Thus, baseball players do not talk about throwing, catching, or hitting: they actually do it. A programmer cannot just read manuals: they have to actually write code. A manager can't just read or listen to lectures about management, they have to engage in the process.

This isn't to say that reading or listening to a talk isn't a valuable method of learning: in fact, a talk is one of the most time effective ways to communicate information to a large group of people. Even there, however, some level of audience involvement is important: be that taking notes, asking questions, or participating in a guided discussion of the material. Passively sitting in your seat while the information is poured into one ear only causes it to pour back out of the other. Similarly, marking up a book, adding highlights on your Kindle, or taking notes as you read all help to increase retention and the ability to use the material. The more we are engaged both mentally and physically, the better we learn. Later in this chapter, we'll look at ways to accomplish this with games.

The quantity of the material to be learned is also a factor. Most subjects are too big to digest in one sitting. We need time to absorb the information, think about it, and adjust our existing knowledge to accommodate the new information. The more we know about something, the easier it is to learn more: the old information provides a foundation and a context for the new. The most difficult part of learning a martial art, for example, is usually the beginning, when everything is new and different. As you progress, it gets easier because you now have context for the information. Thus, learning often requires breaking the information into chunks, learning and practicing each chunk, and then putting it all together. In driving a car, we learn to start and stop before we learn to parallel park; if you don't know how to stop reliably, parking can be exciting. Some people never master the art of packing the trunk.

Information is learned best when practice and training can be spread out over time. Trying to cram too much in at once is rather like cramming for a test: you might remember it for a brief period, but it doesn't stick. Repetition is key: a small amount of repetition every day is more effective than a great deal of repetition once a week. Trying to learn it all at once also runs into problems of concentration and physical stamina. In one rather amusing incident, a martial arts instructor told one of his students that to master a certain technique he would, "have to do it one thousand times."

The student didn't show up for class the next day, nor the day after. Finally, he limped into class, clearly in pain.

"Sensei!" he said, "I did it. I did the technique 1000 times!"

"Idiot!" exclaimed the instructor. "Not all in one day!"

Making sure that the material to be learned is relevant and engaging is also important. In Chap. 4, we talked about how leaders need to build competence, relatedness, and autonomy in their followers. The more relevant and engaging the material is, the more it helps with all three of these factors: learning, particularly with others on your team, builds relatedness. Even taking classes sponsored or paid for by the organization helps build a connection to the organization particularly when the person has a chance to use those newly developed skills. Improving skills also increases feelings of competence, at least once the student begins to master the material. Increased competence, in turn, makes it possible for the person to act more freely; in other words, increased autonomy. A further benefit is that expert power is increased. In many organizations, that can further lead to enhanced referent power and potentially legitimate power as well.

Finally, we need to look at feedback. Just as with any other part of organizational life, effective feedback is essential to maintaining interest. Feedback allows for on-the-fly adjustments during the training process, as well as more effective goal setting. Ongoing, dynamic feedback is best of all, an objective we can accomplish through certain types of serious games.

The longer people have to wait for feedback, the less useful it is. Finding out days, weeks, or months later that your leadership was ineffective or you attempted the wrong solution to a problem isn't particularly useful: the longer the time that passes, the more our perception of the feedback is colored by wishful thinking, the self-serving bias, and the fundamental attribution error.

Particularly in the area of leadership and other soft skills, feedback needs to be rapid enough that the details of the situation haven't been forgotten. Optimally, the leadership exercise will incorporate feedback into its structure so that prospective and actual leaders learn not just the appropriate techniques, but also how others are responding to how they manifest those techniques.

What is Organizational Learning?

Our discussion thus far has focused on individual learning within an organizational context. How, though, does an organization learn new skills?

An organization is, in a very real sense, not an actual physical entity. It is a conceptual construct held together by bonds of common purpose and culture. As we already know, culture is in the minds of the people who make up that culture. Learning, as we already discussed, is a change in behavior. Organizations achieve lasting, permanent behavior change when the lessons being taught are incorporated into the culture and organizational narrative of the organization: in other words, when people not only learn the lessons being taught, but also view those lessons as part of being successful in the organization. Culture is the residue of success, after all, so when we enable people to learn new skills, give them opportunities to exercise those skills, and demonstrate that those skills, or other lessons learned, are routes to success, we start to encode that information in the culture. The more visible those successes, and the more they are publicized, the faster they will be encoded.

People can exercise their skills publically or privately. They can be successful in their own little corner of the world, or their successes can be shown to others. If we want the organization to learn, that is, to change large-scale behaviors, we have to show the successes. If the goal is to spread a particular methodology, then the information the organization disseminates needs to explicitly connect the new methodology with success. If the goal is to teach flexible problem solving, then what gets publicized needs to be the exploration, experimentation, and loss cutting behaviors that enable flexibility.

A key part of organizational learning is moving from people using their skills individually to using them together. Remember that the point of an organization is that it is a community with a purpose: to accomplish that purpose requires that people learn to work together smoothly. In other words, we want to create the high performance teams we discussed earlier. Just as an individual baseball player's ability to hit, throw, or field are important parts of the game of baseball, it is the ability of the team to coordinate those behaviors and support one another that makes or breaks a team.

Organizational learning is thus the act of spreading success throughout the relevant portions of the business. This is an aspect of organizational growth and change. It is usually a gradual process, although we will look at ways of speeding it up. First, though, we need to understand the role of accreditation in cementing learning and status and in defining something as a success.

Accreditation Ceremonies to Acknowledge Learning

"It's like he only respects people who wear purple t-shirts. Now that I have a purple t-shirt, he respects me, even though he's the one who gave me the purple t-shirt!"

This comment was made by my wife upon receiving her black belt in jujitsu. She was referring to our instructor at that time. The achievement involved an elaborate ceremony culminating in the elevation to the rank of black belt. This ceremony was intended to inform everyone present that the student had now taken on a new role, with new responsibilities and power. What was particularly interesting is that amongst perceptions being shaped by the ceremony were those of the instructor who was awarding the belt and those of the student receiving the belt.

As we've discussed, learning is a permanent change in behavior. Along with that change in behavior is an increase in competence and status. Part of making the change permanent is the act of recognizing it: the act of accrediting the completion of a learning experience or, indeed, any change in status, is the final step in making it real. While one might argue that completing a course has physical reality, this is missing a critical component of the process: part of how we decide what is valuable is by looking to see what the organization cares about. What makes the acquisition of a particular skill valuable in a particular organization is that the organization recognizes the value of that skill: my clients care about my expertise in organizational systems, not my black belt in jujitsu. The act of accreditation is telling everyone that this person has just completed this process and achieved this status that we value and want others to respect and emulate.

 At root, an accreditation ceremony is a very simple thing: there is the person being recognized, there is someone who declares their accomplishments and states why she believes those accomplishments are representative of the person's character, and there are one or more witnesses. The person performing the accreditation must be someone who is recognized as an authority capable of making a valid accreditation: being declared a black belt by a seventh degree black belt instructor is meaningful; the same declaration from your mother maybe not so much. The inverse of an accreditation ceremony, a degradation ceremony, follows the same pattern. Indeed, some accreditation ceremonies sometimes begin with some act of degradation, before triumphantly ending in accreditation. College graduations or the awarding of medals at the end of a sporting event are accreditation ceremonies. When Lance Armstrong was stripped of his seven Tour de France jerseys, we were witnessing a degradation ceremony.

For all its simplicity, an accreditation ceremony has tremendous power. By publicly making a statement about a person, the granter is putting their own authority and reputation behind the newly accredited "graduate." The greater the authority and reputation of the granter, the more powerful the ceremony: this is why some college degrees are perceived differently than others. Graduating from MIT or Harvard or Princeton carries with it a much greater degree of status than graduating from Wossamatta U. Of course, consistently granting status to people who then do not live up to the implicit promises conveyed in the accreditation ceremony will eventually destroy the granter's own referent power and their accreditation will become meaningless; conversely, getting it right builds referent power. When those who follow us are successful, we are then held in higher regard, be that as parents, teachers, managers, directors, CEOs, businesses, or colleges.

Because people strive to be consistent, once you stand up and accredit someone, it becomes very difficult to go back on that. Thus, the perceptions of the person doing the accreditation are shifted by the act of accrediting. Because the accreditor is a recognized authority, the way the person receiving the accreditation views herself will also be shaped by the event. Markers of status, such as diplomas, provided during the ceremony extend and reinforce the power of the event. This is why, after physically receiving the black belt, the performance of the student improves: the symbol is a visible reminder to them of their own skill, a marker of competence. As we have already discussed, increasing perceptions of competence improves actual performance.

The witnesses serve to validate the event and provide social proof that it happened. When in doubt, we check to see how others are responding and having others responding favorably makes the event more real. Because the witnesses within an organization are conditioned, by their membership in the culture, to respect the symbols of accreditation, they further reinforce the event by treating the new graduate in a manner appropriate to their new status. This may include forms of deference such as letting them move to the front of the lunch line, or addressing them by titles such as "Professor," "Doctor," or "Sensei," presenting them with special clothing, or a better office, etc. The proverbial corner office is meaningful only because and only when we make it a marker of status.

In any organization, accreditation increases expert and referent power. Even when granting legitimate power, such as a promotion to manager, the public act of accrediting the new manager is an important part of confirming their status. Without that public recognition of status, the new manager is forced to rely more heavily on the cruder exercise of reward and coercive power. It is often harder to be a manager in an organization that does not perform the visible act of recognizing and confirming the status change. It's the difference between people following you because they want to or because they feel they have to.

Because accreditation ceremonies are communal events, they also serve to build connections between members of the group. When a member of a team is recognized for an accomplishment, that recognition can increase the cohesiveness of the team; it can, but does not have to. Another part of what makes an accreditation ceremony work is that the culture views the act being accredited as praiseworthy. As Atari discovered, highlighting individual achievement in a highly team-oriented culture can backfire quite badly.

Accreditation, and degradation, ceremonies optimally match with and reinforce the culture. If they contradict the values of the culture, they will trigger a cultural immune response. People won't believe the ceremonies and will resent the accreditation, viewing it as unjust or unfair. Over time, this reduces trust, motivation, and connection to the organization. It is important, therefore, when accrediting someone's new status, that the reasons for the accreditation be stated and connected to the organizational culture and narrative. Accrediting people who are engaging in pro-organizational behaviors then feeds back into the culture, creating organizational learning. Conversely, when someone is acting in ways damaging to the organization, it is equally important, or perhaps more important, to act quickly to change the behavior or strip that person of their status. Stripping them of their status can include removing them from the organization. Otherwise, as we discussed in the section on dealing with jerks, the bad behavior will eventually infect the culture. Once that happens, it is extremely difficult to remove.

One of the challenges in designing appropriate accreditation ceremonies is finding the appropriate balance between making them too rare and difficult to obtain, and so easy that they have no value. When a martial arts master once boasted that his instructor was so tough that only 10 people in 50 years ever got black belts from the man, the reaction of a great many people was, "Wow, that guy must have been one crummy teacher!" Conversely, if all you need to graduate is a pulse, who cares? The accomplishment has no meaning: parents who have seen their kids "graduate" from pre–pre-school to pre-school may have had this reaction! While hitting the exact middle of these two extremes is quite difficult, anywhere in the general vicinity of the center will work well enough. Managing the difficulty of gaining accreditation is an ongoing, dynamic process. When the process becomes rigid, it also loses its value.

Using Serious Games for Learning

Gamification, or the art of using games in a business setting, is becoming extremely popular. Turning things into games promises to revolutionize productivity, training, and also wash dishes. Okay, maybe the dish washing is wishful thinking. Unfortunately, so is much of the promise of gamification. Fortunately, however, there are also some aspects of using games that are very promising. The key is to use games correctly: highly competitive games are far more likely to do harm than good in organizational settings. Internal competition, within a team or within a business, creates a short-term boost. Over the medium and long term, however, competition leads to lower productivity, factions, and silos. Schein observes that the damage caused by internal competition can take years to reverse.

The good news, though, is that certain types of games do lend themselves extremely well to training and improving organizational performance. At the most basic level, the "video game" model of points, badges, and leader boards can create some excitement and increased interest. Without the glitz and action of video games, though, I have serious doubts how long this approach can maintain interest. On the other hand, certain types of serious games can prove extremely beneficial. It should be recognized at this point that the term "serious games" is not synonymous with computer games; the original concept of serious games had, in fact, nothing to do with computers. We will be looking at a variant of that type of interactive, face-to-face game here: while computers might be used to supplement the game, the objective of the game is to maximize human contact and interaction. Particularly in areas such as leadership and team development, person to person interaction is what it's all about.

How do we apply serious games to business training or organizational development and organizational psychology? We need look no farther than the legend of King Arthur.

What do King Arthur and a modern CEO have in common? Oddly enough, a great deal. Leaving aside the obvious point that King Arthur had Merlin the court wizard, and the modern CEO has his technical wizards, the two are actually facing similar problems. Granted, the modern CEO is somewhat less likely to be hit over the head with a sword or be eaten by fire-breathing dragons. On the other hand, King Arthur didn't have to worry about lawsuits or crashing computers, so advantage Arthur. When you strip away the scenery, the problems, methods, and solutions aren't that different. When you put the scenery back in, you have an opportunity to learn a great deal through the experience of being King Arthur. Not only does the story of King Arthur contain numerous lessons for CEOs, how Arthur trained his workforce has lessons for training leaders and team members today. Through appropriately designed serious games, we can learn those lessons without facing the unfortunate consequences that Arthur faced.

The first connection between King Arthur and a CEO is that both of them require a highly skilled workforce in order to accomplish their goals. King Arthur needed to recruit the top knights to sit at the Round Table. The CEO needs to recruit top people to sit around the table and develop the products and services that the company needs to be successful. How does he know what to do? How does he hone his skills? We've already discussed what needs to be done to hire effectively; appropriate training games are how people can learn to do it.

As fans of the story will recall, even when Arthur drew the sword from the stone, he still had to fight for his kingdom. As an untested 15 year-old, he needed to inspire his troops to go up against some of the toughest, most famous kings in the land. The CEO needs to inspire his company with the full knowledge that the competition ranges from tiny startups to behemoths like IBM or GE. King Arthur couldn't win through brute force or simply by fencing just a little bit better: his troops were outnumbered. He needed to employ superior battle strategies and tactics. Similarly, most companies are competing against numerous opponents, more than a few of whom have far more resources than they do. Even when you are a behemoth, you can't take on everyone. Quite simply, you can't win by doing the same thing only maybe a little cheaper. You need to develop innovative products and services that create both markets and loyalty, possibly displacing an existing competitor along the way. Building an innovative environment doesn't just happen. It too takes training and practice.

As we all know, King Arthur's court was not without its share of interpersonal problems and politics, Lancelot's affair with Guinevere and Mordred's betrayal being the most famous. Arthur himself handled these situations poorly by not confronting the various parties early and dealing with the situation when it was small and easily managed. That inaction cost Arthur his kingdom and his life.

John Gutfreund, CEO of one-time investment bank Salomon Brothers, ignored the actions of a rogue trader and lost his kingdom: he was forced to resign his position at Salomon and the company was nearly destroyed. Unfortunately, it's not easy dealing with such problems and the natural instinct for many people is to hope the problem will go away. It takes facing such problems regularly to develop the skill and confidence to recognize and deal with them early. Appropriately designed games allow that to happen without creating an unpleasant working environment.

King Arthur also had the problem of training the next generation of leaders. The knight business is a tough one. Getting onto a horse in full armor isn't easy, and when dismounting involves another knight with a spear, well, there's going to be some workforce attrition. Even worse, during peacetime, there was the problem of making sure the knights kept their swords, and skills, sharp. King Arthur solved that problem through holding tournaments. The tournaments of the King Arthur stories were the pseudo-battlegrounds in which knights honed their skills and kept themselves ready for war. The skills they practiced, horsemanship, swordplay, archery, gymnastics, were the much in demand skills of the day. Given that the tournaments were often bloody, and people were often injured or even killed during them, one could describe them quite fairly as serious games. Modern sports are the present day incarnation of the serious games of the past: fencing, kendo, judo, gymnastics, and pentathlon, to name but a few. Each of these sports once represented the battlefield skills of the elite warrior. Masters of these sports learn early that success comes from being fully involved and from testing their skills under pressure. In the days of King Arthur, if you weren't fully involved, you would likely end up fully dead.

Fortunately, in today's business environment, sword fighting is strongly discouraged and paper cuts are rarely fatal. In the constantly changing environment of today's competitive landscape, it's hard to know which skills will be needed when. The serious games of today need to focus on a different set of skills from King Arthur's time, but skills that are no less critical: leadership, negotiation, teamwork, confronting problems, public speaking, improvisation, persuasion, decision making with incomplete information, and remaining calm under pressure. Like its predecessors, the modern serious game must fully involve participants, forcing them to solve actual problems within the engrossing and absorbing context of the game. Just as King Arthur didn't want his first clue that there was a problem to be losing a war, a business doesn't want its first clue that people are not prepared to meet the demands of the business to be defeat in the marketplace. In real life corporate situations, feedback may take weeks or months. By the time it is clear that something is not working, it is difficult to identify cause and effect. The modern serious game must have meaningful, in-game consequences for actions. Players need to have the experience of making decisions and living with the results within a few hours or days.

As we have already discussed, all businesses need to provide leadership to their members, motivate employees, and negotiate with individuals and organizations. The problem lies in practicing the necessary skills in an environment that does not feel artificial. Because people learn best when they are enjoying themselves, a well-constructed serious game will provide an entertaining scenario with sufficient challenge that players cannot easily "game the game." When people are having fun, they are engaged. Players get caught up in the game and as a result deal with the problems that come up much as they would in real life. Whether a player gives up in frustration after encountering an obstacle or comes up with an out-of-the-box solution, you can see how they will perform on the job. Because of the immersive nature of the game, participants are fully involved, a key component of learning.

Unlike King Arthur's time, however, the consequences of failure within a serious game are never fatal. By creating a fantasy environment, in this example, King Arthur's court at Camelot, it is possible to design games that free people to practice different scenarios and explore different strategies without risking either the company or their careers. Serious gaming enables businesses to practice and hone the skills of their employees before the critical situation in which those skills are needed. Employees also have the opportunity to experiment and make mistakes in an environment in which there are no financial consequences to the business. Employees who need additional skill training can be identified before they fail on the job. Employees who demonstrate significant aptitude in unexpected skills can be further developed so that the company and the employee can fully benefit from their talents. As an extra bonus, participating in an enjoyable activity that also increases competence increases motivation and loyalty to the business.

Fortunately, serious games of this nature are not a pipe-dream or wish-fulfillment. Known as predictive scenarios, these games provide participants with exactly the sort of play environment in which experimentation and mistakes are safe and encouraged. In short, an environment that provides the necessary experiences to produce real learning. By presenting the problems in a fantastic setting, players are emotionally "given permission" to step outside their normal roles and the expectations others have for them: that freedom is critical to enabling people to explore and make mistakes. The more fantastic the scenario, the more real the behavior of the participants. The more realistic the scenario, the less real the behavior of the participants.

When I ran a Pandemic Flu predictive scenario in Washington DC a few years ago, many participants from DHS, Homeland Security, and other government organizations, found it difficult or impossible to separate their fictional roles from their actual roles. That lack of separation prevented many participants from engaging with the scenario because they were afraid of looking bad in front of their colleagues or superiors. I've observed similar results with overly simple scenarios, where participants spent the entire time debating whether or not the scenario was factually correct.

On the other hand, when I run *Long Ago and Far Away*, a predictive scenario my wife (a clinical psychologist) and I developed, a very different dynamic appears: instead of being the embattled CEO, someone is the king. Instead of ambitious vice-presidents, there are devilish dukes and evil earls, wicked witches and malevolent sorcerers. The problems of leadership, negotiation, team building, and motivation are the same, but the scenery is very different. At the end, players are debriefed and learn what actually worked and what only appeared to work: more than one person has discovered that a coercive style of leadership produced short-term gains, but long-term losses as other players revealed what they had withheld. Others learned that their supposedly unerring instincts for whom they could and could not trust had led them to distrust exactly the people most dedicated to helping them. And still others learned that when you truly empower someone, it's absolutely amazing what they are willing to do on your behalf! The fantasy nature of the game also allows for controlled competition, maximizing the benefits while minimizing the destructive nature of competition within a team or organization. Predictive scenario games manage the competition through the figurative masks participants are wearing; at the same time, the intensity of the experience creates bonds of friendship and cooperation across the organization.

Orientation and Community Building

As we've already discussed, your organizational narrative is a critical piece of attracting the right people: those who care about your organization and its purpose. Once you've got them, though, you have to keep them. No matter how excited someone is by the narrative and vision of your organization, that's only the beginning. Sometimes, such as when dealing with mergers and acquisitions, you won't even have that: all too often one company acquires another only to see key employees of the acquired company depart shortly thereafter. Few things are more frustrating than to acquire a company in order to gain access to its talent and then watch that talent walk out the door. The traditional golden handcuffs of stock options and retention bonuses can help slow this down, at least until said bonuses are collected.

If we want something that will actually work to keep people, we need to go back to one of our key emotions that leaders need to foster: relatedness. It's not enough to connect new members of the organization to the vision and purpose; they also have to feel connected to the people around them. New hires who feel isolated and apart from the group do not perform well and typically do not stick around. New hires who feel connected tend to work harder and are considerably more committed and loyal. Teams acquired through mergers are more likely to stick together. This is both good and bad: when one member leaves, often many of the others will follow.

Optimally, the goals of any new employee orientation should include the following:

- Inform new members of the rules and processes of the organization: should your desk be clear and locked every night or is it acceptable to leave out what you are working on?
- Tell them how to be successful in the organization: in some organizations, informal conversations in the hallway are normal, in others that same behavior is considered rude and unprofessional.

- Build strong, positive relationships with one another and with existing members of the organization.

Although most organizations tend to focus primarily on the first and occasionally on the second, the third is the most critical. In fact, if we do the third well, the other two will almost solve themselves: if new members feel connected, they will also be more open to imitating the behaviors they observe and they will be more willing to ask questions.

Fortunately, we can use many of the principles of organizational learning to help increase relatedness. As we've already discussed, learning improves when people are engaged and having fun. What is particularly interesting is that how they regard their colleagues in the learning activity is also affected by the intensity and enjoyableness of the activity. When people are engaged and having fun together, they develop more positive feelings toward those around them. Conversely, when people are bored, unhappy, or disengaged, they develop negative feelings about those around them. Properly applied, this knowledge lets us rapidly forge connections to other members of the organization, building motivation and loyalty in the process. The stronger the social web that pervades your organization, the easier it is to not only retain top talent, but also attract new talent as well. Strength builds on strength.

All too often, unfortunately, new employee orientation is a sterile affair in which a manager or HR representative goes through a set of procedures and expectations. While this information may be important, that's orientation in only the most basic sense. It's really just bookkeeping. At least take the person out to lunch at the end! That way you get at least some small sense of connection out of it. Better yet, conduct orientation in cohorts: that way new employees feel something in common with other members of the organization. It is best if those other members are people they are working with or see around the office, but just building a cohort helps considerably.

It's even better, though, to take employees off site for a day or two and do something enjoyable. Once again, though, we have to hit the balance between competition and cooperation, between challenge and fun. We also want the activities to involve the use of the social skills people will need on the job in order to work together. By now, you may be thinking about ropes courses and trust falls and other such nonsense. As nice as they sound, they don't work. Think of it this way: a trust fall is meaningless exactly because almost any normal person would act to catch someone falling off a log. Having participated in trust falls, the only trust required is that I have to trust that the group behind me is minimally competent to interlace their hands and is not composed of psychopaths. If the first point isn't true, they'll have fallen on their faces long before we get to the trust fall; if the group is composed of psychopaths, I'm an extra in a bad horror movie. Ropes courses are similar: they sound good on paper, but they just don't work. The skills people are using in a ropes course are not the interpersonal skills they need in the office. Indeed, if ropes courses had lived up to their early promise, we'd see them used in that most competitive of realms, professional sports. Sports teams are always looking for any advantage to maximize the effectiveness of training. I know of no successful professional sports team that uses ropes courses in place of practice.

Here again, we come back to the concept of predictive scenario serious games. Other experiential activities can also work, but often lack the appropriate level of immersion and intensity. The more highly educated and creative the people you are dealing with, the more important it is that activities have a significant level of social and intellectual challenge.

We already looked at how predictive scenarios can benefit existing members of an organization. When bringing in new people, the predictive scenario serves to introduce them to other members of the organization, build connections, and can even start them off with a sense of competence and the admiration of their peers. An advantage of predictive scenario activities is that older members of the organization can participate along with the new members, building "inter-generational" connections. Because new members can be cast into critical roles in the scenario, we get around the problem that people tend to preferentially interact with those whom they know best. And, of course, everyone is engaged together in an absorbing and intense activity, which helps each person build positive views of the others.

Accreditation ceremonies can be used at the end of the orientation to formally welcome new members into the organization. In this case, it's not so much that you are recognizing some great accomplishment in this situation; rather, you are celebrating the end of an intense experience and celebrating the fact that these people have just joined the organization. This sort of recognition, particularly when coupled with an immersive, powerful experience, will build loyalty, commitment, and motivation, and go a long way towards providing a strong foundation of autonomy, competence, and relatedness.

 You can control the first impression a new member has of your organization. Think about what you want it to be because it's going to last.

Organizational Change as Organizational Learning

In Chap. 1, we discussed the fundamentals of cultural change. Specifically, we talked about techniques for building motivation for change and the belief that the organization could change. We can now expand upon that by applying the principles of organizational learning to organizational change.

To begin with, let's recognize that organizations are changing all the time. The entire process of learning is ongoing and continuous. There are times, however, when we need the change process to be rapid and specific: new habits and new ways of working need to be adopted quickly. Building motivation for change is really only one piece of the process, although a pervasive one.

Just as the beginning of the learning process needs to connect to the end, before a change process can begin, it needs to be connected to the end. Remind people of the vision and organizational narrative: what are your overall goals? How are you benefiting your customers? How will this change flow out of your organizational narrative and help bring the vision to life? Alternately, how will the change extend or expand the existing vision? Just as individual learning works best when people can see how they will benefit and will gain greater autonomy and competence, so organizational change works best when people can see how they and the organization benefit and improve their abilities to carry out the organization's vision.

Just as it helps people learn when they can see what more advanced students look like, organizational change works better when you can show people what the future will look like. Provide clear images of what it means for the organization to change. If possible and appropriate, use professionally prepared videos of what the organization will be like after the change is completed. When employees of a company see people who look like them operating in new ways, it becomes easier to learn those new ways of operating. Observational learning is very powerful: in one study, people who were so snake phobic they made Indiana Jones look like a reptile lover did nothing more than watch other people play with snakes for a couple of hours. At the end of that time, practically all of them were also willing to play with snakes.

Remember that part of learning is understanding what our goals really mean and connecting each step. When we ask, "What are you doing by doing that," we are asking how each step connects forward to the next step. We can also work backward from the end point, identifying the key steps along the way. Often, this is an easier way to figure out how to make the change process work. It has the added advantage that working backward lets us identify important decision points and helps us understand how our decisions at those points will shape people's actions and beliefs. This is, in a nutshell, the process of strategy building. Strategy is, in essence, the art of looking forward and then reasoning backward. The more effectively we can articulate our strategy, the easier it is to keep people focused on making the changes happen. Keep in mind that in most voluntarily chosen learning experiences, people are starting with an end result in mind and engaging in some amount of that same backward reasoning to figure out how to get there.

We talked a great deal in Chaps. 3–5 about teams, leadership, and motivation. Teams reinforce one another: when team members train together and learn together, the lesson is constantly echoed back and the team's bonds become stronger. Conversely, when people train apart from their teams, the team bonds are strained. Given the choice between demonstrating new behaviors or acting like the rest of the team, most people chose the second. Thus, organizational change will work best when the team learns the new methods and approaches together, so that no one feels like they are no longer part of the group.

As with any learning process, new routines, processes, or tools need to be practiced until they feel natural. As we've already discussed, until a skill is automatized, it is often hard to see the advantages: the new skill is relatively inefficient and awkward feeling compared to the current practiced, but outmoded, methods of working. While it's hard to break an old habit, it's easy to create a new one. The new habits and routines need to be practiced until they become the natural, default behaviors.

As we have already discussed, mistakes are a necessary part of learning. They are also a necessary part of any significant organizational change. Just as with any other form of learning, making and recovering from mistakes is what builds confidence and comfort with the change. Providing opportunities to practice, including practice areas or simulations, can help with this: there's a reason why pilots use flight simulators!

Accreditation ceremonies, again as we've already discussed, help cement learning. Celebrating the successes along the way, recognizing the significant milestones, is a form of accreditation. Each time you celebrate a significant step, you are joining together as a group to recognize you are succeeding. As with any other accreditation, that group recognition helps reinforce the sense of progress that is important to any long-term project; indeed, part of the accreditation should include reviewing how far you've come. The more people feel they are making progress, the more enthusiastic they will become. The less progress they feel they are making, the harder it will be to keep them focused on change. Success and failure each feeds on itself.

Finally, when the process is complete, remember to celebrate that success as well; after all, you've earned it. You've created a new normal. Now you just have to cement it in. Highlight the challenges and the successes. Don't minimize the obstacles you faced. You want people to walk out of that final accreditation ceremony feeling that they were successful in an extremely difficult undertaking: done right, the entire change process should leave your organization feeling more competent, with greater trust and hence more room for autonomy, and simultaneously more strongly connected than ever before.

Wrapping It Up

It's easy to think of organizational learning as little more than having people take classes. When this is all you do, you miss most of the value of the learning process. Done well, organizational learning is a powerful means of keeping your organization a vibrant, exciting, productive place to be.

Questions to Consider

1. What is organizational learning?
2. In what ways does your organization learn?
3. What learning opportunities do people have in your organization?
4. How are the learning opportunities your organization provides building competence? Autonomy?
5. Relatedness? How do those opportunities tie into the organizational narrative?
6. What accreditation ceremonies have you witnessed? Why did they work or not work?
7. What is the value of new member or new employee orientation? How are you going about it? What could you change to make it more effective?
8. How can you apply organizational learning to making the process of organizational change more effective?

Chapter 9
The Myth of Productivity: Measurement, Goal Setting, and the High Performance Cycle

Once upon a time, there was a light bulb. This light bulb was quite a remarkable light bulb: it was praised far and wide for its incredible efficiency. This light bulb gave off no waste heat. This light bulb did not contribute to global warming. It had no carbon footprint. It did not rely on fossil fuels. Truly, it was an amazing light bulb, and visitors came every day to see this remarkable light bulb.

One day, though, a traveler coming to see the light bulb in action was delayed by an unfortunate flood that closed several roads. He did not arrive until well after night had fallen. Much to his surprise, he found the light bulb sitting in a pitch dark room.

"Why aren't you giving light?" asked the traveler.

"Give light!" replied the light bulb in shocked tones. "You must be joking. If I did that, I would use fossil fuels. I would have a carbon footprint. I would give off waste heat. I would no longer be efficient."

"But isn't the purpose of a light bulb to give light?" asked the traveler.

"I've always been told to be efficient," replied the light bulb with a shrug. If you have never seen a light bulb shrug, it is truly a wonder to behold. The traveler would have been amazed, except, of course, that the room was too dark for him to see the miraculous event.

Once upon a time, there was a software company named "Soak, Inc." Soak's product relied upon a very complex database server. One day, the VP of Engineering stormed into the office and declared, "The server is too slow. We need to speed it up."

From that day forth, every effort was focused on improving the speed of the server. Other issues were deemed insignificant beside the one, critical, goal of performance. Engineers who dared to raise other issues were publically humiliated for wasting the company's time. Bugs that did not relate to performance issues were deemed "optional." People who spent time reviewing the optional bugs and trying to fix them were warned that their insubordination would cost them their jobs if it did not cease immediately.

Eventually, Soak developed an amazingly efficient server. It was fast and robust and was ready to demonstrate to potential clients.

S. R. Balzac, *Organizational Psychology for Managers*,
Management for Professionals, DOI: 10.1007/978-1-4614-8505-6_9,
© Springer Science+Business Media New York 2014

The demo started out remarkably well. The server did not crash, causing some to believe that this could not actually be a demonstration of a software product. Indeed, the server performed flawlessly. All would have gone well indeed for Soak had not someone noticed that the data being delivered by the server didn't make sense. Yes, what the server had gained in performance it had lost in accuracy. In other words, it was incredibly good at very rapidly delivering useless or incorrect information.

When the engineers were questioned about this unfortunate oversight, they shrugged and replied, "We were told to be efficient."

While it is not nearly as amazing to see an engineer shrug as it is to see a light bulb shrug, the effects are much the same.

At Soak, a goal was set, a metric for success was defined, and that metric became the sole determinant of progress. Goals are extremely powerful tools: the best thing about them is that you accomplish them. Unfortunately, sometimes the worst thing about goals is that you accomplish them. At Soak, they accomplished their goals. A dead light bulb is extremely efficient, but not useful. Similar observations can be made about the server.

Before leaping into setting a goal, especially a goal to solve a problem, it helps to understand the actual problem and to understand what the actual symptoms are. Rather than create useful goals, they fixated on a symptom. That did not, however, actually change anything.

At Soak, the VP stated that they were trying to solve the problems his company was facing as rapidly and effectively as possible. They were setting goals. They were Taking Action! Taking action is certainly helpful, but it is even more helpful to be taking the correct action. Since it's not always possible to determine just what the correct action is, it becomes even more critical to listen to the feedback and questions from the people who are charged with actually executing the action. The engineers knew that something was wrong, but no one was willing to listen to them. As we will discuss shortly, a key aspect of successful goal setting is understanding the feedback you're getting.

I realize that many of you reading this are probably chuckling to yourselves and thinking that this scenario could never happen at your companies. The folks at Soak said the same before, during, and even after it happened to them. The light bulb had no comment.

Productivity seems like such a simple thing. Somehow, though, it never is. As we have already discussed, cognitive shortcuts such as the Halo Effect can influence how productive we perceive someone to be. Ultimately, the only real way to measure productivity is through understanding goals and knowing how to construct goals so that they will actually get you what you want. Otherwise, you may just end up with a dead light bulb.

What is Productivity?

One of the challenges in measuring productivity is that we all too often conflate our methods of measuring productivity with productivity itself. As one IBM manager put it "You did a great job. But you made it look too easy, so I'm not giving you a raise." Apparently, this manager measured productivity by how unhappy his employees were, or something equally nonsensical.

Other measures of productivity include the mighty 40-h work week, which always seems to stretch. The 40-h week as a measure of productivity is, as we've already touched upon, itself a cultural artifact. When an assembly line job involves mindlessly turning screws or pulling levers, then a mechanical equating of time spent on the job with productivity at least has some vague basis in reality. In our increasingly technological society, the concept that time equals productivity is at best simply inaccurate, at worst counter-productive, a concept we will return to in future chapters.

Part of the challenge in measuring productivity is that we are often drawn into valuing the things we can measure, rather than figuring out what we really value and measuring that. It's easy to measure the passage of time, so people use that. At one company, employees figured out they could up their managers' perceptions of how hard they were working by spending extra time in the evening surfing the web. No additional work got done, but the various managers all rated the employees as more productive.

Circling back for a moment to our discussions of leadership and motivation, recall that the key emotions of leadership are autonomy, relatedness, and competence. A team works best when the leader can foster these emotions in her followers. An assembly line has no autonomy and the illusion of relatedness: everyone is acting together, but they are doing so independently. That's not really relatedness though, merely synchronization. Fans of Madelaine L'Engle's classic novel, "A Wrinkle in Time," might well remember the planet Camazotz where everyone must act alike and do everything in the same way at the same time. On Camazotz, those are the legal laws. They are also a terrible way to build effective, enthusiastic, and productive teams. It's time to step away from these outmoded beliefs and recognize that real productivity comes through coordinated behavior in pursuit of common objectives in a manner that balances the freedom to work in whatever way you see fit within the needs of the team and the organization. A critical piece of achieving this coordination is understanding and setting effective goals.

Why Set Goals?

Properly designed and applied, goals are very powerful tools for increasing productivity. Ironically, for all the talk about goals, for most of the past century our knowledge of goals was little better than the concept that "goals are good." It wasn't until two psychology professors, Edwin Locke and Gary Latham, started to look seriously at goals in the 1960s that we began to have solid research on the topic. It wasn't until they published their ground-breaking paper on goal setting in 1990 that we had the beginnings of a coherent, coordinated approach to setting effective goals.

By identifying what is important, goals help focus our attention and energy. Having set a goal, it becomes something that is difficult to get out of our heads;

indeed, the more we care about the goal, the more our thoughts are pulled toward it. Similarly, goals reduce our tendencies to be distracted: we learn to ignore the things that don't matter while we focus on the things that do.

With practice and developing skill in goal setting, goals trigger us to develop other goals. A large goal can stimulate us to learn new skills or develop new competencies in diverse areas of knowledge. We will discuss some strategies around effective goal setting and goal decomposition, or the art of breaking goals into smaller goals, later in this chapter.

Recall that our organizational narrative starts with an organizational vision: in other words, a large, exciting goal. Goals help define our organizations: the more vivid and unique the goals, the more unique the organization. Microsoft, Apple, Google, IBM, Amazon.com, Starbucks, Michael Kors are all companies that at least started out with unique and exciting goals. Conversely, every law firm I've ever looked at has virtually identical goals, and every law firm looks much like every other law firm.

Goals also increase our sense of self-efficacy, or our belief that we are capable of controlling the world around us. The more goals we accomplish, the more our sense of control grows; the greater our sense of control, the more we are willing to attempt. The momentum of success is very powerful, as we will discuss when we get to the high performance cycle. With proper goal setting, even the momentum of failure can, jujitsu style, be reversed and turned into valuable information that feeds success.

A key powerful aspect of well-constructed goals is that they provide feedback. Imagine driving to a new destination, one you've never visited before. Road signs, landmarks, your GPS are all providing you with information that tells you how close you are to your goal, how far you've come, even whether you're on course! Feedback, as we've discussed several times so far, is a vital component of maintaining focus and motivation. Failure, in this context, is merely another form of feedback: Edison's proverbial, "I learned a thousand ways to not make a light bulb." When we interpret failure as feedback, it becomes valuable information that helps us further refine and direct our goals, increasing, rather than decreasing, our focus and energy.

Quite simply, human beings are built to not waste energy. That doesn't mean that we're always successful in that objective, but it is our default. Whenever we embark on any project, be it product development, building a business, training for a marathon, seeking a black belt in judo, writing a book, etc., we look for feedback that we are making progress. If we get that feedback, our enthusiasm is reinforced and we continue on. Indeed, the clearer and more continuous the feedback, the more enjoyable the process of goal pursuit becomes.

Conversely, if we don't get that feedback, eventually our enthusiasm starts to flag and we start questioning our decision to embark on that activity. This is why so many projects are begun with such enthusiasm, and then swiftly peter out: without feedback, interest wanes. For all that some martial arts masters decry the colored belt system as childish, it provides valuable, visible feedback of a student's progress. Military rank insignia serve a similar purpose. Those martial arts that do not provide colored belts tend to have fewer students overall and a smaller percentage of students progressing all the way to black belt. Granted, some people will go longer than others without receiving feedback. Indeed, there are some people who don't know when to quit: if, like Edison or Jobs, they eventually succeed we hail them as heroes; if they fail, we dismiss them as fools, as exemplified in the old joke:

> They said Edison was crazy. They said Einstein was crazy. They said the Wright brothers were crazy. They said Amos Schmedlap was crazy!
> Who is Amos Schmedlap?
> My uncle. He was crazy.

If your goals are not providing you with feedback, then those goals are not properly constructed! And, to be completely accurate, Edison did receive feedback: every failure was a form of feedback that helped him know he was making progress. Feedback doesn't mean success, although that helps. Feedback means feedback.

Finally, we do not want to set too many goals. The power of a goal to focus your attention swiftly declines when multiple goals are warring for space in your brain. Four or five large goals are usually plenty. If that doesn't sound like much, recognize that those few large goals can easily generate dozens or hundreds of smaller goals. This can swiftly become overwhelming. We'll look into strategies for how to manage and organize goals later in this chapter. First, though, we need to understand more about what goals are.

What are Goals?

We talk about goals a great deal. Every January I receive numerous articles touting the benefits of setting goals, and assuring me that if I just set goals then everything will magically work out Just Fine (tm). I've lost track of the number of times I've walked into a company and asked people, "What are your goals?" only to receive blank looks in return. Occasionally, I'm told that the goal is to make money. At least they have an answer; it's not a very good answer, but it's a starting point for discussion.

Let's start by recognizing that making money is not a goal. It's not even an outcome. Making money is a form of feedback: it's one of several measures that can tell you if your strategies are working and your company is producing valuable goods or services. Focusing on the measurement instead of on the goals and approaches that enable you to make money leads to poor strategy and short-term optimization at the expense of long-term growth. That's not to say that making money isn't important: for many organizations and individuals it is a vital component of continuing to do what you want to be doing. It's merely not the overall goal and, as we've already discussed, it's also a terrible way to produce long-term motivation.

What about those New Year's resolutions that everyone talks about at the beginning of the year? Sadly, those are not goals either. They are, at best, good intentions. The problem is, an intention is not a goal; an intention is a statement of desire or a wish or a dream, but it is not a goal. As we will discuss later in this chapter, intentions can be used to help execute goals, but they are not goals. Intentions are too vague, too hard to measure, and too lacking in structure to be effective goals.

Rather, we need to think about goals as a combination of desired outcomes, processes or strategies to achieve those outcomes, and learning and discovery. Indeed, like Gaul, goals can be divided into three types:

- Outcome goals—these are our desired results.
- Process goals—goals set to produce behaviors that will lead us to our desired outcomes.
- Learning goals—developing new skills and obtaining new information to help us with our process, outcome, and learning goals.

Let's look at each of these goals in more depth.

What are Outcome Goals?

As we all know, if you want to find a pony under your Christmas tree, all you have to do is set a goal that there be a pony under your Christmas tree and it will show up. Okay, well, maybe not. Of course if things really did work that way, there would be a lot of surprised ponies out there, and even more surprised parents of small children whose goal was to get a pony.

Outcome goals are the things we want to achieve. They might include building a successful product, winning an athletic competition, winning the lottery, and, yes, finding a pony eating your Christmas tree. All of these outcome goals have one thing in common: we can't actually control the outcome. This is most obvious with the pony, although that hasn't stopped generations of kids from whining and begging their parents. The lottery is similar: although we can take the step of buying a ticket, there is no further control over the outcome. The odds of winning any significant amount of money in the lottery are hundreds of millions to one, and nothing you can do will significantly change those odds.

How about winning an athletic competition? Well, now we're on to something, right? After all, we can set a goal of winning a tournament. We can, but again, we have to look at what aspects of the goal we actually have control over. We typically don't control our opponents and we don't control how well they've trained. In fact, the only things we can control are our own training and the strategies we execute during the competition. None of these things guarantee that we will win, but they can make it more likely.

What about building that successful product? Surely that's something that is under complete control? Sadly, once again, it's a worthy outcome but not one we can fully control. We can control how much product research we do, we can control whom we hire to build the product, we can control how knowledgeable we are about team development, leadership, motivation, and decision making. We cannot control our competition nor can we control the economy. We can't even control whether or not some critical employee quits at just the wrong moment in our product development cycle.

The problem with outcome goals is that so much of the goal is outside of our control: the bigger the goal, the more uncontrollable factors there are. That's not necessarily a bad thing, but it is something we need to be aware of. Outcome goals are powerful tools for inspiring people and giving people a common objective to shoot for. Well defined outcome goals that tie into the organizational vision and narrative are critical for focusing effort and creating a sense of purpose. We simply must avoid the trap of focusing solely on the results that we are after. Focusing too intently on results makes the results less likely.

We see this most easily in sports. As we discussed in Chap. 4, those swordsmen who focus most on results are less likely to win. Indeed, like some sort of Zen paradox, the greater the focus on outcomes, the less likely you are to obtain those outcomes. Athletes who focus on process, vision, and strategy, on the other hand, tend to win more often and win more difficult competitions. This is because an obsessive focus on results prevents us from getting the feedback we need to actually accomplish our goals: with outcome goals, the feedback doesn't come until the end, when it is often too late. We will return to this when we look at strategy development.

Outcome goals, to be most effective, need to be decomposed into process goals, learning goals, and, yes, other outcome goals.

What are Process Goals?

If outcome goals are what we want to accomplish, then process goals are how we are going to do it. Process goals reflect those elements of the goal equation that are under our control: for example, the judo player might rehearse different throwing combinations, the fencer different combinations of blade work. A business might explore different methods for improving the quality and speed of software development: for example, they might try Extreme Programming before discovering that it really doesn't work all that well. A writer might arrange her day to have uninterrupted chunks of time in order to be able to concentrate most effectively.

Process goals are the beginnings of strategy: while outcome goals only give us feedback at the end of an activity, process goals give us feedback during the activity. Real-time feedback is what permits real-time course correction. Real-time course correction is what enables us to discover that we should have made a left at Albuquerque before we end up in the middle of the Sahara desert.

The intent of process goals is to focus our behaviors into directions, which will give us control over those aspects of our outcome goals that we can control and improve our odds in those areas that we can't control. For example, Jesse Livermore, the legendary stock market wizard, recognized that he could not control the direction the market was going. However, he could control whether or not he was in the market, and developed rules, or process goals, which told him when to buy or sell. Executed properly, these process goals maximized his odds of turning a profit: indeed, Livermore's profits when he covered his short positions into the Crash on Oct 29, 1929 were reputed to be on the order of $100,000,000.

In sports, when an athlete attempts a move and it doesn't work, the athlete can switch to a different move. A business that conducts market research is doing the moral equivalent: they are testing different approaches or different product formulations and using that feedback to guide their goal-directed behavior.

Process goals are your battle plan. While it may be true that no battle plan survives contact with the enemy, having a battle plan lets you know when you've made contact.

Process goals can be decomposed into outcome, process, and learning goals.

What are Learning Goals?

Learning goals are the goals we set to obtain new knowledge or information, develop new competencies, and devise new strategies. As we discussed in the previous chapter, part of successful learning is tying the beginning of the learning process to a valued ending. Learning goals help create that connection, in part because learning goals are often tied to other, valued outcome goals. Learning goals also help direct our attention to the most important aspects of what we are attempting to learn. Of course, that flip side of that is that if we focus on the wrong lessons, we will learn the wrong lessons. Learning goals are also key components of managing successful organizational change, where new skills and new ways of working must be learned. Formulating change in terms of learning goals can be an effective way to break the change process down into manageable and easily digestible chunks.

Learning goals can be a powerful supplement to our process goals. Just as process goals provide the how to the outcome goal's what, learning goals help us to interpret the feedback we get from our process goals. Thus, we can start with process goals and make a list of the possible results that we might get, identifying what each result means. Our learning goals let us then explore the course of action that is dictated by our results; if we get a result that we didn't anticipate, understanding that result also becomes a learning goal and a form of feedback! Thus, a business might anticipate several possible results from customer focus groups for a new product, and base different marketing strategies around those possible results. If they get a completely different result, that tells them that they need to understand what just happened!

Learning goals can be decomposed into outcome, process, and additional learning goals. That's basically what we did when we discussed training.

What About "Do Your Best?"

I often hear the argument made that the effort involved in effective goal setting is really unnecessary so long as people just "do their best."

The problem with "do your best" is that "your best" is an arbitrary term. There is no real way to measure it or even know when you've arrived. Each person has their own view of what "best" means. Thus, I've often heard managers telling employees, "You call this your best work? This is terrible!" Of course, this "feedback" is of absolutely no value as it fails to provide the person with any information that she can use to change or improve her work. Conversely, I've also seen many an engineer respond to a deadline by saying to their increasingly frustrated managers, "But it's not done yet. It could be better!"

For an organization, "do your best" lacks any coherent focus or vision. It produces muddied priorities instead of a common objective. Common goals help bring teams together and provide a means to adjust course when something doesn't work as expected; "do your best" is more likely to produce argument and blame when the team runs into an unexpected problem. In a "do your best" environment, clearly failure is the result of someone not "doing their best!" Everyone should just "try harder!" This is a sure recipe for overwork, exhaustion, burnout, and low productivity. Of course, since everyone is busy running around in circles frantically trying to "try harder" and "do their best," it looks like a lot is getting done: remember that motion does not equal progress. Accomplishing goals equals progress.

The whole point of goals is that they give us a way to decompose a task into logical pieces, organize those pieces, and attack them in a systematic fashion. Goals provide us feedback so that we know how far we've come, how much is left to do, and when we've arrived at our destination. "Do your best" does none of these things. Overall, people, and businesses, with clear goals out-perform those who are simply attempting to do their best roughly 99.9 % of the time. But, since autonomy is an important motivating factor, you should feel free to bet against those odds if you really want to.

How Do I Construct Effective Goals?

The rules for chess are relatively simple. The strategies for playing chess are complex. Goals are similar: the concepts are fairly straightforward, but actually setting goals is as much an art as a science. The major problem most people have with setting goals is that they don't take the time to really think through what they want to accomplish. They fall back on the (in)famous SMART (Specific, Measurable, Achievable, Relevant, Time-bound) formula, and then wonder why it didn't work. While the formula is a good mnemonic, the mnemonic doesn't really tell you how to use it.

What Does Specific Mean?

The trick is to start at the end: what are you *really* trying to accomplish? When someone says they want to "get in shape," do they mean run 2 miles? A marathon?

Bicycle? Play tennis? Lose weight? When a business says it wants to ship a product, again, what is the outcome they are seeking? What product? Who will buy it? Why would they want it?

This is where it is particularly important to consider the larger ramifications of the initial specific goal. I have seen plenty of people set the goal of running a marathon, or the equivalent, succeed, and then swiftly return to old habits of exercise and eating. I've seen businesses get so focused on shipping a product that they left themselves so exhausted and disorganized that they couldn't capitalize on their successes.

The best thing about a goal is that you might accomplish it. Sometimes, though, the worst thing about a goal is that you might accomplish it: for instance, the business that set a goal of 15 % growth. They achieved it, but could have hit 25 %.

In setting our specific goals, therefore, it is helpful to return to the "what are you doing by doing that?" exercise we discussed in previous chapters. Are we looking at outcome goals? Process goals? Learning goals? Are we trying to run a marathon or are we trying to make significant changes to our exercise, eating, and sleeping habits, with the marathon being a way of checking our progress? Are we trying to ship a single product or are we trying to build an innovative organization capable of creating a series of world-class, exciting products? There are plenty of one hit wonders out there, but very few Apples.

What is Measureable?

When we talk about progress toward a goal being measureable, what we are really talking about is knowing what sort of feedback actually matters and knowing how to recognize that feedback. There are usually many different ways to measure progress; time on task is a popular one. It is not, however, always a meaningful one. In particular, the idea that more time spent on a task equals greater progress or greater value is simply false: if your car is in the shop, what is more important to you, having it back quickly or having it back in a week or two? Since most of us are not experts on cars, we tend to associate longer time with greater quality, but that's not necessarily true for cars any more than it is true for anything else. At the same time, as it were, speed is not always valuable either: you can't bake a cake much faster than what the recipe calls for.

In measuring progress toward a goal, we need to avoid the trap of valuing what we can measure, rather than identifying what we value and then figuring out how to measure that. In one company, technical support was measured by how many and how rapidly they closed support tickets. Several members of the tech support staff figured out that if they simply annoyed callers sufficiently, those callers would give up. This enabled them to close support tickets very rapidly indeed, and get commensurately high ratings. At a certain psychiatric practice, staff members were evaluated on the quality of their paperwork, not on client outcomes. It wasn't long before the organization was filled with people who were very good at filling out forms, but not so good at treating the complaints their clients had.

While a big part of measurement is figuring out how much we've done, we also need to be able to determine how much is left to do and how we'll know when we're done! Don't assume that you'll know it when you get there, because we often get somewhere and then argue about where that is. Knowing how to recognize a successful outcome is pretty important! Conversely, how we measure progress also needs to provide feedback if something isn't working out as planned. Good feedback, or good measurement, doesn't just tell us if we're on course, it also tells us if we're off course. Feedback mechanisms that don't do that can't really be trusted.

Part of measurement is distinguishing between "perfect" and "good enough." Blockbuster products, be it the IBM 360, Microsoft Windows, the Kindle, iPhone, or iPad, to name just a few, did not ship when they were perfect. They shipped when they were good enough: good enough that people would use them. Good enough that people enjoyed having them, or, in some cases, at least found the gain exceeded the pain. Good enough that people were enthusiastic enough to ask for more, allowing the companies to continually improve their products. Perfect products are the ones that never actually ship.

What we measure shapes what we focus on and what we focus on shapes the outcomes we will get: as we discussed at the beginning of this chapter, a dead light bulb is very efficient. One of the best ways of measuring progress toward a goal is through ticking off the subgoals along the way. We will look at that further when we discuss goal decomposition.

What is An 'Achievable' Goal?

The difficult we do at once, the impossible just takes a little longer.

When we talk about a goal being achievable, we really mean a couple of things:

- Can this be done at all?
- Can this be done in the time we have available with the resources we have available?

While it isn't necessary to be able to definitively answer both of these questions before proceeding toward the goal, we do want to have some means of determining the answers at some point. Sometimes it may be obvious. For example, 6 months is ample time to train to run a marathon, 6 days not so much.

It is important to look at the size of a goal: how big is it? How major an undertaking? Huge goals often look impossible until we break them down. It's like the old kid's joke, "How do you eat an elephant?" "One bite at a time." As we take each bite, what feedback are we getting? For example, we might learn that elephants taste better with ketchup.

As we start to break down a goal, we can start to identify the resources we'll need. That may include learning goals to acquire new skills or knowledge or it may require enlisting the help of others. Time itself can be considered a resource in this context; we'll talk more about time in Chap. 10. For now, though, while we want to be optimistic about what we can achieve, we want to be slightly pessimistic about how long we expect it to take us.

How Can a Goal be Made Relevant?

The effectiveness of a goal is directly related to how much it matters to you. The more you value a goal, the more you'll feel a sense of accomplishment when you successfully execute that goal. Personal satisfaction, enjoyment, and self-efficacy all increase dramatically for a relevant goal, and may not change at all if the goal is not relevant.

One of the ways organizations can make goals relevant is by tying them to the organizational vision and narrative. The more the goals seem to flow out of the culture of the organization, the more relevant they are: remember that if you're doing things correctly, the members of your organization have already bought into your vision and narrative. If they haven't, well, difficulty making goals relevant is merely the symptom of a much bigger problem!

Helping people see how goals are going to directly affect them is another way of making them relevant. When people don't see how they will benefit from the goals, then they tend to not care. When people see how the organization's goals and their goals are connected, the goals become very relevant. Techniques such as stock options and profit sharing are attempts to create that tie-in. However, those are both outcome-based solutions and are dependent upon a great many external factors. It helps to create ongoing process-based ways of building relevance through the different types of feedback that people receive.

As we've already discussed, an important aspect of motivation is your own excitement and enthusiasm. Similarly, when you the leader are honestly excited and enthusiastic about a goal, your followers will be more excited as well. Remember that you are the barometer of feelings for your team. If you don't seem to care, neither will they. If you care, so will they.

It can also help to show how a goal will make a difference to the world, even if only in some small way. How does this goal matter? At a small company, this is often fairly easy. At a giant company, it can be much harder to convince people that their actions will result in anything but a rounding error on a balance sheet somewhere. If necessary, shrink your target and focus on the importance to the team, department, or division rather than the company as a whole: how will this goal matter to us, here and now?

What About Time?

Time is a funny thing. When it comes to goals, time is a way of checking progress and forcing us to impose some organization on our goals. Time often forces us to assign a completion date for a goal. This is a good thing: goals without completion dates will often languish, ignored, and, if not forgotten, at least put off indefinitely. Just think about those countless household projects that never seem to get done: annoying as the status quo may be, there is never any urgency. Even in the office, there are always things that we talk about doing "eventually." Eventually, however, either never comes or abruptly turns out to be tomorrow.

In an interesting feedback loop, the decision to assign a deadline to a goal is part of how we decide how important and relevant it is, and the importance and relevance of a goal is part of how we decide what deadline, if any, to assign to it. Once a deadline is assigned, the relevance does increase. How much it increases depends on how close the deadline is: the closer the deadline, the greater the perceived importance. This can cause problems with large goals, since they also need more time to complete. We'll look at how to handle that problem shortly. We will look at time in depth in our next chapter.

Goal Setting and Strategy

Understanding what a goal is, while important, is only half the battle. The next problem is understanding how to set effective goals and use goals to build strategy.

Goal Decomposition

I've mentioned several times the concept of creating subgoals and how large goals generate a great many smaller goals. This process is known as goal decomposition. Goal decomposition is critical if we're going to accomplish anything large or significant: a black belt in a martial art, a college degree, shipping a product, building an innovative organization, or implementing successful organizational change, are all large goals that must be broken down into pieces in order to have any reasonable chances of success.

When breaking goals down, it helps considerably to start at the end and work backward to the starting point, rather than work forward from the starting point to where you want to go. Working backward, a technique known as reverse goal chaining, does two things:

First, working backward creates implicit agreement for each step. As you define a step, it's clear how that step moves you forward; after all, you just stepped backward to define the step! If you can't see how to move forward from a given step, that alerts you that you're taking too big a step. You can address that issue immediately, or at least put in a goal that when you get to point X you need to evaluate how to move to point Y. Because you are working backward, the logical progression is easier to see and there is less debate about whether that step will get you where you want to go. Instead, the implicit agreement that you're building makes it easier to generate overall agreement to the entire goal chain; this is extremely valuable when you need to convince your team to buy into the goals! People are more likely to listen with an open mind instead of arguing the validity of each step in the process.

Second, reverse goal chaining is a very elegant way to transform your goals into a well thought-out strategy for accomplishing those goals. Strategy is, in a very real sense, the art of looking to your end point and then reasoning backward. As you work your way backward, instead of fighting over the validity of the step, you can instead consider how each step influences or changes the world around you and how those affected by your actions might respond. In what way might a competitor react to your actions? How can you anticipate and prevent that? A chess master builds his strategy often at an almost unconscious level, but they do work backward. They are then playing toward various board positions that they know will move them to victory. Intervening board positions are the subgoals along the way to the final board position. At the same time, the other player is seeing and responding to each move, potentially forcing the strategy to evolve and adjust. Fencers do the same thing, leading their opponents into patterns of moves so that the opponent becomes predictable. Smart businesses try to force their competitors into untenable positions as well.

As you work your goals backward, you also need to address the question of close and distant deadlines. Technically speaking, we are looking at Proximal Goals and Distal Goals.

Proximal goals are the goals that are right in front of us. Those are the goals we are doing today.

Distal goals are further off in time. Those are the goals we are working toward tomorrow.

Proximal goals build upon one another to bring us to our more distal goals. At any given moment, our proximal goals tend to be the most relevant since, after all, they have the most immediate deadlines. Sometimes, though, a proximal goal is just not that interesting or personally relevant by itself. In that case, our distal goals help remind us of the importance of those proximal goals: the proximal goal of practicing falling feeds the more distal goal of learning to throw, which feeds the goal of passing a belt test, which feeds the goal of learning the next set of techniques toward the ultimate goal of a black belt. Even a student who doesn't much care to practice falls will still do so if they value that end point sufficiently. Because the path to the end point is broken down and visible, it's easier to imagine achieving it.

When a business tells me that their employees have no sense of urgency, one of the first things I look at is how they've broken down their goals: are milestones all big and distant? Quite frequently, the problem is that the goals and rewards are all distal and there are no proximal goals to get people started.

Goal Momentum

Another advantage of proximal and distal goals is that they help you build goal momentum. Remember the importance of feedback: we use feedback to tell us that we are making progress and, by extension, to tell us that we are not wasting our time and energy. Goals have intertia: people who accomplishing goals tend to keep accomplishing goals; people who are not accomplishing goals tend to keep not accomplishing goals.

When goals are all big and distal, it's hard to get started. Many a would-be author never manages to actually write their book: all they can see is the finished product and it's so big and so far away that they just can't even begin. When we construct our goals well, our proximal goals enable us to get started. As we accomplish those goals, we experience success. Those initial successes help build our belief that we can succeed. It is always good to start a project with some easy goals exactly so that you can start to build that momentum! Think of it as warm-up: if you take off running without warming up, you can easily end up flat on your back with a pulled muscle. If you hit your team with a huge goal at the start, you'll spend most of your time convincing them that they can do it and keeping their spirits up. If you start slowly, before long you're going pretty fast. The success of a large project is not based on how fast you start, but how smoothly you accelerate.

Once you are moving, remember our discussion of motivation. It's important to take breaks. Use significant milestones to recognize progress and review how much you've done. It is always more motivating to see how far you've come rather than how far you have left to go! Even at the half way point, focusing on the half undone is discouraging; focusing on the half that is done is encouraging. Just because the two are mathematically equivalent doesn't mean they are emotionally equivalent for anyone other than *Star Trek*'s Mr. Spock.

Plan to Fail

I have to confess to being very tired of the old aphorism, "If you fail to plan, you are planning to fail." Planning to fail is actually a worthwhile exercise, while failing to plan is simply a good way to waste time and energy without any benefit at the end. Failure is a surprisingly useful tool, at least for those who are not afraid to use it.

Seeing how your plan is failing can give you vital information on how to shift focus, allocate resources, and generally adjust your strategy. On a more subtle level, we won't fully trust a plan that fails to consider failure: we need to have confidence that our plans or our feedback systems will alert us to something going wrong in order for us to believe it when things are going right. I've frequently seen companies abandon working plans simply because they had never determined how they'd know if something was going wrong and therefore concluded that something must be going wrong no matter how much evidence they had that their plans were working!

More broadly, though, the difficulty is often a misunderstanding of what it means to plan. I've worked for companies that tried to plan projects out 2–3 or more years. While this is possible in a very broad sense, details matter, and you can't plan details that far in advance. Instead, you have to plan the steps in front of you. Part of the plan is to pause periodically and review the plan. What worked? What didn't work? What are the next steps? Developing an effective strategy is not something you do once and then execute blindly; you have to constantly adjust as circumstances change. The beginning chess player tries to play out a sequence of moves and is paralyzed when the opponent doesn't respond as expected; the chess master has a plan and constantly adjusts his strategy in response to his opponent. You need to plan far enough, but not too far: this may sound like it contradicts the concept of reverse goal chaining; not at all. It is simply the case that the more distal steps are going to be vague until you get close enough to see the details. Good strategy requires a certain comfort with ambiguity and the ability to periodically evaluate, adjust, and adapt any plan.

Interestingly enough, the beginning chess player usually can't explain his plan, while the master can. The beginner's plan sounds like, "I have a plan: I'll do this, and this, and this, and that's how I'll win." The chess master, on the other hand, is likely to treat you to a detailed discussion of his thinking processes and chess strategy. The first is easy to say and easy to listen to, but is fundamentally useless. The second is hard to articulate and takes a lot of effort to follow, but actually does have a chance of working. Part of the reason it works is that the chess master has contingencies built into his strategy: he's already considering that his opponent might do something unexpected and is mentally prepared to handle that. The beginner, by assuming that each step simply needs to be executed in the proper sequence, is locking himself into a rigid mindset. Chess strategy or business strategy, the results are same.

Fundamentally, failure is a form of feedback. In fact, this is exactly what you want failure to be: a means of testing out different strategies and figuring out which ones work best. Used this way, failure can be very helpful. Indeed, without such productive failures learning and strategy development is impossible.

However, sometimes the cost of failure can be somewhat higher. If Billy's goal is to cross the street safely 75 % of the time, what about the other 25 %? Even if we raise the expectation to 99 %, that one failure can negate all the successes: getting hit by a car can ruin your whole day.

It's all too easy to confuse the two types of failures and businesses do it all the time. They are afraid to fail when that failure would give them valuable information and they take risks that sound good but where one slip causes you to lose everything.

How do we tell the two types of failure apart?

Pay attention to how decisions are being made. Making sequential decisions, while often a good way of breaking problems down, can also create the trap that while each individual decision seems good, the totality is a disaster. A slightly different version of the sequential decision problem is making multiple decisions where any one of them can cause you to lose everything. In the classic example of the law firm of Stark, Rave, and Madd, no junior partner has made it to senior partner in decades. Failing to make senior partner means that they have to leave the firm and start again elsewhere. After the most recent round of performance reviews, in which they are rated 1-10, the ten junior partners complain. Mr. Madd himself tells them that they can all be promoted to senior partner; they should meet and decide the criteria for promotion.

Initially, the junior partners are all set to all be promoted. Then someone suggests that, in order to maintain the quality of the firm, only those rated 2 or higher should be promoted. This passes 9-1. Okay, so nine get promoted, that's still pretty good. But then someone suggests that only those 3 or higher should be promoted. This too passes 9-1: everyone rated 3 and up votes for it, and the guy rated 1 vote for it as well. He looks better if he's not the only one who doesn't get promoted. Only the number 2 guy objects. So it continues, with the cutoff set at 4, 5, 6, etc. Eventually, someone suggests that the cutoff be 11 or higher. That's right, it passes 9-1. Each individual decision looked good until you lost everything.

As I was writing this chapter, I was informed about the train wreck at the Banjo Corporation (the name has been changed), and given permission to include them as an excellent, albeit messy, illustration of this phenomenon: the company hired an engineer to come in and "clean up" their software. The person accomplished this, in true Efficient Light Bulb fashion, by effectively lobotomizing it. At the same time, a demo of their pre-lobotomized software presented to a potential client led to an almost euphoric response: the client was overjoyed, saying, "Wow! This is better than we'd imagined. We are revamping our entire approach in order to use your software." Then began the debate about which features actually should have been removed from the software and which ones need to be there. For any given feature, no one could definitively state that that specific feature is critical. Even the client was more focused around the total package rather than any individual component. The net result was that each feature was debated, argued over, and many of them were left out for apparently logical and good reasons. The end result, though, was missing the elements that the client most wanted. Now, it's clear that there were a number of failure points along the way: failure in decision making, failure in not properly defining what it meant to cleanup the software, failure in how they communicated with the client, the list goes on. Each decision they made seemed to make sense, but left them in a mess. Moreover, none of these failures provided any useful information to improve future decisions or help direct resources.

Essentially, to make failure useful we must first be open to the concept of failure. If we're not, we are already in deep trouble! Next, we must have some clue about what we are trying to find out. If we try X and X doesn't work, what could that mean? The traditional answer, "It means you guys didn't work hard enough!" is a cop-out. If that's really what's going on, either you need to reread this book or your team isn't very competent. Go back to Edison and his light bulbs: each failure provided him with information he could use to further refine his next attempt. More recently, in the 1990s, Palm, the maker of the original Palm Pilot, invited testers to walk around carrying various sized pieces of wood in order to figure out what people would be comfortable with. Most of these experiments were failures in the sense that people didn't like the size or the shape; each one helped them narrow down their search space. Effective failure is about testing ideas and seeing what breaks.

Another way to determine if you're failing correctly is to try to explain your strategy. Remember, the chess master's strategy is complex and contingency-based. Similarly, you'll know that you're prepared to learn from failure when you can explain your strategy in terms of alternatives and possibilities instead of a rigid belief that each step must work. The latter leads to groupthink.

Ultimately, we're looking at feedback systems: how do we know we're succeeding, how do we know if we're off course? What does failure tell us? What have we learned? What is the feedback telling us? 3 M's ubiquitous Post-It notes are an example of when exploring the lessons of a failure generated a dramatic success. Even the yellow color of the notes was an accident: the lab next door had some yellow paper they didn't need, so that's what the team developing the Post-It notes used.

The High Performance Cycle

Earlier in this chapter, we discussed the concept of goal momentum and how that ties into motivation. You'll also recall our discussions of how to use rewards as feedback that people are helping to realize the goals of the company and that people tend to seek increasing challenge. Finally, in our discussions of the organizational narrative and leadership, we looked at the importance of autonomy, relatedness, and competence. Properly structured goals can bring all of these elements together into one extremely powerful system. Locke and Latham of goal setting fame dubbed this system the High Performance Cycle (HPC).

Basically, the HPC links goals, job satisfaction, and commitment to the organization into one virtuous circle. Accomplishing goals leads to internal rewards, such as feelings of competence and self-efficacy, and external rewards, such as bonuses, promotions, and recognition. Provided that those rewards are structured as feedback, not as the goals themselves, the rewards foster job satisfaction. Job satisfaction, in turn, leads to greater commitment to the organization and its goals; in other words, the goals become increasingly relevant. Increased commitment, or goal relevance, leads people to take on ever more challenging goals, and thus the cycle repeats.

Each turn of the cycle gives people an opportunity to build their competence as they accomplish goals. Even if a goal fails, if that failure is structured as feedback, it is still useful. It becomes a learning experience, assuming that the term "learning experience" is taken seriously and not just used as an excuse. Because people are working together toward mutually agreed upon and relevant goals, we are building relatedness. As people work together, they develop increased trust and better communications, growing and developing as a team. This is the process of team development, as we discussed in Chap. 3. As the team progresses along the stages of development, increased autonomy becomes possible and the team becomes stronger.

Now, you might reasonably wonder how the HPC gets started. After all, what about new companies or new members of the organization? How do they get caught up in the cycle? There are two ways: first, the organizational vision and narrative provide an entry point into the HPC. When people get excited by the vision of the organization and decide that they want to be part of that vision, they are implicitly accepting at least some of the goals of the organization. That's the beginning; that's what gets them started on the cycle. Provided that start experiencing some successes to help feed their sense of job satisfaction, they will be drawn in. On the other hand, if they dive in and don't experience any successes or don't feel like they are helping to advance the goals of the organization, loyalty might remain but commitment will weaken.

Let me draw a distinction here between loyalty and commitment. People can be loyal to an organization for many reasons: they like their boss, they like their co-workers, they've been there for a long time, they've sunk a lot into the organization, they believe in the organization's vision, they feel a social obligation to not quit, and so forth. As should be obvious, not all forms of loyalty create commitment. If we have loyalty but not commitment, it's hard to get the HPC to work: you don't have the sense of goal relevance. Conversely, if we have commitment but no loyalty, we have people who are more easily drawn away to other organizations: only the current proximal goals are really relevant; there is no long-term relationship. Early successes and properly structured feedback, as we've discussed before, help cement both commitment and loyalty.

The second way we get the HPC started is through the enthusiasm of the leaders and other members of the organization. Enthusiasm is contagious and is even easier to spread than the flu. When new members see the enthusiasm of those already present, they are more likely to become enthusiastic themselves: that's part of why new hire orientation is so important. Building social connections and allowing people to get caught up in the excitement of the business is a powerful tool. The trick is then to focus and direct that enthusiasm, bringing us back to goals.

Flow

An additional benefit of the High Performance Cycle is that it contributes to Flow, a phenomenon identified by psychologist Mihaly Czikszentmihalyi (pronounced "Cheeks sent me high." There's a reason everyone calls him "Big Mike."). A Flow state occurs when we are engaged in an activity in which our skills match the difficulty of what we are doing. When that match occurs, we can become so totally absorbed in our activity that all of our physical and mental energy is devoted to it. We become virtually immune to distraction. If you've ever been so involved in what you were doing that you lost all track of time, and suddenly "woke up" to realize that hours had passed and you were starving, then you've experienced Flow. If the work is too easy, we don't experience Flow; we get bored instead.

Conversely, if we perceive the work as too hard, we frequently slip into anxiety and worry, reducing our performance and potentially causing us to slip into a vicious circle of worry leading to poor performance leading to more worry and thus poor performance. We will look more deeply into this issue when we discuss stress in Chap. 11.

How powerful is Flow? I once watched a small, elderly, Judo master hobble, barely able to walk, to the mat. As she stepped onto the mat, the years seemed to fall away. One moment this woman could barely move; the next she was throwing to the ground 300 pound men who were easily 50 or 60 years younger than she was. When she finished and stepped off the mat, suddenly she was an old woman again. Judo had been part of her life for so long that when she did it, there was no room in her brain for anything else, even the limitations of her body. Imagine how powerful your teams would be if you could achieve even a small fraction of that!

One of the biggest benefits of Flow is that it is an extremely enjoyable experience. Although we might feel exhausted at the end, we also feel a profound sense of exhilaration and competence. Not only does it feel good, it leaves us feeling good about ourselves and about being committed to a cause we can believe in. As such, Flow is a powerful motivational tool indeed. A caveat, however, is that even something as enjoyable as Flow can be overdone: remember that a major risk for Stage Four teams is burnout. Too much time spent in Flow, even though it might feel good, can leave us exhausted and drained to the point where the team structure starts to come apart. Breaks are critical!

Some Final Thoughts on Productivity

It is very easy to get caught up in measuring things that are easy to measure. It's easier to see motion than results. Motion for the sake of motion doesn't mean a whole lot though: going around in circles always ends you up in the same place no matter how fast you go. It's moving purposefully in a desired direction, with all the pitfalls and branches along the way, that really matters. In other words, set effective goals and use them well. Get away from measuring hours and learn to focus on learning, strategy, and results and you'll see productivity really take off.

Questions to Consider

1. What are the benefits of the different types of goals?
2. Why do outcome goals get you stuck?
3. How can you use failure to create innovation?
4. What are the benefits of effective strategy development?
5. How do goals guide, inform, and direct strategy?

6. How can you tell what you can control and what you can't?
7. What are the risks of process and learning goals?
8. What goals do you see at play in your organization? What does that suggest about your culture?
9. What is your process for setting goals with your employees?

Chapter 10
Master of Time and Space

*Where oh where has my little week gone, where oh where has
it gone?*

It's Thursday afternoon and that big project is due at 5 pm. There's no way you can
finish it in the time you have available. No problem, you can just go to the time bank.
All your life, people have been telling you that it's important to save time. Well, just
like you've put away money for a rainy day, you've saved quite a lot of time. Now
you just need to withdraw some of that time and use it to finish the project.

What do you mean that didn't work? When you save time, shouldn't you be able
to withdraw it when you need it? Unfortunately, that trick never works. Even Doctor
Who, the main character of the popular British science-fiction series about a wandering
Time Lord, can't manage that one. That's the problem with time: no matter how much
we save, it's never there when we go to make a withdrawal. We all get sixty seconds to
a minute, sixty minutes to the hour, and 24 h in a day. Time passes whether we use it or
abuse it. The only choice we have is how we use the time, not whether we use it.

We have so many gadgets now for measuring time: clocks, watches, iPhones,
the list goes on and on. But measuring time is not experiencing time: we have
thermometers that tell us what the temperature is, but whether we feel warm or
cold can depend on many factors other than just the number on that thermome-
ter. 45 degrees in January can feel downright warm, and 55 in July might seem
blessedly cool. Time is similar. Our experience of time passing is very different
from what the measurement of time might tell us; this is why productivity and
time are not the same! While we might measure time by the ticks of a clock or the
dropping of grains of sand through an hourglass, we experience time as a series
of events. When we have nothing to occupy our brains, time seems to stretch end-
lessly, each second ticking by with the excrutiating slowness of an overwritten
sentence. Watching paint dry is so painful exactly because nothing much is happening. Conversely, when we are engaged in something that fills our brains, time
seems to race by. When we look back, though, on a day filled with activity, it often
seems like a very long time must have passed. Two people can experience the passage of time in the same situation very differently. Some athletes will view their
opponents as moving very rapidly, while other athletes, who trained to manage
their perceptions in ways that change their sense of time, will see their opponents
apparently moving in slow motion. The second are far more likely to win.

S. R. Balzac, *Organizational Psychology for Managers*,
Management for Professionals, DOI: 10.1007/978-1-4614-8505-6_10,
© Springer Science+Business Media New York 2014

What it boils down to is that we do not experience time or perceive time by the passage of seconds on our watches. We perceive time through the passage of external events: day and night, the waxing and waning of the moon, the changing of the seasons, and so forth. Those who have spent time in a windowless conference room or office may have noticed that feeling of disorientation that occurs when you step out at the end of the day and realize just how much time has passed: working for IBM in the late 1980s, in the winter months I would often arrive at the office before it was light and leave after dark. Spending the day in a windowless office meant that by the end of the day, I felt extremely confused about what time it actually was. Spending the day in an office dealing with a constant barrage of interrupts produces a similar disorienting effect.

At the same time, as it were, how we feel about time can change our perceptions of the world around us. In one classic experiment, divinity students about to give a talk on the Good Samaritan had their sense of time manipulated: while still in their dorm rooms, some of the students received a phone call stating, "Where are you? You were supposed to be in the chapel 5 min ago!" Other students received a phone call stating, "Although we have plenty of time, we'd like everyone in the chapel a few minutes early."

On the route between the dorm and the chapel was an apparently sick or injured person. Those divinity students who thought they were late went by that person, in many cases without even noticing him lying there. Those who did notice assumed that someone else would take care of it or figured that maybe the person wasn't that sick, or something. Conversely, those divinity students who thought they had plenty of time were far more likely to notice the sick person and take appropriate action. Feeling rushed reduces our ability to see the world.

Just as our perceptions of time influence our behavior and how effectively we work, pursue goals, and interact with others, the physical space we are in matters as well. Space creates associations and triggers for our behavior; the right space can make us feel safe or in danger, critical or creative. The same space at different times can also trigger different reactions. Fundamentally, we humans are creatures of our environment. We can't completely ignore our surroundings when looking at organizational psychology and behavior. Rather, we need to understand how space matters and how our interactions with the space around us can serve to reinforce or undermine our organizational culture, narrative, learning, motivation, perceptions of fairness and justice, and goal setting. Even our perceptions of leadership can be affected by how space and time are handled.

What is Time?

> [time] is more like a big ball of wibbly wobbly, time-y wimey... stuff.
>
> The Doctor, "Blink"

Doctor Who aside, perhaps the best definition of time is that it is nature's way of keeping everything from happening at once. Unfortunately, that doesn't stop us from trying to do everything at once! Even more unfortunately, this approach triggers that feeling of being rushed and reduces our ability to get things done. It helps, therefore, to view time as a framework within which we organize our tasks and plan out how to accomplish our goals. This means adopting more of an event-based view of time rather than the clock-based (or duration-based) view most of us are accustomed to. In this context, a schedule is a way of organizing and viewing time such that people and resources are in the right places at the right times and flowing from event to event.

What is an Event-Based View of Time?

We are accustomed to scheduling ourselves based on the clock:

7:45 pre-meeting meeting
8:00 am Project planning meeting
9:00 am Customer meeting
11:30–12:30—Lunch
12:30–2:00 Work on presentation
2:00–4:00 Brainstorming meeting

And so forth through the day and week. We learned this in school and we do it at work. The problem, though, is that a lot of work needs to be done in ways that don't always lend themselves to such precise structures and many activities are not always totally one hundred percent precise in their start and stop times. When you have to coordinate a great many people and resources, you need to have a more precise, structured approach to time: colleges, for example, have to manage student schedules, room utilization, professor availability, etc. But that structure comes with a lot of overhead, and is not always all that useful. While we don't want to completely eliminate structured time, we also don't want to be totally controlled by it.

A recent article in the NY Times discussed joint military training between the United States and Japan. When asked what the most difficult part of the training was, the Japanese commander commented that he was initially put off by the fact that the US Marines did not have a set schedule. Japanese military exercises are conducted with, "the precision of a Tokyo subway." Eventually, the Japanese commander realized that the American troops had learned through real combat experience that things do not always, or often, go according to plan. Flexibility is essential. Rigidity leads to defeat.

Do any of the following scenarios sound familiar?

I was going to start the report at 3 pm, but the meeting ran late, and by the time we finished it was time for the conference call. Then I wasn't sure what to do next.

I got done early, so I figured I could relax a bit before starting the tests. Then, suddenly, it was late!

> I allocated an hour for that call, but it took 2 h and now my schedule is completely wrong!

> I allocated an hour for the call, but it only took 30 min. I decided to get a cup of coffee and I lost track of time.

Each of these scenarios represents a clock-based schedule. For many people, having the schedule break before it even has a chance to get going is very upsetting. Even without that issue, duration-based schedules can be very stressful because of the difficulty in hitting the times.

Event-based schedules, on the other hand, pay less attention to specific durations and focus more on the overall flow of activities. The idea is to let each activity be the trigger for the next one, such that it's not such a big deal if something runs a little long or a little short.

An event-based schedule might look something like the following:

Arrive at the office
Get cup of coffee
Clear email
10 am Product design meeting
Lunch
Work on presentation

<break>—Where the break is some predetermined activity with a known duration and logical stopping point. Visting Facebook is a bad idea. Reading a chapter of a book or taking a walk might be just fine. You have to experiment and find out what works to clear your brain and recharge your metaphorical batteries. We'll talk about this in more depth in the next two chapters.

You'll notice that as much as possible we're not really focusing on exactly how much time any single activity takes. We care more about using each activity as the trigger for the next activity. This doesn't mean we're totally free of time concerns: we still need to finish projects by deadlines and we need to sleep at night. However, focusing more on the flow of events and less on hitting specific time points removes the "OMG I'm already behind!" problem. It also takes into account the fact that we are generally not that good at predicting how long something will take: roughly 99.9 % of projects take longer than their worst case scenarios. As Boston's Big Dig so amply demonstrated, taking as it did 20 years instead of the predicted 10, Murphy's Law reigns supreme. When I pointed this out in a talk once, a member of the audience became quite irate and launched into a tirade about how one can very accurately predict how long a project would take by using various statistical techniques. That particular manager was legendary for consistently and reliably overshooting every deadline. Murphy's Law is not impressed by advanced statistical techniques!

Therefore, the trick to designing a good event based schedule is to pay attention to how long things are *actually* taking (I said we're not totally free of time!) as opposed to guessing how long things *should* take. You may have to adjust things around if, for example, you find yourself finishing work at 2 pm one day and midnight the next. Wild schedules are not a recipe for success; in fact, the less predictable the day, the less productive we tend to be.

Long-term projects need to be slotted into the schedule as they come up. Sometimes we can anticipate them, sometimes projects happen in response to unexpected events or opportunities. Since it's not always clear how much time a long-term project will take, you'll need to put checkpoints into the schedule so that you don't forget to evaluate progress.

Remember to have a "planning" event in the schedule, where you organize what you'll do when for the coming week. This can help manage the clutter of meetings, phone calls, project reviews, and other things that need to happen on a fairly regular basis. Don't forget to bound unpleasant tasks, as we discussed in Chap. 5.

It can also be very helpful to put in "worry time." Block 15 min or so (long enough, but not too long—you have to experiment!) on the calendar once or twice a week for worrying. Intrusive thoughts are your brain's way of reminding you of something important (or at least of perceived importance). Frequently, the simple act of noting down the worry on the calendar as part of the agenda for your worry time is all it takes to contain it until you have time to sit down and address it. It can be hard, especially for newer managers, to give their team the space necessary to make mistakes and learn to communicate effectively. Setting aside worry time gives you a structured way to monitor that progress without getting caught up in the crisis of the moment.

How can I Use Event-Based Schedules to Accomplish Goals?

In Chap. 9, we talked briefly about the time component of goals. Without a deadline, goals are not seen as particularly important. If we want a sense of urgency around our goals, we need to put a target date on them and we need to have check points along the way to monitor our progress. But if we become overly specific about scheduling every piece of the goal, we find ourselves back in a clock-based schedule, with all the hassle and headaches that entails. One of the problems with a lot of goals is that components are at least somewhat open-ended. It's one thing to go out and run on the track for an hour; a software design project may not be at a logical halting point after an hour, making it extremely hard to stop and move to the next thing. Instead, we need to treat goals as events, and use events to trigger our goals. We do this by using implementation intentions.

Now, having read Chap. 9, you might be thinking, "Are you nuts? Didn't you just tell us that intentions are not useful?" Well, it's certainly true that intentions are not goals and should not be confused with goals. However, properly constructed implementation intentions can help us accomplish our goals. Implementation intentions are a way of linking an arbitrary event to a piece of a goal, linking one piece of a goal to another piece, and linking one goal to another. We can even use implementation intentions to link a goal to a break and a particular leisure activity to a goal as a way of making sure that when we stop, we then start up again. One of the biggest advantages of implementation intentions structured into an event-based schedule is that it becomes very easy to develop the habit of executing the steps in order without having to decide what to do next. When we have to think about the next step, that's when we become the most vulnerable to distraction. Implementation intentions become the metaphorical cotton in the ears that protect us from the siren song of Facebook and other common time sinks.

We've already seen how to construct an event-based schedule. To add implementation intentions, or action triggers, we say or note down on paper, "Once I pour my coffee, I will sit down at the computer" and "Once the computer boots up, I will open Chap. 10 and write," and so forth. By making the connections explicit, we make them more powerful. We "know" exactly what to do when the appropriate trigger occurs. Writing out the schedule helps considerably, since it means we don't have to actually remember as many things when we're busy.

Implementation intentions can also be connected to triggers in our environment: "When the coffee cart comes around, I will close the file I'm working on and make the phone call to Bob," or, "On Wednesday night after dinner I will review the design for the new Tate GPS." The more specific the implementation intention, the better. Specific triggers are easier to activate. More general triggers are easier to delay: "After dinner, I will..." is more easily put off from dinner to dinner. Sometimes our implementation intentions are conditional or based on an ongoing experience: "Once I find my way home from wherever this stupid Tate GPS took me, I will fire the person who designed it!" (don't be surprised; he who has a Tate's is lost).

Any external event can trigger an implementation intention. The best events are those that require no effort on our part to notice. Thus, "When I look at my watch and see that the time is..." is not a good trigger. Looking at a watch requires us to make a conscious effort to remember to do that and then think about the time. It's better to trigger off something automatic, like the lights dimming or changing color, the mail being delivered, or that annoying guy who never varies his schedule an iota walking by. Since we so often work in environments with artificial lighting, you do want to be careful about using "it's getting dark outside" as a trigger, unless you can control the lights. Having the lights automatically clicking on is a good trigger, or having software on your computer that changes your screen brightness according to the position of the sun is another. Even reminders on your smartphone can be very effective, although they tend to be more useful when you want to transition activities at a very specific time.

Some people find it helpful to use objects as triggers: "when I see the Perkins file in the morning, I will..." Like having too many goals, too many such triggers will cause confusion rather than triggering the desired behavior. You don't want to trigger five behaviors and then have to choose. You want one thing to trigger and then it triggers the next thing, and so on.

It's worth noting that successful athletes use implementation intentions all the time. When a fencer trains to respond to different attacks by their opponent or a judo player to different throws, what they are doing is setting up a very rapid implementation intention. Teams do it as well, although that does take significant practice since several people's responses must be coordinated. Some athletes will even use implementation intentions to decide ahead of time how they will feel if certain events take place in the competition: "If I find myself down on points, I will be energized, relaxed, and focused," or, "If another runner passes me, I will imagine a rubber band pulling me forward and snapping me past him." As silly as some of these intentions may sound, rehearsing them works. The event triggers the feeling or the action.

In my own consulting practice, I've helped people develop implementation intentions and event-based schedules to organize their time and increase the effectiveness. One particular example, the Insurance Salesman Who Could Not Make Phone Calls, is illustrative of the concepts of organizing for time and emotion.

In this particular situation, an insurance salesman contacted me for help because he was finding it increasingly difficult to make phone calls. He was acutely aware of the fact that the people he was calling really didn't want to be interrupted and he was becoming convinced that they really didn't want what he was selling. The traditional solution to this problem frequently involves years of psychotherapy or a battery of self-esteem workshops. Neither was actually necessary. The actual solution involved designing an event based schedule with appropriate implementation intentions and taking advantage of existing habits and routines.

This particular salesman happened to be a serious tri-athlete and described himself as being at his most optimistic and energized right after his morning run. Thus, the schedule that we developed ended up looking like this:

Event	Implementation intentions
Morning run	After my morning run I will make ten phone calls
Make ten phone calls	If follow-up is called for, I will enter that on my calendar
	After I hang up the phone, I will cross off the name and make the next call.
Shower	After my shower, I will make ten phone calls
Make ten phone calls	If follow-up is called for, I will enter that on my calendar
	After I hang up the phone, I will cross off the name and make the next call.
Lunch	After lunch I will make ten phone calls
Etc...	

After we finished refining this schedule, his first reaction was, "You must be kidding! That's it?"

Three weeks later, he said, "I can't believe it! This worked. I didn't believe it at first, but I've just had the best week of my career."

Simply by eliminating the need to constantly stop and think, "What should I do now?" and instead using events and implementation intentions to make each step almost reflexive, the opportunity to become anxious, worried, or discouraged was eliminated. Initially setting up such a schedule does take some effort, but it's worth it. Don't expect it to just happen automatically.

Corralling the Wild Schedule

As we've seen, our subjective sense of time and what we're doing with our time is often prone to error. This can make getting control of our schedule more than a little challenging. Fortunately, there is a way to approach the problem.

What needs to happen is that you need to figure out what you think you're doing and then what you are actually doing. Recognize that this process is not a quick one: it usually takes a couple weeks to gather enough data. It may take longer. If your response to that last sentence was something along the lines of "oh, I just don't have the time to do that!" well, that is, as they say, diagnostic.

Start out by getting a calendar, either paper or electronic, and putting your entire schedule into it. Put in the schedule you really believe you have.

Look at your schedule. Do you have time included for planning? One of the big mistakes in scheduling is not blocking time out to plan the week. You may not always need that time, but it's worth putting it in. If nothing else, it forces you to review the week ahead and make sure everything fits. If you're going to have changes to your normal schedule, it helps to review that ahead of time, especially if other people are involved.

Do you have time scheduled to review what you've done during the week? Many schedules lack a defined time to review progress and celebrate successes. It's also important to see what didn't work so that you know where you need to make changes. At the very least, if your week was disrupted by some external event (e.g. the flu), you need to figure out when you'll catch up on anything that needs catching up on. Reviews should be at least weekly, more often if needed.

Look at your various tasks and projects. Have you listed only the due dates? Are there reminders to work on the pieces? Have you broken the tasks up into pieces? If there's a major presentation coming up, is there a reminder ahead of time to prepare for it? Have you built in slush or is your schedule tight as a drum? The latter is recipe for disaster: something always goes wrong, takes longer than expected, or doesn't work quite right. It's surprisingly disorienting when your schedule gets disrupted that way and suddenly you have to figure out on the fly how to rearrange everything.

Okay, you've done all that. Now we get to the second part of the puzzle: identifying the schedule you really do have.

Over the course of 2–4 weeks, record where you are spending your time. Start building up a picture of how long things actually take, as opposed to how long you think they should take. Maybe you've forgotten to include travel time to customer meetings, or waiting in the long line of cars to pick your kid up at school. Perhaps some tasks routinely take longer than you think they should. Note all that down. Also note down the dead times. Finally, note down how you feel at the end of each day.

The next step is to evaluate the data you've collected.

Do your schedules match? Are you doing what you think you're doing? Or are you finding that the schedule is too aggressive and stuff isn't getting done? Are you feeling burned out and short-tempered at the end of each day?

Look over the schedule. Is there dead time on the actual schedule that wasn't in the model schedule? Can you do something during those times? Can you shop while your kid is at her music lesson? Can you bring a laptop and write while waiting at the fencing class? Or maybe what you really need is to take that 15 min and close your eyes and meditate instead of trying to squeeze something in.

If you're ending every day exhausted and upset or burned-out, you may be trying to fit in too much or at least haven't included enough down time.

Pay attention to how you work, how you manage time. Are you someone who can drop what you're doing and switch tasks or walk out of the office when the reminder bings? I can't... my calendar is reminding me to make two phone calls right now and I'm having trouble switching tasks ☺. However, I know this, so I have slush built in around exactly when I make the calls. I can wait until I hit a logical break point on this chapter.

That done, let's get back to the topic at hand... if you're someone who is slow to switch tasks, build in time to allow that to happen. It takes less time to plan to take the time you need than to not plan in the time and take it anyway. As we've discussed, when you start feeling rushed, things become more difficult.

Are some tasks taking much longer than it seems like they should? Is this because you've underestimated the difficulty of the task or because the task is being stretched out? If the former, you may need to block out more time, and, if necessary, cut less critical tasks. If it's the second reason, what's causing the delay? Are you forgetting to bound unpleasant tasks? Remember, when you don't bound them, they stretch to fill the time available. It's when something unpleasant is limited in duration or in number of events that we are quick to get it done and over with.

Finally, are you trying to fit ten pounds of stuff in a five pound sack? If your schedule is simply too full, you will need to prune it. Packing the day to the point where you're constantly stressed out and running full out just to keep up is not a recipe for success: remember that too many goals dilutes focus. It's okay to back off and focus on fewer things. Multi-tasking is an illusion that really only serves to slow us down.

The Illusion of Multi-Tasking

Computers are wonderful devices. They can do multiple things at once, right? Well, maybe not. Computers put on a credible illusion of doing multiple things at once, but it's a trick. What the computer is actually doing is switching very rapidly between different applications. Most of the time, this creates an illusion that multiple things are happening at the same time, particularly since the computer takes advantage of the time when we're reading a webpage or writing text to devote some time to the things we're not actually looking at. Thus, that webpage loads in the background or the game we're playing is waiting for us to make a move when we switch back to it. Multi-tasking is similar to the illusion of moving pictures:

we're actually looking at a series of stills going by very very fast; our brains fill in the illusion of motion. Of course, if you try to open too many applications on your computer, it will start to slow down and, much like a cheap Hollywood set, the trickery starts to show.

Our brains multi-task in a manner very similar to that of a computer: we switch from one task to another. Unlike computers, our brains are not optimized for this process. As one friend of mine discovered when he moved from engineering to management, the process of context switching is tiring and error-prone. His job required him to be a manager who also wrote code. However, it wasn't a situation where he managed for half the day and then devoted his time to software. Rather, he was writing software unless interrupted with management tasks. This left him mentally drained at the end of each day and more prone to making errors on both tasks.

"But wait," I hear you cry, "this can't be true. Athletes do multiple things at once: just watch them! Heck, I do multiple things at once when I drive my car! Steering, accelerating, braking, shifting, adjusting the radio, all while watching the road, are all part of driving."

Indeed, there is some truth to this claim. Under some very specific conditions we can do more than one thing at a time. When we train a skill to the point where we can do it in our sleep, then it becomes possible to do more than one thing at a time. Thus, a fencer trains their feet to move correctly while they are thrusting with their sword; a basketball player can run, dribble, and pay attention to the other players. This automatization of behavior allows the athlete to focus on overall strategy and on the behavior of their opponents. That part of the game cannot be delegated!

Similarly, while we can multi-task low-level, routine behaviors, we cannot multi-task the parts of our jobs that require concentrated thought. When we try, that just prevents us from focusing effectively on the task at hand: it takes us time to sink into a task, and if we change tasks or keep distracting ourselves before our concentration has time to fully deepen, we never work at peak effectiveness; we end up more tired for less output.

What about Speed?

One of the questions that often comes up is, "Why not just move faster? If we just packed more into the day, wouldn't we make better use of our time?"

Do any of these statements sound familiar?

No matter how fast I work, my to-do list ends up longer at the end of day.

The faster we go, the more deadlines we miss.

We just can't work fast enough to fix all the errors that crop up.

Everyone's rushing around, but no one is stopping to think!

Speed is a funny thing. It certainly looks very impressive watching a master chef chop food or a martial arts expert go through a form. I recently watched a fencer defeat opponent after opponent with his extremely fast swordsmanship. The one person who beat him that weekend didn't do it by moving faster; rather, she moved rather slowly. However, somehow she was in the right place at the right time often enough to win.

Sometimes, speed doesn't always get you want you want!

I was once asked for advice on an organizational change project. The project was running behind schedule and they wanted to know how to finish on time.

"Slow down," I told them.

"Are you crazy? We're already behind!"

There are several problems with speed. In this particular situation, the more deadlines they missed, the more rushed they felt. The more rushed they felt, the more keyed up everyone was. The more keyed up they were, the faster they tried to work. The faster they tried to work, the more problems they had. Similar to fencing, or pretty much any other sport, trying to rely on speed wears you down. When we rush, we become less able to focus, more likely to make mistakes, and less able to come up with creative solutions to problems. Like the fencer, we may become unable to change a losing strategy before it's too late.

With large projects, particularly one involving organizational change, the faster you go, the longer they take.

The first and biggest challenge in any change project is getting everyone on the same page and moving forward together. If you move too quickly, you'll find that some people were left behind. Now you have to metaphorically circle back to get them. If you don't, you'll quickly find that they're slowing down everyone else through misunderstanding, lack of coordination between groups, or outright opposition to the program. The quick thing to do is to simply announce the change and expect everyone to jump on board. As more than one management team finds out, that only means expending a great deal of time and effort before finding yourself back where you started. The slow approach is to take the time to get everyone to buy into the idea that change is necessary. Once you've done that, you have effectively convinced everyone to be in the right place and at that point it's the right time to move forward.

One of the inevitable truths of big projects is that nothing ever works quite the way it's supposed to the first time. When you rush, what could have been at most a minor annoyance becomes a major problem. First, it's more difficult to recognize errors and adjust the strategies you are using. Like the fencer, the harder you try, the worse it gets: events are happening too quickly to process well and thus errors grow before anyone stops to think. Second, when you move too fast you tend to overshoot your target. When you're trying to coordinate the behavior of a large number of people, even a small overshoot can cause big delays as you get everyone back on track. In the change example, management was in such a rush to implement the new departmental structure and flow of control, that they found themselves with a company full of very confused, angry employees. Some didn't like the changes at all, found them pointless, and were resisting as much as they could. Others were simply confused and didn't know which procedures to use.

Slowing down and addressing everyone's concerns would have solved the problems. The people who didn't see a need to change could have had their concerns addressed, and those who were simply confused could have had their questions answered. Ultimately, that's exactly how we brought the project to a successful conclusion; unfortunately, not before a great deal more time and energy were wasted in pointless rushing about.

In the end, speed is not about how fast you can move. It's about how often you have to stop and go back, versus how well you can be in the right place at the right time. It's amazing how fast you can go and how much you can get done when you're not rushing.

What is the Momentum of Time?

As we discussed when we looked at the High Performance Cycle and goal setting, goals have momentum. In a more precise sense, success has momentum. When we are succeeding, we feel better about ourselves, our work, and the organization we are a part of. How we manage time plays a major role in our perceptions of success.

As we saw earlier in this chapter, when we feel rushed, our perceptions narrow. We don't see things that are right in front of us. We will even miss things that matter deeply to us: when they felt rushed, our divinity students speaking on the Good Samaritan completely missed their opportunities to live up to the content of their talks. In business settings, people in a hurry will spend days, weeks, or sometimes months not noticing the solution that is staring them in the face.

Whenever we are running behind our schedules, we end up feeling rushed. Being behind schedule might trigger people to work hard, but they do so at the expense of working smart. When we are behind schedule, every minor problem becomes a major disaster. It's just one more thing that is preventing us from hitting our deadlines and getting the job done! As a result, we tend to respond with quick fixes and overly simple solutions just to get the problem to go away. At one software company, when the product team was clearly not going to make the deadline, the director of engineering grudgingly allowed them another 2 weeks. They still weren't ready, so he did it again. This proceeded for about 3 months! Half of each two week chunk was spent undoing the quick fixes they'd implemented in their frantic race to finish during the prior 2 weeks, and the other half was spent instituting a new set of quick fixes! The constant feeling of pressure meant that no one had time to think or consider any solution that took more than a few days to implement. In three months of being behind schedule, they probably made about 1 month worth of actual progress! Had they just extended the schedule by 6 weeks or 2 months right from the start, they would have finished a lot sooner.

Conversely, when a team is running ahead of schedule, people are much more energized and creative. The feeling that there is time available means that people feel they have more space to consider alternatives and look for lasting solutions to problems. Unexpected problems become challenges rather than disasters. When a team is ahead of schedule and team members work long hours because they are excited, they are choosing to put in that extra time. When the team is behind schedule, team members are often pushed to work long hours to try to catch up. The choice is no longer really theirs.

Fundamentally, being behind schedule means feeling that we don't have control of the situation and our time. Being ahead of schedule means feeling that we do have control of the situation and our time. The more control we think we have, the more motivated and focused we are. Individuals and teams that feel in control work harder and produce higher quality results than those that feel that they don't have control. Thus, a team that is ahead tends to pull further ahead and teams that are behind will often tend to fall further behind until the inevitable triaging of incomplete work allows them to declare themselves done.

Going back to the High Performance Cycle, when we complete goals with a burst of effort and blast across the finish line after being triumphantly ahead of the game, we feel a much greater sense of satisfaction and internal reward. The external rewards also tend to be greater in that situation. When we stagger across the finish line after completing the equivalent of the Bataan Death March, we just feel exhausted and relieved. Internal rewards are lower and satisfaction is lower. It's the first case that really builds high performance.

Build schedules that you can beat with hard work. If you consistently finish with lots of time left, then your goals are not aggressive enough. If you are always falling behind, then you are too aggressive. Pay attention to the feedback that you are getting as you set deadlines and see if you are making them. It takes a certain amount of effort and practice to make your schedules appropriately challenging but not impossible, particularly because we tend to routinely underestimate the difficulty and time requirements of most tasks: just think about Boston's Big Dig or that latest home remodeling task you still haven't finished. Remember that you want to start with easy goals so you can experience early successes and quickly move out ahead of the schedule: that will set the tone for the entire project. Starting with success gets momentum on your side.

The Final Frontier

Space, the final frontier.
Captain James T. Kirk

To be fair, Captain Kirk was talking about a different kind of space than what concerns us here. It may seem a little odd that a book on organizational psychology would be concerned with space; fundamentally, however, we are creatures of our environment. We respond to what is around us and how we perceive the space we are in can affect our moods, our creativity, even our perceptions that our team is worth our time. How people feel about the space they are in can influence whether or not they believe a leader is authentic!

Imagine that you are going to rent an office: you approach the building and see peeling paint and dead trees outside. How does that shape your impression of the building? What will your clients think when they see it? What if you were going to visit a doctor whose office was in that building? Perhaps you're already beginning to have doubts. Sure, she has great recommendations, but could someone competent really work out of a building like that? Of course, once you step inside you might find a brightly lit, professional office, but first you have to get that far.

Well known psychologist Martin Seligman once observed that as the chair of the psychology department at the University of Pennsylvania, he interviewed many people who went on to become quite famous in the field of psychology... somewhere else. Why were none of the candidates accepted? Reviewing the applications, he and the rest of the faculty found something wrong with each candidate and consistently felt that their strengths just weren't strong enough. Eventually, Seligman noticed that they were holding all their candidate reviews in a gray, windowless, conference room. When he tried holding the meetings in a brightly lit, colorful space, suddenly the candidates' flaws didn't seem so bad and their strengths were considerably more obvious.

Our moods and our environment feed off one another. It's hard to be discouraged on a bright, summer day, and hard to be excited when it's cold and gray outside. Similarly, when our work environment is gray or boring, we tend to be less trusting, less creative, less open to new ideas, and less cooperative. We spend more of our mental energy just trying to be vaguely cheerful, and less on actually getting the work done. Conversely, when we are in open, brightly lit spaces, we tend to be more willing to trust and cooperate with others, happier, more energetic, more creative, and considerably more open to new ideas and experiences. If successful innovation and brainstorming requires that we suspend disbelief and open ourselves to off-the-wall ideas—and that is exactly what they do require—then we need to construct our environment to encourage that mindset.

Teams in Space

Like individuals, teams are also affected by the space they are in. One of the characteristics of high performance, stage 4, teams is that they have a defined work space. The exact nature of this space will vary according to the specific nature of what the team is doing, but part of how we "see" team cohesion is through the space we are in: the feeling that the team has a place to be helps the team form its identity. When team members are physically spread throughout the organization, it is harder for the team to come together: their identity as a team is more diffuse, less precise. This can be even worse for virtual teams: rather than engaging in actual teamwork, they are really performing something more like parallel play. This can certainly work, particularly when the task can be divided into unitary pieces and assigned to different members of the group, but it is not a high performance team. Conversely, once a team has developed a strong identity as a team, proximity isn't quite as big a deal.

Overall, teams coalesce better when members are in proximity to one another and when the team has a defined area. Whether this is a wing of a building or merely clustering people together, the results are pretty much the same. When different groups are intermingled, there is more confusion and less of a sense of team identity. Basically, the interface between two or more groups should be distinct.

Go back to our discussion of silos and spaghetti in Chap. 1. When the borders between groups are vague and intermingled, you start to get spaghetti organizations. It's easier to take information out of context: people chat with those around them, without really thinking about the context of the information they are discussing. A message meant for marketing might well be misinterpreted in engineering and vice versa. In each case, the message might well have been delivered in the context of the team's primary responsibilities; stripped of that context, the meaning changes.

On the flip side, when the interfaces between groups are difficult or hard to cross, you get silos. Locked doors or separate buildings are two obvious examples, but sometimes it's just the attitude expressed toward those who "don't belong here." In New England, it's customary to give directions in terms of the landmarks that used to exist: "Go straight down the road and turn right where Jack's barn used to be before it burned down in '92. Then continue to the..." and so on. This form of direction giving is something of a code to see who belongs and who doesn't. When groups become too insular in their space, they stop communicating effectively. Mingling is good; you just don't want the space intermingled.

Particular types of space can also signify status. It's often the case that the people on higher floors are seen as higher in status than those on lower floors. Teams with better office space are seen as more important to the organization. It's important to recognizer the status assumptions in your organization and balance that against the needs of teams to communicate with other teams. We'll discuss that further in a moment.

Remember that a leader and her team are symbiotic. When the leader's office is separate from the rest of the team, the connection between the leader and the team is weakened. It's harder for the leader to maintain trust and build referent power: they don't seem like part of the team anymore. This forces the leader to rely more on external power, that is legitimate, reward, and coercive. For a leader to be most effective, it's important that their "home base" be with the team, even if the constraints of the job require that they spend a lot of their time elsewhere. Of course, even if the home base is with the rest of the team, never being around will take its toll. Although it's been said of King Richard the Lion-Hearted that he became one of England's most popular kings precisely because he was always off fighting in the crusades, for most leaders absence does not make the heart, or their team's feelings for them, grow fonder.

Control Over Your Space

As we've discussed in several chapters, the feeling of control is important. One of the key messages of the organizational narrative is autonomy: how much control do members of the organization have over their schedule, how they do their work, even when and where they work. Leaders need to foster a sense of autonomy and control amongst the members of their team for the team to achieve the highest levels of productivity and performance. We seek to exert control over time, and we seek to exert control over the space we are in. One easy, and powerful, way of doing this is putting a picture of a spouse or other important person on your desk, as we discussed in Chap. 5. However, that is not the only option.

As much as possible, we want to let people have control of their personal space; indeed, we want to make sure they have personal space to have control over! Not having a fixed working area is disorientating. You don't really feel like part of the organization. Even when you have a fixed working area, be that an office or a cubical, how much control you have to arrange it to your liking or decorate it with personal effects varies from organization to organization. If you want everyone to think alike, a good first step is to make sure everyone's office looks exactly alike. Of course, they will also tend to be less engaged and less likely to commit to the really difficult goals. Giving people control over their space makes them more engaged and helps them feel that they have more control over their ability to solve the organization's goals. Control, or its lack, in the small areas of organizational behavior spreads outward to the big areas that businesses really care about.

It is also worth noting that wide open working areas and the lack of even the illusion of privacy can reduce people's feelings of control. While there are some organizations where this is inevitable due to the nature of the work, much of the time cubical farms and pods are unnecessary and counter-productive. What they save in short-term costs they make up for in reduced concentration and increased distractibility. It's hard to feel in control of your space when you can hear everyone talking or tapping on keys. However, since cubical farms seem to be the norm in more and more organizations, constructing them to maintain at least some illusion of privacy, if not the real thing, will help increase people's sense of personal control. We will revisit the concept of control in the next two chapters.

Proximity and Communications

Communications technology is truly amazing. We can carry in our pockets a device that has more computing power than you could pack into a house a few decades ago and that device can even make phone calls. We may not even have to dial the number: if you happen to own an iPhone, you need do nothing more than tell Siri whom to call and Siri places the call for you. What Siri, and its equivalents, cannot do is figure out who you need to call and when you need to call them. This is no doubt an interesting technical problem, made even more complex in the cases where the person you need to talk with isn't someone you even know.

An article in the NY Times in Dec 2012 made the observation that when you put R&D and Manufacturing near one another, you get unexpected connections. Manufacturing can give feedback to research and vice versa, and this feedback happens rapidly. MIT researchers are now studying the shocking revelation that people who are physically near one another will often talk to each other.

Okay, I'm being a little bit sarcastic here (but it is true that MIT researchers are studying this). The trap that we often fall into is forgetting that "Manufacturing" or "Research and Development" are not entities. They are merely convenient labels we use to identify different organizational functions. Manufacturing does not talk to Research and Development; the people in the manufacturing division talk to people in R&D. Despite all our technology, we tend to think about and connect most easily with the people around us. If manufacturing and R&D are located near one another, casual conversation and connection is easy, to say nothing of more formal communications. We don't want them intermingled, for reasons that we've already discussed: they are different functions and need to have the space to forge a sense of identity. Neither do we want them so separated that they cannot easily communicate: that creates silos. It doesn't matter if the silo is across town or in another country, it is still a silo!

Now, you might be thinking, how hard can it be to communicate? After all, those folks in R&D just have to call those folks in manufacturing! What's wrong with them? The problem is that when we're separated into silos, we don't know whom to talk to! Even if we have a name, without a connection to that person, it's hard to make that call and get them to listen: they are busy, we are busy, and exploratory conversations get swept aside in the rush to meet deadlines or deal with day-to-day business. Pretty soon, both parties forget. There is a real truth to the old saying, "Out of sight, out of mind!"

Building relationships with other people is a human activity. We can maintain relationships over a long distance and many years with our technology far more easily than ever before. What technology cannot do, however, is create relationships out of nothing. For that, we need human contact. We can initiate and reinforce those contacts through orientation and learning tools such as serious games, we can increase the probability of contact through the physical layout of our offices and plants, we can bring people from different parts of the organization together in various offsite locations, but no matter what we choose, we must create the opportunities for those contacts to occur. Once they do occur, we need to periodically refresh and reinvigorate them. Even professional relationships need reinforcement!

I was recently asked how to determine the ROI of holding a meeting to bring people together from different parts of the organization. This is the wrong question to ask. It is the equivalent of asking an athlete to determine the ROI of any individual workout. One workout is pretty much meaningless. If you happen to miss a trip to the gym or a run around the track, nothing much will happen. But if you stop going to the gym or stop running, after a few weeks or months, you'll notice a difference! It's the habit of exercise that matters, not any specific workout. Similarly, it's the habit and ease of making connections throughout the organization that matters. It's the flow of information that leads to problems being solved and innovation taking place. You can decide how much that is worth to your organization!

Meetings: Where Time Goes to Die

A black hole is something so dense that both time and space seem to stop as you get closer and closer to it. A chapter on time and space thus would be incomplete without taking the time to look at that great organizational black hole, the Meeting.

See if you can identify the actual science fictional elements from the following description of a scene from the original *Star Trek*.

Captain Kirk and his officers are sitting around a conference table aboard the starship Enterprise. *They are looking at screens set into the table, on which information is being displayed. Occasionally someone taps a screen to get more information. Kirk and the others conduct their meeting, periodically referring to the displays.*

Now, the *Enterprise* is certainly fiction. We don't have any starships, despite the more optimistic predictions from the TV show.

The touch sensitive video screens were certainly science fiction back in the 1960s. Today, they're almost quaint. We've moved well beyond that, with our iPhones, iPads, laptops, and tablet computers. So, no points there.

The real science fiction in this scene isn't the array of gadgets or even the starship. It's the fact that not one person is using the screen for anything other than business. No one is checking email, no one is Tweeting, no one is browsing the InterstellarNet, and no one is playing Angry War Birds. Everyone is actively engaged in the meeting and no time is being wasted. Now that's science fiction! Granted, these meetings usually occurred when the *Enterprise* was about to be destroyed by Romulans or something, which is an important clue.

I've occasionally heard the argument that meetings can be completely eliminated. Not so. All organizations have something to talk about: the challenge is in prioritizing the topics so that you aren't wasting people's time. I frequently encounter organizations suffering from the tendency for one part of the organization to assume if they know something, everyone else must know it as well. In this case, the lack of occasional meetings is harming progress.

There are times when it can be very valuable to spend some focused time working on a problem with other people, exchanging ideas, or brainstorming. Not all information is easily conveyed over email. In businesses that have no meetings, the greatest danger is that time will be wasted trying to figure out what to do and critical information will never be communicated. Sometimes, it really is helpful to meet and **quickly** review priorities and make sure that business critical issues are being managed properly.

The first, and perhaps most important, thing about preventing meetings from eating up the day is to recognize the feedback you're getting. When you start a meeting and everyone is already nose deep in an iPhone, that's feedback. The trick is to recognize what it's telling you. Some possibilities include:

- Participants do not see the point of the meeting.
- Participants are not interested in the topic or material being discussed.
- Participants do not see how the meeting is relevant to the work they're doing or the deadlines they are facing.

- The meeting is lacking in focus or does not have clear objectives.
- You are boring.

Let's take the last one first.

Sadly, not all presenters are the most interesting people on the planet. Some speak in a monotone. Others don't know when they've made their point and keep talking. Still others don't respect the schedule. Naturally, if you're reading this, that clearly doesn't apply to you. However, not everyone listening to you realizes that. Therefore, it helps considerably to pay attention to your own presentation style so that you can be sure to get through to those who might otherwise assume that you are going to bore them. On a related note, it's equally important to moderate discussions so that one or two vocal people cannot dominate the meeting. When that happens, everyone else feels like their time is being wasted.

Why are you holding your meeting? On *Star Trek*, there's always a good reason for the meeting: for example, figuring out to avoid being eaten by a giant space amoeba. While it is unlikely that you are facing a similar threat, nonetheless there needs to be a point to the meeting. What is the goal? At the end of the meeting, what do you expect to have accomplished? If the answer is that you simply wanted to convey information to people, or have people share status updates, perhaps emails would better. After all, do the status updates really need to be shared at that moment in that place?

Along with the point of the meeting, it also has to feel important to the people you want present. They need to know that being there matters to them. This can be surprisingly tricky: far too often people assume they need to be present when they don't. Since there are times when, surprising as this may seem, attendance at meetings is used as a gauge of employee engagement, it's not too much of a stretch to realize that people might be attending the meeting to avoid being seen as disloyal. You can avoid this unfortunate misperception by having a clear agenda for the meeting and making that agenda known ahead of time. Only having the relevant people present speeds things up considerably.

Another advantage of a clear agenda is that the purpose and time requirements for the meeting are known ahead of time. This allows your employees to better plan their schedules. A documentation review session might be held for a specific period of time, while a brainstorming session might be more open-ended. Of course, even then it's best to not "go until you are done." Rather, define the duration in advance and also clearly define how you'll know when you're done. If you find that people can't agree on how they'll know when they're done, you need to resolve that before you hold your meeting! Go back to our discussion of decision making in Chap. 3 and understand where your team is at. In the case of meetings, a specific end time is often quite valuable in focusing attention and effort. Remember, when it comes to meetings, all's well that ends, so respect your end time!

On the topic of decision making, remember that how your group makes decisions won't improve just because you're in a meeting. If anything, it might get a little worse. One of the worst problems is revisiting the same decision over and over in every meeting. It just sucks the life out of everyone, sort of like Dracula returning from the grave to bite again and again. Take the time to bring people to consensus: the point at which each person feels they've been heard, have had their say, understand the choices, and can support whichever one is decided upon. If you don't accomplish that, you'll quickly find yourself spending far more time revisiting the decisions than you spend on building the consensus.

I'm occasionally asked when is the best time to start a meeting. Early? Late? Mid-day? The answer is that the best time is the time you specified. When people know when a meeting will start, they can plan accordingly. They walk into the conference room with their brains already focused on the meeting. If you don't start on time, you create an opening for them to become bored waiting and get sucked into their smartphones. Once that happens, it's much harder to get their attention back than if you'd not lost it to begin with.

Where you hold your meetings is also important: as we've discussed, the physical ambiance of the room will affect how people approach the topic under discussion. Most businesses have conference rooms for routine meetings. That can be fine in many situations, but it's not always the best layout. It's all about the mindset you want to instill in people. Some of the entrepreneur bootcamps I've attended have would-be entrepreneurs brainstorming in comfortable lounges with white boards off to the side. Quite often, sitting side-by-side instead of across a table encourages people to be more collaborative. Aboard the *Enterprise*, the meeting rooms are pretty boring; the fact that anyone could come up with a creative idea in those rooms is also science fiction!

A productive meeting is often science fiction, but it doesn't have to be!

Wrapping it up

It's easy to get caught up in the idea that time and schedules are immutable forces. They are not. Time is a resource and a tool. It is the thing that forces us to organize our goals and think through our strategies. The secret to having a lot of extra time in the day is to use implementation intentions and event-based schedules to eliminate the time wasted trying to figure out the next action. Saving 10–15 min even three or four times a day adds up very quickly!

View your schedule as a living document. It's something that you will constantly adjust according to the situation, especially at the beginning of a project. The less you know about potential difficulties down the road, the harder it is to plan: so don't. Instead, plan to plan. As you move forward, you can revise and project the schedule further and further into the future. However, never lose sight of the fact that no matter how skillful you become at using your time, there is still a limit to how much you can pack in.

Similarly, using space appropriately is a simple way to improve the information flow in your business, develop better communications, and increase innovation. Pay attention to what your culture says about space, and change it if you need to!

Questions to Consider

1. When are you moving too fast?
2. Consider a situation in which moving too fast led to careless errors. What would you do differently?
3. What is your actual schedule? How does it compare to what you think it is?
4. In what ways is your physical layout interfering with communications between departments?
5. What can you do to make meetings in your organization more productive?
6. What are some signs of an overly optimistic schedule in your organization? What can you do to avoid that?
7. How can you take advantage of event-based schedules to increase productivity?

Chapter 11
Organizational Stress: A Two-Edged Sword

There is an old and hoary claim that if you put a frog in boiling water, it will immediately jump out, but if you put it in cold water and slowly increase the temperature, the frog will sit there until it cooks. In fact, this happens only if the frog is equipped with little frog cement galoshes rendering it unable to jump: frogs are too smart to be boiled alive. They leave long before the water gets hot enough to cook them. Why, then, does this story have such longevity?

In my experience in the high-tech world, I often find that people are sitting in some very hot water indeed. One might think that they would have noticed the warning signs as the heat increased, but apparently not. In fact, they are tolerating, or even accepting as normal, conditions that leave outsiders shocked. Rarely did conditions start off as bad as they became; rather, they became worse and worse over time until the water was boiling. This can make it difficult to recruit new talent or to keep the people whom they do manage to hire. It also means that a tremendous amount of effort is being expended on merely surviving the environment and preventing burnout instead of on productive activities.

It appears, therefore, that while frogs have the sense to get out of the hot water, people do not. Now, most people are smarter than frogs. What is going on?

For one, frogs do not show off how well they can handle being boiled alive. At many companies, however, what frequently happens is that dealing with an unreasonable situation is seen as a sign of toughness or dedication to the company. Overtime, a culture develops which celebrates and perpetuates that purported toughness. In jujitsu, I hear all the time from people who tell me that they had to give up falling because they just could not tough it out anymore. In fact, it almost invariably turns out that they never learned to fall correctly in the first place and that's why it now hurts too much to continue. Assuming that they just had to "tough it out" prevented them from recognizing and fixing mistakes early, before they were ingrained as bad habits.

Now it is certainly true that overcoming a difficult or stressful situation feels good: it increases feelings of competence and self-efficacy. There is, however, a difference between overcoming and enduring. Mountain climbers overcome

S. R. Balzac, *Organizational Psychology for Managers,*
Management for Professionals, DOI: 10.1007/978-1-4614-8505-6_11,
© Springer Science+Business Media New York 2014

challenges, they do not merely endure them. Enduring is fine, so long as it moves you toward a goal. Unfortunately, what far too many people choose to endure is, in fact, not moving toward anything except burnout and failure.

Another issue is that people respond to a situation by checking to see how others are responding: if it looks as though others are tolerating the situation, the instinctive response is to attempt to tolerate it as well. Thus, each person assumes that he or she is the only one uncomfortable, while, in reality, no one is happy. Ironically the harder team members work to avoid letting down the rest of the team, the more the team lets down its members and the company.

Of course, in true frog-boiling tradition, if the situation gradually worsens, we often do not realize just how bad it is getting. It is not until the environment undergoes a major change or we take a vacation that we realize just how dysfunctional things are. Like sitting in an awkward position, it is often not obvious how sore you are until you move.

So how can you recognize that you are being boiled alive and what can you do about it? To answer that, we first have to understand what stress really is, and why it is necessary for success.

What is Stress?

I hear all the time about stress reduction and the importance of eliminating stress from your life. The problem is, if we eliminated all the stress, we would also eliminate all progress and success. Stress is healthy, in the same way that food is healthy: we need it pretty much every day, but too much can give you a belly ache or cause other health problems. It is not necessarily the food per se, it is the quantity or quality that kills you.

Stress, at root, is anything that gets us moving, be that thinking, feeling, or acting. When a stressful event occurs, we experience physical and psychological reactions. It is the combination of the stressful event along with our reactions to it that we need to know how to use to our best advantage. It is when we do not use stress to our advantage, or when it gets out of control, that we start experiencing the negative effects of stress: illness, distractibility, reduced team performance and organizational commitment, loss of creativity, and so on. In order to really understand how stress works, though, it will be helpful to look at cavemen and the starship *Enterprise*.

Let us turn the clock back 20,000 years or so and consider Thag. Thag is a hunter, a member of a nomadic band of hunter-gatherers. In Thag's line of work, the biggest risk is being eaten by something that disagrees with you. On a typical day, Thag wakes up in the morning, grabs his trusty spear, and heads into the primeval forest to hunt. He probably does not have a cup of coffee, there being a notable lack of Starbucks in the forest primeval and besides, Thag has not yet invented money.

So far, this has been a fairly low stress day for Thag. There is enough stress, specifically hunger or the needs of his family, to get him up and out hunting, but nothing too extreme. This is about to change. As Thag makes his way through the forest, birds chirping ominously in the background, a tiger suddenly springs out. Now the stress level skyrockets. Thag's heart starts beating faster, his breathing comes more quickly, and the blood is really flowing in his veins, which, in point of fact, is where he would like to keep it. Under the surface, as it were, epinephrine and norepinephrine (the chemicals formerly known as adrenaline and noradrenaline) are released into Thag's blood. Energy is routed from nonessential functions, such as digestion, healing, and the immune system, to Thag's muscles. In little more than a heartbeat, Thag is ready to fight or run.

But wait! Since when are digestion, healing, and the immune system nonessential? Without them, we are not going to be particularly happy or healthy. Fundamentally, if you are looking at a hungry tiger, or, more to the point, if that hungry tiger is looking at you, neither fighting off the flu nor digesting your last meal are particularly high on the priority list. Your goal is to live long enough to worry about the flu otherwise that last meal really will be your last meal.

Why not run or fight and also maintain digestion, healing, and the immune system? Well, to answer that let's jump from the distant past to a not quite so distant future. Whenever the starship *Enterprise* is attacked by Romulans, Captain Kirk orders full power to weapons and shields. That makes a certain amount of sense: when someone is trying to blow you out of space, you do not want to put half power to the shields. Sometimes, though, full power is just not quite enough. When that happens, as it so often does, Kirk orders emergency power to the shields as well. At that point, Mr. Spock usually observes that such an action will mean taking power from life support, which never stops Kirk but does serve to make the scene more exciting (which is also a form of stress, albeit a pleasant one at least when it is happening to someone else). Basically, the *Enterprise* may be big, but it is not infinitely large. It has only so much power. That power can be put in different places, shifted around as necessary, but there is still a finite limit to how much there is. Most of the time life support, or long-term survival, is a pretty high priority. However, when confronted with hostile Romulans, the short term need to not be vaporized takes priority.

On *Star Trek*, this is known as a Dramatic Moment. For Thag, however, it is more commonly known as the Fight or Flight response. Confronted with danger, the stress triggers Thag's body to fight or run. Like the *Enterprise*, Thag's body is finite. He has only so much energy to go around.

Overall, though, this mechanism serves Thag extremely well, especially if he is a trained hunter. With the fight/flight response activated, Thag's attention is marvelously well focused on that tiger and, if he is forced to fight, he will hopefully slide into his trained behaviors. Under the sort of stress that activates fight/flight, we do not really think about what to do, we merely act. We tend to default to trained actions, if any, provided that the stress levels are not too extreme. Crank that fight/flight response high enough, and eventually even training collapses, leaving only panic. Should Thag panic, he is cat food. The good news is that the better trained he is the less likely the fight/flight response will get out of hand. It is all a matter of control: the better trained Thag is the more control he thinks he has, and the more control he thinks he has, the more moderate the threat appears. Assuming Thag survives the encounter; he will have the chance to rest and recuperate on his new tiger skin rug. Whether he successfully fought off the tiger, killed it, or ran away, once the encounter is over, his body can return to normal. Just like on *Star Trek*, once the Romulans are defeated, they can lower the shields, turn off the phasors, and turn the food replicators back on.

As should be clear, despite the tongue-in-cheek tone, stress can be very beneficial. Without it, Thag would not have survived the day. More generally, and less dramatically, normal levels of stress help us in countless ways. Exercise is a form of stress; when we exercise, we put stress on our bodies, and our bodies respond by building muscle, increasing endurance, and becoming more cognitively capable (yes, that is correct. Exercise does more for our brains than all those silly brain exercise apps ever do). Exercise even triggers our bodies to produce more stress resilient neurons. When we want to learn a new skill, be that fencing, jujitsu, programming a computer, developing our creativity, or giving a speech, the learning experience creates stress and we respond to that stress by growing and becoming more capable. When we have a deadline coming up, knowledge of that deadline generates stress; we respond to that stress by focusing our attention and increasing our effort. In each case, we are experiencing a mild activation of our fight/flight response, which helps us rev up to the right level of physical and cognitive activity for the task at hand.

Of course, there is a catch. There is always a catch. You did not seriously think there was not, did you?

The most significant factor is that Thag was one of those people who never threw anything out. He had a pretty effective way of handling stress, and he liked it so much that he passed it along to his children. They liked it too, or at least found it sufficiently useful that they kept it and passed it along. When we fast-forward to today, we find that our physiological responses to stress are not significantly different from those of great-great-great-great-,etc.-grandfather Thag.

Now, it may seem a bit odd that Thag's stress response mechanism, the fight/flight response, has not changed much in the millennia that have passed since Thag fought his tiger. In terms of human evolution, the past 20,000 years or so is but the blink of an eye. Give Thag a shave, haircut, and a nice suit and he could run for Congress or appear on *Star Trek*. Despite all of our technological advances, the basic human simply has not changed all that much. Thus, faced with modern stressors, our stress response is often activated incorrectly and then remains active for longer than is healthy.

In today's world, we are unlikely to run into a tiger on the street, and the thing jumping out of the closet is most likely your cat or a small child yelling, "Boo!" No matter the cat's opinion, it is not a tiger. However, when we get startled in that fashion, we still break out in cold sweat, our heart beat accelerates, and the adrenaline starts to flow. More to the point, though, we do not need to be startled to trigger our fight/flight response. Having your computer crash just before you hit "Save" on that report you spent all day working on, a fight with the boss, heavy traffic driving to that important meeting, a car spinning out of control in front of you, unexpected bills, late projects, being trapped in a phone menu tree, concern about the health or safety of a close friend or loved one, are all forms of stress. Each of them triggers the same fight/flight response: when a demand in placed on our body or mind, we respond to that demand in the way that millions of years of evolution have prepared us to respond.

Unlike in Thag's day, however, most of our modern stressors cannot be solved in the simple, direct fashion that worked so well for Thag. Faced with a tiger, Thag stabs it with a spear or he runs away. In either case, Thag gets to use all that energy his body is providing. Today, though, that approach is rarely quite so effective. While drop kicking our laptop across the room might feel satisfying at the moment, in the long run it is likely to only increase our stress levels. And, no matter how much we might dream, bringing a spear to work is going to attract some very strange looks, many of them from men in blue uniforms or white coats. Nor do we get to run screaming from the office. The net result is that we are all revved up with nowhere to go. Instead of helping us focus, we end up physically and mentally tense, unable to concentrate because we are "looking" for danger.

One of the interesting, and in this case irritating, factors in how we deal with stressful situations is that we use our own stress response to help us recognize when we should be having a stress response! In other words, it is not just that our fight/flight response activates when the tiger appears; it is that if our fight/flight response is activated, we assume there must be a tiger around somewhere. If we cannot find the tiger, we rev up even more. As you might imagine, having our fight/flight response activate even before we are consciously aware of the danger can buy us those critical fractions of a second that can make the difference between life and death. The price for that capability, however, is that our modern stressors can trap us in a vicious cycle of increasing stress responses. This is not good; once we rev up past a certain point, performance collapses. Even without that, we are not built to have our fight/flight response active for long periods of time. Remember that when we are directing all our power to the weapons and shields, there is not much left for life support. When fight/flight is active for long periods, it interferes with healing, digestion, blood pressure, and sleep. Long term, we become more vulnerable to sickness and injury: anything from indigestion and distractibility to more serious problems such as reduced attentional capacity, high blood pressure, and heart disease. On a very short term, practical, level, stress has the potential to short-circuit everything we have discussed in earlier chapters about team development, motivation, goal setting, and the organizational narrative. Highly stressed people will often be compliant, but they are not actively committed to the organization's goals, thus killing the High-Performance Cycle. When the water is boiling, creativity, cooperation, and effective problem solving are amongst the first things to go: stressed out people are more critical, more impulsive, more easily irritated by trivial incidents. Indeed, one of the hallmarks of too much stress is when trivial issues quickly escalate into intense, pointless conflict.

The other sneaky problem with stress is that stressors are not independent of one another. Stress is cumulative: it does not take a major traumatic event to push our fight/flight response into overdrive. A great many small stressors add up to a large stress response. The daily hassles of life, frustration at work, a distressing political, or economic climate, can all help trigger our stress response and keep it active even when there is no immediate physical danger. Thus, that one additional request you are making of your employees might not seem like much by itself, but can trigger a major outbreak of bad temper or collapse performance if it comes after a series of major changes or reorganizations or during a period when everyone is frantically working to hit a deadline. I am still amazed when a company ramps up the stress level right around Christmas: so many people are already stressed out around the holidays that adding to it does not help.

The trick to dealing effectively with stress is in understanding how to maintain the right level of stress: we want people to feel excited and engaged. When the levels of stress are appropriate, that is exactly what happens. When they get out of hand, though, is when individual and organizational performance breaks down. We also need to understand how to manage stress: Olympic athletes, after all, thrive under conditions of extreme stress. They have learned the trick of being physically revved up and mentally relaxed, giving them the best of both worlds and enabling them to perform at an incredible level.

When is Stress Destructive?

"Are you a damsel in distress?
Dis dress, dat dress, just help me."
—Bullwinkle Moose & Natasha Fatale.

Stress is very much one of those things about which we can truthfully say, "Can't live with it, can't live without it." While we are capable of handling very large amounts of stress and responding quite effectively to the demands upon us, too much for too long is a sure recipe for unbaking your team and burning out the members of your group or organization. It is also the case that whether or not the stress is good or bad depends on context: being around other people revs us up. When it comes to brainstorming and bouncing ideas off others, this can be a very good thing. However, when it comes to complex problem solving and tasks requiring deep concentration, the presence of others can turn from energizing us to distracting us. In addition, there are certain types of stress that are more destructive than others: it is not just the raw amount of stress that matters, but the nature of the stressful event.

Loss of Control

Recall our discussion of the cultural immune response from Chap. 1. A cultural immune response occurs whenever we have a mismatch between a member of the organization and the organization's culture. In most cases, this results in the mismatched person either leaving or adopting the values of the culture. However, when the mismatch is the leader, things are not so easy. In that case, members of the organization are caught between what they "know" is right, because that is the way things are done, and that this new leader is telling them to do. If they stick with their beliefs, they risk losing status, including their jobs; if they follow the leader, they will often feel they are betraying their comrades, values, and mentors. This puts people in a very unpleasant, and hence very stressful, situation. That, in turn, means that the fight/flight response is activated. The reason many people quit at this point is that they feel that they cannot effectively fight, so running is the only option. If they choose not to do that, out of loyalty to the company, a bad economy, or anything else, they are now stuck. For most members of any large organization, leadership issues are, as the expression goes, above their pay grade. This leaves them feeling like they have very little control over the situation.

Indeed, when we look at what most events that produce destructive stress have in common, we see that they almost always involve feeling out of control. Consider our discussion of speed in the previous chapter. As we observed, moving too fast causes a number of problems around coordination and error correction. As experienced athletes know, speed also shifts our perceptions in ways which can dramatically increase our feelings of stress and lack of control.

As you will recall from our discussion of time, we experience time by the passage of events. When we move fast, we will often feel as though time is passing rapidly, and this causes us to rev up more and more in an attempt to keep up: the faster that tiger is moving, the faster Thag wants to move in response. Unfortunately, as our fight/flight mechanism revs higher and higher, we quickly become highly distractible: we try to look everywhere at once, instead of focusing where we need to be, which further increases our feelings of stress. Thus, the fencer is easily fooled by an opponent's feint, the programming team goes rushing from one bug to another, never quite managing to finish fixing one problem before running to the next, or the management team continually shifts strategies whenever something superficially more attractive comes along. One particular organization routinely announces ever more elaborate reorganizations of its senior management structure, and everyone rushes around to implement the new regime. In the end, though, nothing changes.

The faster we go, the less time we have to think and consider our responses; the less time we have to think, the more we just react; the more reactive we are, the less we are in control of the situation. The less we feel in control, the more stressed we feel, which causes us to further rev up, which increases our distractibility, completing the vicious circle.

This same erosion of control occurs in a more insidious, and considerably more devastating, fashion when organizations get caught up in the myth of 20–20 hindsight. Let me be clear: there is an important, albeit subtle, difference between conducting an effective postmortem on a project and engaging in the hindsight trap. Unfortunately, while most organizations think they are doing the former, they are usually doing the latter.

The hindsight trap can be best described by Dr. Watson saying to Sherlock Holmes at the end of the mystery, "It is so obvious once you explain it!" Holmes famously does not reply by saying, "Elementary, my dear Watson," though one might imagine that he is at least thinking it. The fact is, though, that what Holmes is doing is not elementary or obvious, as evidenced by how few readers can actually figure it out. In fact, being able to look at an apparently random collection of clues and figure out how they fit together is incredibly difficult. However, because after the fact it seems so clear, we are vulnerable to the hindsight trap: we assume that because hindsight is 20–20, foresight must have been 20–20 as well.

In rereading the Sherlock Holmes stories recently, I realized that Arthur Conan Doyle does play fair most of the time: he reveals the clues to the reader, or at least he reveals the fact that there was a clue in such a fashion as to provide the reader the information he needs to figure out what is going on. For example, there are times when Holmes is taking advantage of knowledge not readily accessible to the reader, such as Holmes' encyclopedic knowledge of mud or cigar ash, but that is not the point: it is a sufficient clue that Holmes is interested in the mud or the cigar ash. Despite this, it is extremely hard to figure out the solution to the mystery before Holmes reveals it. Once revealed, though, it is equally difficult to imagine the pieces fitting together any other way.

Now, if this phenomenon was limited to Sherlock Holmes mysteries, it would be rather thoroughly insignificant. Unfortunately, it happens all the time:

"I can't believe she didn't see that coming!"
"How could he have not noticed the problem ahead of time?"
"Were they even paying attention?!"

When something goes wrong, be that in a marketing campaign, a client engagement, developing an app, or launching a new online service, the reasons are almost always obvious… in hindsight. Like a Sherlock Holmes story, once the ending is clear, we cannot imagine any other arrangement of the pieces. Thus, we assume that not only is someone responsible, that person or that team must have been incompetent, indifferent, or careless, because they did not recognize what we now know to be completely obvious. Ironically, what I have observed over and over is that when someone does point out the potential problem in advance, they are first laughed at for being too nervous and then when the problem is clear to everyone, castigated for not pushing their point more aggressively!

On the flip side, when someone does successfully anticipate and forestall a problem, their efforts are not taken seriously. After all, the problem was obvious, so why did it take them so long to figure it out and prevent it? Clearly, they were not working all that hard!

The net result of both of these manifestations of the hindsight trap is that self-confidence and the feeling of being in control are both eroded. This is a very bad combination, because eroding self-confidence makes us less likely to take actions that might demonstrate control, and reducing control also reduces our self-confidence. As we can see, getting caught in the hindsight trap is a very destructive form of stress. In particularly severe situations, the hindsight trap can produce such a strong focus on the past that it leads to organizational stasis or passivity. No one is willing to make a decision because they are too afraid of being second-guessed for it later. The decision to do nothing is viewed as the safest course.

Taking this a little further, we can now understand why fear based motivation sooner or later causes trouble. Fear activates our fight/flight response: just ask Thag! Fear focuses our attention on the source of the fear; if we cannot easily find the source, then our attention is very likely going to be grabbed by anything which we think might be the cause. In the first case, when people are afraid of the boss, they are not focusing on the goals of the organization. Rather, they are focusing on pleasing the boss, or at least avoiding his wrath. While this can be a tremendous boost to the boss's ego and self-esteem, it does not do much for the employees. Their sense of control is now based not on their actual ability to address problems and accomplish goals, but on the far more nebulous ability to manipulate the boss. Cooperation, creativity, problem solving, and the high-performance cycle all suffer in this scenario. In the second case, where attention is grabbed by whatever seems to be causing the fear, we again see a loss of control. In this case, the organization or the team spends its time and energy focused on the wrong things, and hence fails to adequately address the actual challenges in front of them. Constantly seeking to change something that does not matter will sometimes briefly create an illusion of control, similar to constantly pressing a "Walk" signal that does not actually work. More likely, though, is that the wrong focus leads to repeated failures to change the situation, and a steady erosion of both individual and team confidence.

As we discussed earlier in this chapter, our own stress response is one of the signals that tells us that we are in danger. When we feel threatened, we look for the threat. If our attempts to identify the threat and make it go away fail, we first start to see the people in other departments as the source of the threat, and eventually our own colleagues as well. Fear is not that precise an instrument! In a very real sense, it does not matter if we are physically afraid or afraid of being embarrassed or losing status, the reactions are the same. If anything, our fear of embarrassment or loss of face is often greater than our fear of physical harm!

Thus, when fear takes over, cooperation and teamwork suffer. People start to fight over little things, as they attempt to exert control over something. When we feel out of control, we seek to take control of what we can in whatever ways we can. When we do not know what to do, we do whatever we can, whether effective or not, whether appropriate or not.

What Was That Again?

Related to the various ways in which people can feel like they do not have control is the problem of role ambiguity. Recall that in early stage teams, people are often uncertain of their goals and of their exact role in the group. This sort of ambiguity is stressful: it calls into question how we fit into the group, which, in turn, calls into question whether we fit into the group. As we have discussed, exile from the group is a powerful threat; indeed, social exclusion can actually cause us to feel physically cold.

Although role ambiguity within a group can be dealt with as the group matures—indeed, must be dealt with for the group to mature—other forms of ambiguity are not always so easily resolved. Matrix organizations, in particular, run into problems where employees are being given contradictory instructions by different managers. Even in organizations with more traditional lines of control this problem crops up. Having policies in place to provide clear instructions on how to resolve these conflicts are critical to avoiding unnecessary ambiguity and the attendant stresses.

Another popular form of ambiguity is policies in the trusty employee handbook that do not match what is actually being done: at one startup, the employee handbook had a very clear "no alcohol" policy; meanwhile, the CEO routinely brought in beer for the staff. The handbook was revised. Although this particular example was funnier than anything else, these areas of ambiguity do create tension: people are unsure how to behave and whether or not to follow the rules.

As we have already discussed, organizations are communities of people united for a common purpose. In carrying out any nontrivial purpose, there will always be areas of ambiguity. Removing the unnecessary ones makes it possible for people to focus on the important areas of doubt and uncertainty.

One Life to Live

Another area of destructive stress is everyone's favorite problem: conflict between work life and family life. The problem here lies in the basic premise that we have two lives: a work life and a family life and that these are somehow two separate existences. Perhaps if you are James Bond you get to live twice; the rest of us do not have that luxury.

One of the biggest sources of frustration for employees is this illusion that these lives are separate. When we ask people to sacrifice family for the sake of the organization, we are putting them into a very stressful situation. In part, we are forcing them into a form of role ambiguity: they are being forced to play two roles at once or choose between two very important roles. We are also forcing them into a mental state where they are doing one thing but thinking about the other: a form of multitasking. This is a very bad place to be. Not only does it reduce performance, it also interferes with job satisfaction. As you will recall from our discussion of the High-Performance Cycle, reducing job satisfaction reduces commitment to the organization, which interferes with goal accomplishment, better known as productivity.

Taking the time to respect people's lives outside the organization is a powerful tool for building loyalty and commitment. Indeed, as we have discussed, time is a powerful gift. Sending people home a little early if you are running ahead of schedule or accepting that quarterly report a little late so that Fred can attend his kid's soccer game are extremely effective methods of reducing that work/family conflict. Flexible work from home policies is another good approach. When you make it easy for people to manage the demands of work and family, you build loyalty and increase satisfaction with the organization. That, in turn, feeds the High Performance Cycle.

What is Happening with the Stress Response?

We have talked a great deal about activating our fight/flight response and about various forms of destructive stress. However, that still leaves unanswered the big question of exactly what is happening? Exactly how does stress affect our concentration and why is some stress good? To understand that, we need to know a little bit about how our brains work and how we decide what to focus on.

Imagine the letter U flipped upside down, as in Fig. 11.1. This is known by the very creative and imaginative name of "The inverse-U". It has nothing to do with standing on your head, a different form of inverse-you. What psychologists and athletes have all found is that our focus and performance tracks with our arousal according to the inverse-U. Arousal is simply how revved up or energized we are at any given moment. As we can see in the figure, when we are at very low arousal, for instance, asleep, our focus is very low. Performance is about nil, unless you are involved in some form of competitive snoring. As demands, such as the alarm clock, are made on us, our arousal level increases along with our ability to focus on and perform various tasks.

One of the advantages of increasing arousal is that we become better able to focus on the things we care about and tune out the things we do not care about. When we are sleepy, it is hard to keep our mind on what we are doing; we tend to wander off task or otherwise get distracted. This is a common feeling for many people before their first cup of coffee! Eventually, arousal increases to a point where performance is at the top of the curve. This is the optimal level of arousal, as shown in Fig. 11.2. The optimal level of physical and mental arousal varies

Fig. 11.1 Inverse U

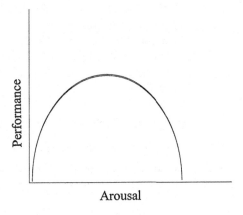

Fig. 11.2 Inverse U–optimal
arousal

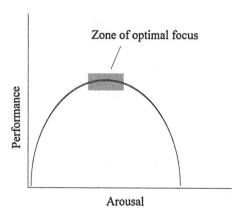

from task to task: it is different for a tennis match than a chess game or for writing software versus giving a speech.

There are a number of advantages to operating in the zone of optimal arousal. The major advantage is that our focus feels almost effortless. We automatically pay attention to relevant information and ignore things that are not relevant to the task at hand. This is assuming, of course, that we know what is relevant and important to the task at hand! How do we know what is relevant and what is not? That is where goal setting comes into play. One of the advantages of structured goals is that they tell us what is relevant and what is not. Thus, well-designed goals combined with implementation intentions and the proper level of arousal generates that optimal level of focus shown in Fig. 11.2. Productivity in this state is at its peak; it will not get any better. In sports, this is known as performing in the Zone; an athlete in the Zone will perform many times better than a similarly skilled athlete who is not in the Zone: it is the difference between winning and not even making it to the podium. The results in a business environment are similar.

An implication of how our brains handle this optimal state of arousal is that, faced with random distractions, it is better to tell you yourself to ignore the distraction than to try to work harder. In other words, if there is noise coming from down the hall or the construction taking place on the office building next door, telling yourself to ignore the noise will be more effective than trying concentrate harder. When you tell yourself to ignore the noise, you are mentally marking it as irrelevant to the task at hand; as we have already discussed, optimal arousal is when we automatically ignore irrelevant inputs, provided we know what is actually irrelevant. On the other hand, working harder or trying to concentrate harder only has the effect of increasing our level of arousal. When that happens, we start to move out of the optimal arousal/performance space and head down the right side of the performance curve, and that is not a fun place to be.

As we see in Fig. 11.2, arousal does not stop once we reach the optimal arousal for the task. If more demands are made upon, if we are interrupted by urgent phone calls or if we are trying to multitask, arousal can increase. It is also possible that the demands upon us might increase arousal so rapidly that we move right over the top of the curve and start heading down the right side.

On the right side of the curve, we are too energized. If we are only a little off the peak, this might manifest as restlessness or difficulty concentrating. As we move further along the right side of the curve, this restlessness only increases. We might find that our heart is pounding or we are sweating or breathing hard, all common experiences when angry, upset, or afraid. Indeed, anger and fear are emotions that will often shoot us over the top of the performance curve and down the right side. The problem is that in this mental state, concentration is extremely difficult. We are too busy looking for danger. We become more prone to making impulsive decisions or acting rashly. Our attention skitters from one thing to another faster than we can process the information, forcing us into a sort of rushed multitasking. That, in turn, just makes the situation worse. If we remain in this state for too long, we overload our ability to switch focus and end up with tunnel vision: more than one driver who ran into a tree later said that they saw the tree coming at them, but could not take their eyes off it or turn away from it. The tree can be figurative: many people have experienced slow-motion "train wrecks" in the office. In fencing, an angry fencer is a dead, or at least defeated, fencer.

Granted, sometimes that heart-pounding, breathless state can feel pretty good: when it feels good, we call it excitement. Some excitement is certainly fine; indeed, we want people to feel excited by their work. However, that excitement can also become an addictive adrenaline high: being behind schedule or starting a project at the last minute can trigger exactly that sort of arousal. It can be productive so long as nothing goes wrong and you have correctly estimated exactly how much time you really need. Get it wrong, though, and the excitement swiftly transforms into panic.

Speaking of Panic

I have two cats. Cats being the creatures that they are, I have only to sit down to read a book and instantly there is a cat on my lap. Regardless of which cat it is, a familiar pattern ensues: first, the cat carefully positions itself in front of my book. Once I adjust to move the book, the cat then carefully positions itself on one of my hands. This continues until I give the cat the attention it is seeking. At that point, it first butts its head against me and then, purring loudly, turns and sticks its behind in my face.

I am sure that there are people who find this end of a cat absolutely fascinating. I am even quite sure that there are contests in which cats win awards for having the most beautiful behind. For cat breeders and cat fanciers, it can be a big deal to win one of these cat trophies. It is a cause for great celebration.

It is not a cause for celebration when our arousal spikes up so fast, or is kept high for so long, that we hurtling down the right side of the performance curve. Instead of a more or less gradual decline in performance, we instead experience a very different form of catastrophe, as shown in Fig. 11.3.

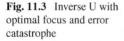
Fig. 11.3 Inverse U with optimal focus and error catastrophe

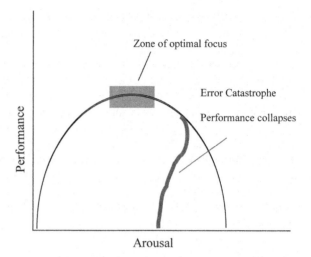

As we can see, instead of sliding smoothly down the curve, performance can collapse suddenly. Whether this collapse occurs depends on a number of factors, including the overall level of stress, a person's overall level of fitness, whether or not you have had enough sleep, how recently you remembered to eat, and so forth. People, who are in good physical condition, are getting enough sleep, and who are remembering to eat despite the stress is less likely to experience catastrophe. They are not immune, but at least their odds are better.

When we are sliding down the performance curve, various centering and focus techniques can be used to stop our descent and move us back up toward the peak; we will look at those techniques shortly. Once we fall off the cliff, however, we have to start all the back at the left end of the curve. In other words, we need to rest and recuperate, at least overnight, possibly for a few days, before our performance will return to its precatastrophe peak. Quite simply, when we are sliding down the right side of the curve, we are drawing on our energy reserves more and more rapidly. When we hit catastrophe, we have exhausted our reserves and we need to recharge.

If we try to continue performance once we have hit catastrophe, we just make things worse. Now we are into error catastrophe, where mistakes compound upon mistakes, and our efforts to fix them only causes yet more errors. Athletes who hit catastrophe generally do not have a choice about continuing: they are often physically unable to do so. If you have ever seen an uninjured runner or cyclist abandon an endurance race that is often what is going on. In the office, however, we are more likely to get into competitive frog boiling. No one wants to be the first to admit defeat and go home, so everyone keeps pushing on even though productivity is plummeting and we are actually making the situation worse. When we are feeling stressed, our instincts are to make the stressor go away; taking a break and sleeping seems counter-intuitive, even though it is exactly what we need. Remember, cognitive short-cuts most often kick in when we are tired or distracted, and lead us into errors. It is also possible to reach a point of such mental fatigue that it almost becomes too difficult to stop and take that necessary break. This is where it is particularly important that the team leader has the judgment and presence of mind to chase everyone out of the office.

A final thought here: I have seen many companies where the idea of going home and getting a good night's sleep was viewed as a sign of weakness. Instead, the teams would push on until they dropped from exhaustion, and then force themselves to continue the next day. The results were never worth it. In the infamous Apollo 13 disaster, with oxygen running out for the stranded astronauts in the damaged space capsule, mission controller Eugene Krantz still ordered the crew to get a few hours sleep before attempting the difficult maneuvers necessary to bring the space capsule back to Earth. Running out of air was less risky than the consequences of attempting a difficult operation on no sleep.

Techniques for Managing Performance

At this point, we now understand that managing stress is really the art of managing performance. Managing performance, in turn, requires that we recognize what sort of performance we are after: do we, like a sprinter, need to perform at an extremely high level for a short time? Or, like a marathon runner or endurance cyclist, do we need to maintain strong, consistent performance for a long period of time? In the course of our day, do we need to frequently deal with unexpected or unanticipated problems that have the effect of distracting us and raising our arousal outside the optimal zone?

The key to using the various techniques for stress management, or, more properly, performance or arousal management, is recognizing that:

1. The techniques are flexible; how you choose to apply them determines the results you get.
2. They take practice. Remember that under stressful conditions, we revert to our rehearsed, trained behaviors. What we have not rehearsed we do not use or it does not work when we need it most. Top performers in all domains practice the skills necessary to maintain that performance. Put another way, the will to win is useless if you do not have the will to prepare.

Remember, when you find yourself always feeling tired or waking up in the morning not feeling rested, that is an important clue that you are draining your reserves faster than you are replenishing them. No matter how much we may feel like we are running around being productive, actual quality performance is rapidly declining under those conditions.

The 90 Min Cycle

As successful athletes all learn, energy is finite. While physics might state that energy is neither created nor destroyed, it can certainly be depleted. Many an athlete learns this lesson the hard way! The key to success in sports is maintaining a constant energy level. Allowing your energy to fluctuate up and down is a recipe for failure: it becomes all too easy to hit catastrophe or rush ahead too fast and sprint when we should be running a marathon. In either case, we end up crashing our performance. The office is no different.

What makes things tricky is that we are not built to continuously expend energy. We shift between burning energy and recharging our batteries. As anyone who has sit in a classroom or made a long presentation has probably noticed, after roughly and hour and half, maybe 2 h, attention is wandering. This is no surprise: as we touched on in Chap. 5, we are capable of maintaining focus for about 90–120 min at a stretch. After 90 min, we need to take a break. As a recent article in the *NY Times* observed, top performers in sports, music, acting, speaking, and other fields typically work for about 90 min before taking a break. When we go longer than 90 min, we are starting to pull on our reserves, a tendency which we exacerbate through consuming large amounts of coffee or other energy drinks. We are also fighting our brain's desire for a change of scenery. This means that we must put more energy into maintaining focus, which increases our arousal and pushes us out of the Zone of the optimal performance. At that point, we become more distractible, and hence need to spend more energy. We can avoid this destructive spiral by taking that break.

The other thing to realize is that we are good for three of these 90 min bursts per day. Now, when I explain this to an audience, I often get looks of disbelief or gasps of horror: after all, the 8 h day is sacred and really dedicated people do far more than that! Whether they are productive, on the other hand, is a separate question! Sadly, just because someone is visibly dedicated to the job does not mean they are really productive, and quite frequently those who are the most productive do not appear dedicated, at least by the superficial measures that are too often used.

The real point, though, is this: three 90 min chunks, with real breaks is most of an 8 h day anyway, so those who feel a deep need to be horrified can relax. Even more to the point, people who train themselves to work this way are often 2–3 or more times more productive than people who are working 10 h days. They are more creative, more energetic, and less prone to making costly mistakes that may not show up for weeks or months.

After that third 90 min chunk, then it is time to switch gears and do the less demanding tasks. Remember our discussion in Chap. 5 about bounding unpleasant tasks; this is the perfect time to do those annoying but less creatively intensive tasks. On the other hand, if we try to do those irritating tasks first, even if we bound them, we will often find ourselves lacking the focus to do the important work later.

In adapting my own working style to the 90 min cycle, I have noticed that at first it really does feel like I am getting less work done. After all, I end up stopping when it feels like I could be done in just a few more minutes. Those few minutes, however, invariably turn out to take much longer, leaving me much more tired. When I stop after around 90 min and take a break, when I pick the task up again it really does only take a few more minutes: the break gave me time to get a fresh perspective. Whether writing this book or shoveling snow, taking a break after 90 min made me more productive and left me feeling less exhausted at the end. I have also noticed that because I am not feeling as drained, I do not tend to overeat at meals. Aside from the obvious benefits, I find I can enjoy dessert more frequently without feeling guilty!

Now, you might be thinking, "But wait! Athletes go for much longer than 90 min at a time! Marathon runners, cyclists, Ironman competitors, and the like, might engage in events that last all day. That is true, but, as always, the devil is in the details. First, successful athletes are constantly eating and drinking throughout the competition; exactly what they eat may vary according to what they are doing, but they are careful to maintain their energy at a constant level. I personally experienced the consequences of forgetting to do that while attending a jujitsu convention one year. I had to skip half the classes I wanted to attend. Second, there is a limit to how frequently they can compete and how many high-level competitions they can do in a year. There is a reason endurance sports are difficult!

Remember, also, that we are quite capable of expending a great deal of energy in one short burst when necessary. The marathon runner might make sprint the very end of the race, just as the business team might engage in an intense "sprint" to meet the deadline at the end of the project. In either case, we are temporarily revving up and draining our reserves to cross the finish line. If we try to maintain that pace on a routine basis, the runner collapses long before the finish line, and the product team produces somewhat less than stellar results. Even in a Flow state, we are expending energy; we are just concentrating so deeply that we do not notice how much. Even something as pleasurable and productive as Flow needs to be used carefully or it will burn us out. Remember that high performance teams are frequently undone by their own dedication and love of their work: they forget to take breaks and once exhaustion starts to set in, team cohesion breaks down.

Finally, after any push, rest and recuperation are critical! The athlete rests in order to compete again at a peak level. Intellectual or creative efforts are no less exhausting, even though it may be less obvious.

Fortunately, most of us are not riding the Tour de France in our office. The more we respect the way our bodies work, the more productive we are and the less likely it is that we will need to engage in a massive sprint at the end.

Make Breaks Count

We discussed on multiple occasions the importance of taking breaks on a regular basis. The question now is what is a break? What makes a break productive?

Fundamentally, a break is a change of scenery, a chance to recharge both physically and mentally. As we have discussed, after about an hour and half, our brains are looking for something new. If we force ourselves to keep going, we are spending more and more energy fighting the tendency to be distracted. An effective break, therefore, is doing something different. If you have been staring at the computer screen all morning writing code, looking at Facebook is not something different. You are much better off walking away from the computer altogether. A change of scenery is a change of scenery; you cannot fool your brain on that score!

On the physical front, healthy snacks and activity are both valuable. Whether we are working with our bodies or our minds, we are expending energy. That energy must be replenished. Although we will often crave sugar and caffeine, that is not enough. The boost we get from sugar, in particular, does not last all that long. We need protein for sustained concentration and performance. However, we also need to recognize that after working intensely for 90 min or so, we will come up for air craving sweets. Fortunately, if we have healthy snacks readily available, we will eat them just because they are there. Take advantage of your natural instincts to increase your productivity.

The better we feel, the better we think. Many of the most productive people in all fields take breaks to exercise, particularly if their work is mostly sedentary. This is especially true of today's knowledge workers. Physical activity is one of the best ways of keeping the brain sharp; indeed, one elementary school in New York State, decided to test this out. Instead of following the national trend to decrease recess time, they increased it. Sure enough, behavior and academic performance improved dramatically. Kids who got to run around were better able to concentrate and more capable of sitting still and working in class.

For those who consider innovation important, taking breaks are crucial! Innovative insights and breakthroughs typically happen when two conditions are met: first, that we spend some extremely focused time working on a problem; second, that we then take a break. It is when to go and do something else that our brains rearrange the pieces in different and creative ways. If you have ever had the experience of staring at a problem for hours at a time getting nowhere, and then having the solution pop into your head while at the gym or after getting a good night's sleep, that is what is going on. It is when we let our brains work on the problem in the background that we often get the best results.

Breaks all too often are viewed as nonproductive time, or time when nothing is getting done. That belief could not be further from the truth. Remember, without the breaks between the notes there would be no music: all we would have is cacophonous noise.

Manage Arousal

Another piece of managing performance is recognizing that arousal controls performance and thus what we are really doing is controlling arousal. The ability to modulate arousal up or down as necessary is a hallmark of skilled athletes. Even chess masters do it! Sure, they may be sitting in a chair staring at a chess board, but they still need to manage their arousal to put themselves in the optimal state of concentration necessary to play at their best.

Just as the fight/flight response spikes our arousal up, sometimes so fast and so far that we cannot think clearly, we have mechanisms we can use to modulate that response and turn down the level of arousal. Remember, once arousal gets too high, we are no longer functioning effectively; rather, we are in a state of panic, the classic "adrenaline dump." You do not need a tiger jumping out at you to get into that state; plenty of companies manage to talk their employees into a fine state of panic. Of course, since panic only lasts so long before we burn through our reserves, what really happens is that they end up alternating between panic and exhaustion. This is neither productive nor useful.

A common, and extremely effective, method of controlling arousal and turning down the fight/flight response is through the practice of meditation. For those who do not like that term, relaxation breathing is the same thing. More and more athletes at all levels, including the Olympics, use meditation to give themselves an edge over their opponents. It is simply the practice of sitting quietly, closing your eyes, and focusing on your breathing, listening to music, or anything else that just lets your mind drift for a few minutes. To be effective, meditation requires daily practice, optimally 15–20 min once or twice a day. In this way you do several things:

First, you develop the habit of relaxation. Having this habit lets you respond more calmly in times of stress, keeping your cool when others are losing theirs. By training yourself to relax, you build the habit and, through practice, make that habit robust under pressure. Being able to relax effectively also means that you are more able to take advantage of downtime and breaks. One of the biggest reasons people do not find breaks or vacations restful is that they do not know how to relax and turn off their fight/flight response.

Second, the practice of meditation is, in a very real sense, an exercise in concentration. When we sit and focus on our breathing, we are concentrating on something that is not particularly interesting most of the time. The practice of concentration in that one area improves our overall ability to concentrate. That, in turn, makes us more productive.

Finally, meditation is a very effective form of break between work cycles. By quieting the mind and shifting attention away from what you were working on, you give yourself that necessary break and increase the odds of a creative breakthrough.

Refocusing

Managing arousal also means regaining control when something unexpected happens. Athletes who are taken by surprise either learn to quickly regain their focus or they learn to lose. Refocusing techniques are used by athletes in a variety of sports, from running and cycling to soccer, tennis, fencing, and judo. Refocusing techniques are designed to be quick and effective; they are intended to keep your performance level high until you have time for a more substantial break. Because these techniques are used by people engaged in sports in which the action is fast and furious, I am always a little amused when people in an office tell me that "there's no time" to refocus. As we have discussed, there is always time. It is just a question of what you do with that time. Unlike a judo match or a fencing competition, if you stop to refocus in the office, you are highly unlikely to be slammed into the ground or hit with a sword. The trick, as always, is to practice refocusing techniques when you are not under pressure so that they will work when you are under pressure.

While there is any number of refocusing techniques, two very effective ones for dealing with stressful situations are "Breathe and shrug," and "Thought-stopping." As we will see in Chap. 12, refocusing techniques are specific examples of a the more general concept of building a success mindset through performance routines.

Breathe and shrug is simply the act of closing your eyes, taking a deep breath, and shrugging or shaking yourself. As you do it, you imagine the thing that is bugging you as a weight that falls away from you as you shrug. In a very literal sense, we "shrug it off."

Thought-stopping is the act of noticing that you are becoming focused on negative outcomes: "I can't do this;" "It'll never work;" "That's just too difficult!" Once you realize this is happening, you imagine taking that negative thought and destroying it, replacing it with a positive thought. Martial arts legend Bruce Lee used to imagine writing the negative thought down on a piece of paper, crumpling it up, and either throwing it away or burning it. Either way, he symbolically destroyed the negative thought and thus freed himself to focus on the positive.

Frog Soup

As we can see, stress can be one of our most effective tools. The key is learning to use it well. As we saw in Chap. 9, performance is all about being able to develop effective strategies and measurable goals. As we see from examining the dynamics of performance, success in this endeavor is not based on what we can do in a few minutes, a few hours, or even a few days or weeks. Performance is determined by how long and how steadily we can work. We get an amazing amount done when we can work in ways that take advantage of our innate productivity cycles! The old aphorism that, "success is a marathon, not a sprint," is not just a good idea, it is the law (at least metaphorically!).

It is when we let stress get out of hand, or when we allow the wrong kinds of stress to dominate the environment, that we start to undermine our natural productivity cycles. Once stress becomes destructive, we rapidly enter a destructive cycle that can transform even the best organizations into miserable places to work. Unlike our mythical boiling frog, which has the sense to know when to jump, all too often we allow ourselves to be trapped in those cycles, not realizing just how bad it is getting.

While the stress and performance management techniques we looked at will help, it is even better to develop the habits of thought and working that prevent destructive stress cycles from occurring in the first place. The more we avoid destructive stress, the more our performance management techniques serve to increase our performance, rather than merely maintaining it. Learning to avoid destructive stress, also known as developing a success mindset, is the topic of our final chapter.

Questions to Consider

1. How can stress be beneficial to your organization?
2. What kinds of stress are destructive? Where do you see those stressors in your organization?
3. How can you apply the 90 min cycle to dramatically increase productivity in your organization?
4. What is error catastrophe? When does it happen?
5. How can you apply stress/performance management techniques in your organization?
6. How is your organizational culture preventing you from increasing performance?
7. How could you use performance management techniques to improve team and leadership performance in your organization?

Chapter 12
The Success Mind: Building Optimism and Focusing Will

"It was a terrible throw!"

This statement was made to me by a student in my jujitsu class. She then proceeded to elaborate on all the ways in which she had executed the throw incorrectly. Her partner, meanwhile, was patiently lying on the ground at her feet where she had thrown him. Observing this fact, I eventually commented that the throw couldn't have been all that bad. After all, it had accomplished its primary objective: putting the other person flat on his back.

In jujitsu, it's easy to perform a technique and then focus on everything wrong with it; after all, a technique can always be improved. The problem, however, is that when you focus on all the problems you lose sight of the big picture which, in this case, was that the technique was successful. Was there room for improvement? Of course there was. That room for improvement doesn't change the basic success, unless we allow it to.

The same phenomenon happens in business all the time. After a grueling marathon of long days and late nights, the team finally ships the product. Rather than celebrate the release, they focus entirely on the bugs that didn't get fixed, or the features that they didn't have time to put in. In one rather egregious case, the director of engineering was busily berating his team for their "lousy" work even as the customers were singing their praises!

As we have discussed in a number of different contexts throughout this book, a focus on success is far more rewarding and, well, successful, than a focus on failure. When we only look at failure, we start to think of ourselves as failures. When we look at success, we think of ourselves as successful. Failure is depressing; success is exhilarating. When we feel like we're failing, our willpower is wasted just forcing ourselves to keep going. We try to make things easier in order to feel a success, any success. When we are successful, we start setting our sights ever higher. Think about the motivation trap and the high performance cycle!

While there are certainly lessons to be learned from failure, and failure is necessary for successful innovation, we also have to take the time to enjoy the

S. R. Balzac, *Organizational Psychology for Managers*,
Management for Professionals, DOI: 10.1007/978-1-4614-8505-6_12,
© Springer Science+Business Media New York 2014

progress we are making and take pride in what goes right. Optimistic people are those who take pride in their successes, who recognize how their efforts made those successes possible, and who keep failure in perspective. Pessimists, on the other hand, focus on how they contributed to failure and tend to view success as being as much about luck as anything else.

Now, people have assured me over and over again that they are optimists! They are not focused on failure, no way, no how. Actions, however, trump words in this case, as they so often do. If you engage in behaviors that orient you toward success, you are an optimist; if you engage in behaviors that keep you thinking about failure, you are behaving pessimistically. When planning is all about avoiding failure, that's inherently pessimistic!

Although pessimists so often seem rigorous and logical, optimists are happier and more successful. An organizational culture can be biased toward either optimism or pessimism; the most successful organizations are fundamentally optimistic. Optimism works.

Of course, it's not enough to just say, "Be more optimistic!" If that were all it took, you wouldn't need this book. Being optimistic is more than just some sort of mythical power of positive thinking. Rather, real optimism, the kind of optimism that gets things done, is based in identifying the positive, building resilience, engaging in behaviors that reinforce our sense of control over the world, and learning to reframe failure into useful feedback. Building an optimistic organization, enjoying success, and knowing how to learn the right lessons from failure, are all skills that take time to develop.

In this chapter, we are going to look at how to do just that. Along the way, we'll see how the different aspects of organizational behavior that we've already discussed fit together to reinforce that message of optimism.

Stop and Admire

As we've discussed in previous chapters, celebrating success is a critical part of building motivation and accomplishing long-term goals. Celebrating success is part of how we know we're on track. One component of celebrating those successes along the way is to periodically pause to admire your handiwork. The basic rule here is this:

You will never admire it more than you do right now.

This requires some explanation. Any complex project has intermediate steps. Those steps are opportunities to stop and take a long, hard, look at your work. Do you like what you see? If you don't, sleep on it. If you still don't like it, you won't like it more when you're done; in fact, the odds are very high that you'll like it much much less. If you ignore that feeling, then each subsequent step is going to remind you of the thing you didn't like, which is only going to to undermine your enthusiasm for the project. When we've worked hard at something and we just don't feel good about the result, that's a clue that something is wrong. It may not be immediately obvious what that wrong thing is, but the odds are pretty darn good that it's there and whatever it is isn't going to just get up and walk away on its own.

When we were remodeling one of the bathrooms in our house, my wife designed and built several ceramic tile shelves, complete with colored glass trim that matched the shower enclosure. She completed the shelves, and stopped to admire them. She wasn't happy with the result. She couldn't really put her finger on why, but something wasn't right. She ended up redoing them. The second time around was not only much better, but once we had the redone shelves to look at, even I could clearly see why the originals didn't work. One very important lesson here is that you can't always tell what's wrong until you redo it; if you redo it and you find you can admire it, it'll also often be obvious what was wrong before.

An important caveat here is that this method works in the context of having defined goals for what you are trying to accomplish. Without goals, you have nothing to measure against. Without that sense of comparison, your ability to admire is likely to be influenced by any number of extraneous factors. As with all skills, this technique gets better with practice.

Practicing Control

We've discussed control throughout this book. You will also recall that in the previous chapter we talked about beneficial and harmful forms of stress. Stressors that decrease our sense of control over our world are amongst the most damaging. Conversely, we can build optimism, commitment, resilience, and motivation, and also increase creativity, by providing opportunties for people to exercise control over their environment and their lives. If you want people to tackle big things, they have to believe that they can control the outcomes for big things. To get people to believe they can control big things, they must have control over small things. It is control over the small that convinces us we can control the large. Conversely, when we lack control over the small things, our attempts to control the big things tend to be halfhearted and we give up more easily when things don't work right away.

An article in the NY Times on 16 March 2013 discussed Google's work environment. One of the points mentioned in the article was that employees could exercise a great deal of choice in how they configured their personal office areas. Basically, employees are provided with the equivalent of high-tech tinker toys and could design their workstation, add a treadmill if they liked to work and walk at the same time, and so forth. Google also does not have a policy about showing up in the office; rather, the article stated that the company assumes that employees and their colleagues will work out mutually acceptable arrangements within their workgroups. While the article highlighted the flexibility and creativity aspects of Google's policies, I was struck by the more subtle, and more powerful, message: you have control. You have control over how you work, when you work, where you work. Because you have control, you know that you are doing the work because you want to do it, because you believe in the company's vision and organizational narrative. If the company forces you to come in, you never really have to decide whether you're doing the work because you care or because you have to. That small difference is quite often the difference between an enthusiastic, successful, high-performance team and being caught in the motivation trap. It is the difference between treating people like responsible adults rather than children; as we've already discussed, how you treat people is what they become.

Google has quite brilliantly created an environment in which people have control and choose to use it in ways that benefits the person and the company. No wonder motivation and creativity are both so high!

If you really want people to buy into your organizational narrative and goals, give them control and make it easy for them to choose said narrative and goals. Not only does the exercise of control make us more optimistic by letting us see that we can affect the world around us, the more we feel we are freely choosing to take an action, the more deeply we believe in our choices. Compulsion generates compliance, but arranging for people to have control and freely choose to use that control to act on behalf of the organization is what generates commitment. You can't force a team into the High Performance Cycle, but you can make it easy for them to choose it.

To give a very practical example of this sort of control in action, I recently had occasion to call Amazon.com's customer service line. My kids and I were watching Babylon 5, and one of the DVDs in the set was bad: moreover, it was the last DVD and the place where it died was in the last 15 min of the climactic final episode of the third season; fans of the show will know just how big a cliff hanger that episode was! It was well past the 30 day return policy. I called Amazon.com and explained to the customer service representative what had happened and how we could not possibly have figured this out within 30 days of buying the complete series. She immediately issued me a refund for that season and I had the new DVDs a day later. She could do this because she had sufficient control over the situation to be able to exercise her judgment and help a customer. Customer service representatives who don't have sufficient control to exercise their own judgment are generally less willing to help out at all; those who feel they can exercise control find ways to make the customers happy.

Make It Easy

It's worth a brief discussion at this point of the concept of making things easy. My first jujitsu sensei used to frequently remind me to not stand my partner's foot when I was trying to throw him. It was frustrating for me and didn't particularly amuse my partner.

All too often, we get in our own way when we want people to do something. There is a big difference between making it hard for someone to say "No" and making it easy for them to say "Yes." When we make it hard to say "No," we are also making it hard to say "Yes" because we are, in effect, denying the other person autonomy or control. When we make it easy for them to say "Yes," we are constructing the situation to produce the results we want and letting the other person freely choose to give us those results. As one Googler in that NY Times article put it, even on days off she comes into the office: there's always healthy food available and it's a more interesting place to be.

Speaking of food, this is another good example of how Google makes it easy for people to make the choices the company wants. Eating healthy food, as opposed to soda, chips, and sweets, is extremely important to maintaining focus, energy, and creativity. Google doesn't want to play Big Brother and tell people what they can and cannot eat. They are happy to provide all the traditional junk food found in many high tech companies. However, at Google, the healthy food and drinks are in front, and the soda and sweets in the back or in the cabinets. It's not hard to get at them, but the easiest choice is to eat what's in front of you.

Figuring out what you want people to do is the easy part. The challenge is in not standing on their feet when they go to do it.

Undermining Control

The powerful thing about providing people control is that it builds their sense of competence and autonomy. They become more likely to tackle difficult projects and are less willing to give up. However, if we approach control in the wrong way, we can easily reverse those effects. It's easy to order people to do something and then tell them exactly how to do it: that's not giving them control. That's micromanaging.

The more serious problem, though, is when you routinely second-guess people's decisions: a form of the hindsight trap we discussed in the previous chapter. Remember that your goal is not to have people make the decisions you would make, but to make the decisions you can work with. As we discussed in the section on feedback, focus on what people did right. When you do have to correct something, make sure you clearly explain why the decision was incorrect and how they can fix it in the future. Avoid doing this unless it really is necessary: frequent correction only undermines confidence and destroys the sense of control. I'm not in control if I'm always wrong! If you are finding that you have to frequently correct people, either you haven't adequately conveyed the goals to them, you have the wrong people, you haven't provided them proper training, or you are too sensitive.

This Ain't No Comedy Routine... But Maybe It Should Be

My son takes Kenpo Karate. At the end of each class, the instructor has the kids bow and then recite the rules of the school, a short bit about effort and character. The kids then remove their belts and leave the mat. One afternoon, though, instead of the head instructor, one of the other black belts was teaching class. As the class drew to a close, the head instructor stepped onto the back of the mat, kneeled down, and bowed with everyone else. Instead of having the kids recite the rules, the black belt teaching the class told the kids to turn and bow to the head instructor. What followed was a moment of pure confusion: some kids started reflexively reciting the rules. Others half turned, then hesitated when they saw other kids not turning or starting to take off their belts. It took the assistant instructor several tries to get everyone to turn around, bow, and then end class normally.

Classes normally follow a very predictable routine. It always begins and ends the same way. Changing that routine, as the instructor found, isn't easy. This is true for all manner of organizational routines. It doesn't matter whether we're talking about kids or adults: routines are powerful. As we discussed in chapter eleven, athletes use routines all the time to help them focus and prepare for competition.

There are fundamentally two different types of routines: routines that we deliberately create and routines that we just fall into. Both types are equally powerful. However, while deliberately building a routine is generally beneficial, routines we just fall into are as like as not to be counter-productive.

Basically, a routine is a series of actions that we perform so often that they become automatic and which often produce a particular mindset. The more we practice the routine, the more rapidly we create the mindset. Eventually, merely contemplating the routine will initiate the mental state, although performing the routine is still essential most of the time if we want it to last. When an athlete executes a pre-performance routine, that routine is intended to get them physically and mentally prepared for competition. Many people create morning routines around breakfast, coffee, and reading the news as a way of mentally preparing to focus on the day's work. My first jujitsu sensei used to tell us that the reason we bowed as we entered the dojo was to leave the day's baggage at the door so that we could concentrate on the workout. If we practiced the routine with that image in mind, it worked. If we didn't, it didn't.

Quite often, though, routines are created less carefully. They just build up over time: for example, the student I described in the opening to this chapter was in the process of building up a routine around her throws. Throw, focus on the negative, produce a negative, pessimistic mindset, repeat. Of course, as she built that mindset, her throws would get worse, there would be more negatives to focus on, and so it went. When this process isn't interrupted, students start dreading the practice of throwing because they've built such negative associations.

I've encountered this phenomenon in jujitsu, and also when conducting seminars on mental skills techniques for athletes in other sports. It comes up in the business world as well: as I alluded to at the beginning of this chapter, in one particularly dramatic example, a software engineering team at one major company would conduct a post-mortem review after each product ship. Unfortunately, as we know from chapter three, group polarization can produce extremes of behavior in a team. In this case, team members all wanted to demonstrate that they were serious and dedicated and open to giving and receiving criticism. It wasn't long before each product ship was followed by a laser-like focus on the flaws, while the very real successes were minimized or ignored. Over time, the ability of the team declined simply because they convinced themselves that they just weren't all that good and eventually product quality followed. Then they really did have something to complain about! Performance reviews are another area in which routines develop over time, a point well illustrated by the number of managers who complain about how unpleasant it is to even contemplate the review process!

There's a reason we want to stop and admire our progress and celebrate our successes: it's all part of building the routine and establishing the positive, enthusiastic mindset. Ship, enjoy, and then move on to the next version. Make that your habit and you'll be more successful. In the end, you can fill your head with thoughts of failure or with thoughts of success. The bad news is that there's only room for one. The good news is that you get to choose which one it is.

Effective Problem Solving

One of the things that world class successful organizations, the organizations that keep innovating and growing and reinventing themselves, have in common is a remarkably effective ability to solve problems. What is interesting, however, is that they don't necessarily get it right the first the time; often, perhaps, but not always. What they are extremely good at is knowing how to solve problems in ways that constantly reinforce their cultural beliefs of optimism and success.

To begin with, problem solving is really a question of goal setting. In this case, it is a goal where the outcome is to make the problem go away. Unfortunately, that's not really enough information to create a specific goal, although plenty of businesses try. There are, however, many ways to make a problem go away at least temporarily. Hence, if that's all you focus on, you end up with a problem that feels like a boomerang in a Saturday morning cartoon: it keeps coming back and whacking you upside the head. Thus, we need to do a bit more work in order to formulate effective goals around solving our problem.

Before we can solve a problem there is one thing we absolutely have to know. What might that be? Whether I ask this of college students or managers, I always get the same response: puzzled looks and then people start yelling out answers such as, "the solution," or "the cost of the problem," or "what resources we need," or a host of other answers. Eventually somebody says, "Don't we have to know what the problem is?"

Exactly. Before you can find a solution, you have to identify the problem. As obvious as this may sound, if you don't know the actual problem, then your solution isn't likely to fix it. There are a great many solutions out there looking for problems.

A problem can be broken down into three major pieces: there is the actual problem, whatever that may be. We don't know what the problem is because we can't actually see it; what we can see are the effects of the problem. That may mean deadlines being missed or angry customers calling to complain or a lack of motivation or difficulty hiring or retaining talent, or countless other things. Those are the symptoms of the problem. Finally, there are the things that occur around the problem, things which attract our attention but which are basically irrelevant to the situation. They look important but they're not. That's known as chrome: the shiny stuff that draws our eye and distracts us from what really matters.

You Look Good in That Car

Familiar line, right? Every car salesman says it, and if you've bought a car, you've heard it. The car salesman wants to get you thinking about how good you look in that car so that you're not thinking about other things, such as the price or those expensive options that you don't really need. That's chrome. That's getting your attention caught up on something that only seems to matter. After 2009's failed attempt to blow up a plane by a man hiding a bomb in his underwear, the initial reaction was to say that since the Underwear Bomber had made his attempt in the last 90 min of flight, passengers wouldn't be allowed to hold carryon items in their hands during the last 90 min of a flight. Fortunately, that rather obvious bit of chrome was dropped fairly quickly. However, even several years later I continue to hear late night comics repeating the joke that, "Since the Underwear Bomber was seated in seat 19F, from henceforth no plane will have a seat 19F." And, of course, a bit of chrome from a different event means we can now carry small knives onboard a plane but not a bottle of water.

The real danger of chrome is not just that it can cause us to buy the wrong car or remove seat 19F from an airplane. Chrome can trap us into focusing on the wrong problem. Once chrome catches our attention, we start to think of it as the problem. Once that happens, we can easily become stuck on that idea: all the evidence starts to persuasively point in that direction. It just seems so easy and so obvious.

While doing some work for a certain medical device company, I was told that a particular manager was "passive aggressive." Why? He allowed someone to eat on the shop floor. The person telling me this was quite convinced that the reason the company was having a problem with its products being returned by customers was due to this "passive aggressive" behavior. He gave me all sorts of reasons why he was correct in his evaluation of the situation. Of course, the manager wasn't passive aggressive. The problem didn't even have anything to do with him: in fact, none of the managers were enforcing the no food rule because they weren't getting support from higher up. That was the real problem. But this particular bit of chrome had struck someone else as "passive aggressive" and everything after that become an attempt to prove it.

Could You Make That Noise Again?

Ever listen to NPR's *"Car Talk?"* For those who might have been under a rock for the past 25 or so years, *Car Talk* features "Click and Clack, the Tappit Brothers," also known as Tom and Ray Magliozzi, taking questions about and giving advice on car repair. In the course of the hour show, they will take several calls, laugh at their own bad jokes, and ask a series of questions such as, "Does it make that noise when you turn to the right or to the left?" "And it goes away above 30 miles per hour?" and, "Could you make that noise again?" I suspect the last question is mostly because they find it hilarious to listen to callers attempting to imitate the odd sounds their cars are making.

What Click and Clack are doing through their apparently random questions is identifying the symptoms of the problem. The symptoms are not the problem; they are merely the symptoms. However, when we understand the symptoms, we are able to gradually identify the problem. Going back to our discussion of goal setting, we are defining and executing learning goals. We are setting goals that will help us answer several important questions:

1. What are the observed symptoms? Exactly what is happening?
2. When do the symptoms occur? All the time? At certain times?
3. When did it start? What changed?
4. Where do they occur? In one location or many? In one product or many? At one customer site or many?
5. How long do they last?
6. What is affected?
7. Who is affected?

Solving the Problem

Once we've identified the symptoms, then we can brainstorm about the causes. Sometimes the cause will be obvious and much of the time it will certainly look that way. Unless the problem is small, the goal of the brainstorming session is not to produce one definitive answer, but rather to identify several likely causes. Wait a day, or at least a few hours, and then come back and examine your potential problems.

Why wait? Simple. When we try to mix evaluation and brainstorming what we get is the functional equivalent of a sodden mass. First generate ideas, then take a break. The reason most brainstorming fails to live up to its promise is that people skip that critical step.

Why generate several possible hypotheses? We don't want to get locked into one answer too early. The goal is to develop habits of problem solving that work with big problems or small ones. Start by practicing doing it right even when you don't need to. In jujitsu, we practice taking the fall correctly all the time, not just when we're thrown hard enough that we need to land a certain way. What you train is what you do. You can always shortcut the process once you're good at it.

When you return to evaluate your different hypotheses, don't look for evidence why each one is correct. You'll find that without much effort; after all, you came up with those hypotheses based on the symptoms you were evaluating. Remember the confirmation bias that we discussed in Chap. 7: we never have trouble finding support for our beliefs! Instead, look for the data that will prove you wrong. In other words, you aren't asking how each potential cause you've identified could cause the symptoms you're observing. This time around, you're asking how the observed behaviors would disqualify your potential solutions: if the team was having problems communicating before Fred was added, then Fred didn't cause the problem. Approaching things this way saves a great deal of time and energy spent chasing down the wrong problem and is a lot easier on Fred than firing him and realizing that the problem hasn't gone away.

At this point, you should have reduced your set of possible causes of your problem to something manageable, like one or two. Now you can formulate more precise goals around each of your possible solutions. If you find that you can't formulate those goals, you probably have identified the wrong problem. Start again. Continue until you can get to this point and build well-structured goals that at least look like they'll move you to a solution.

Now Can I Solve the Problem?

Unfortunately, you still can't solve the problem. There's still just a bit more to do before you dive in and implement your solution. Examine the goals you just developed: how will you carry them out? Which steps can you plan and which steps can you not plan in advance? How will you know if you're successful? This last point may seem silly: after all, if you're successful, the problem will go away! While that's true, it helps to identify precisely what you expect to happen and when. Back to goals and feedback: we want to know if we're succeeding before we get to the end. Conversely, if we are solving the wrong problem or if our solution is flawed, we want to know this as early as possible. As with all goals, we have to define our intermediate steps and identify the factors that will tell us if we're going off course. At the end, we don't want to get bogged down arguing about whether or not we've succeeded: by defining our criteria ahead of time, before we're invested in the results, we avoid the danger of getting somewhere random and simply declaring that to be the finish line.

If the implementation of the solution is going to be carried out by other people, it pays to bring them into the process at this point if we haven't brought them in already. People who have to implement a solution will feel more engaged and committed if they are involved early on in the process of coming up with that solution: respect their competence and build relatedness. On a purely practical level, they are also likely to have expert insights that others may not: I worked once with an architecture firm whose head architect made a point of involving builders in the earliest stages of design. He told me it was because that way he wouldn't end up giving the client drawings for something that couldn't be built.

At this point, you can go ahead and implement your solution. At the end, do a final check: did it work? Since you've already defined the criteria for success, at least in theory this shouldn't be too hard to determine. In practice, it's often a bit messier than it sounds on paper, so be prepared for that. If it didn't work, you have a choice in how to respond:

Option 1: Clearly the failure is someone's fault. Heads must roll!

Option 2: What have learned that we didn't know before? Remember our discussion of hindsight in Chap. 11. Just because something is obvious now doesn't mean it was obvious before. Based on what we've learned, how can we now solve the problem? What else have we improved along the way?

Cultures that focus on blame typically go with option 1. However, the more optimistic and successful organizations choose option 2. That doesn't mean not doing a post-mortem and trying to identify mistakes or failing to refine your processes; it simply means that you're proceeding from the perspective that you have competent, committed people who have no more interest in wasting their time on a wild goose chase than you do. The secret to solving large, difficult problems is accepting that there will be mistakes along the way. The secret to optimistic organizations is that they actually treat those mistakes as feedback and learning opportunities instead of merely giving the concept lip-service.

We'll return to these concepts when we discuss organizational diagnosis later in this chapter.

Difficult Decisions or the Difficulty With Decisions?

Some years ago, when I was getting married, my wife and I engaged in the traditional ritual of the Choosing of the China. After trying to choose between china patterns all afternoon, the thought of being eaten alive by creatures from another planet was looking more and more attractive. Fortunately, it wasn't an available option! By the end of the day, I just wanted the choices to end. I was ready to agree to anything. Indeed, I've often wondered if the reason police shows never use choosing china patterns as a form of interrogation is that it is seen as just too cruel.

In their book, "Willpower," psychologist Roy Baumeister and NY Times reporter John Tierney discuss the phenomenon of will and decision making in great detail. From an organizational perspective, though, there are some key points that we need to consider as they have far reaching effects on organizational effectiveness.

As anyone who has ever had to choose china patterns can attest, the process is exhausting. We can only make so many decisions in a day before we start to feel like our brains are turning to goo and are trickling out of our ears. Part of the problem is that decisions are not always obvious: you'll recall in Chap. 11 we discussed the point that part of focusing on a task is being able to distinguish what is important from what is not. That separation is a form of decision making. Tuning out that annoying coworker in the cubicle down the hall is a decision. Indeed, what Baumeister found is that our decision making and our overall willpower are inextricably linked. The more decisions we have to make, the less willpower we have left for other things, like focusing on a problem or being creative.

Part of why decision making in groups works the way it does is that the energy people have determines the types of decisions they can make. In stage one groups, people are spending most of their time and energy just figuring out how to work together; thus, we end up with directive leadership being the most effective style in that situation. The group members lack both the decision making skill and energy for more sophisticated decision making techniques. As the group members become more comfortable with one another, the combination of learning to work together and increasing skill at decision making enables the group to develop and move to higher levels of performance.

Unfortunately, unlike physical tiredness, the sort of mental tiredness that comes with decision fatigue isn't always so obvious. It's not like we stop making decisions; rather, we just make increasingly poor decisions. When we're mentally tired, we have trouble making the types of decisions that involve risk. We're much more likely to just choose the thing that's easy, which is generally to do little or nothing; to not try that new initiative or explore that new product idea. The planned bold new leap forward at dawn becomes a hesitant shuffle by the end of the day. Whether at an individual or a group level, we are subject to decision making errors of this sort. With groups, though, the poor decision is then amplified by the echo chamber effect of group polarization.

Now, you might be thinking that we've talked a great deal about giving people control and now it seems like I'm implying that giving people choices is a bad idea. Not quite. As we discussed earlier in this chapter, we don't want to stand on people's feet when we want them to do something. We want to give them control over their lives and also make it easy for them to choose to do what is best. Putting the attractive, yummy junk food up front next to the healthy food forces people to make a difficult choice every time they walk into the kitchen. Putting, as Google does, the junk food in the back makes the choice easy even while it still leaves the choice available.

Part of why all day meetings are so mentally exhausting and unproductive is that it takes a lot of willpower to sit in a room and stay focused for hours. Whether you're solving problems or brainstorming, the meeting takes focus and drains willpower. By a rather amazing coincidence, the length of time we can focus before needing to take that break and replenish our energy is about 90 min. After that, performance, willpower, and decision making all start declining more and more rapidly.

More broadly, organizational life is a constant series of choices. The key is to make sure those choices are important ones: make it easy for people to be loyal, committed, and motivated so that they don't spend energy making those decisions. We've discussed in some depth how to do that! When people are unhappy in their jobs, every day is a decision just to go to work. If that's the decision they're making, they have that much less energy available for the really important decisions on the job. When people are prevented from replenishing their energy on a regular basis, they don't become more skilled at operating with low energy; they just become better at making bad decisions.

Letting It Linger

A common decision-making trap is allowing the decision to linger after it's made. This is particularly true with difficult decisions that are not easily reversed. At one company, the decision was made to fire the VP of Software Development. This was a very good decision for a very large number of reasons. But then someone decided that they should really hire someone to take his place before they told said VP that he was being fired. This man was not stupid. He could figure out that something was up even if he didn't know exactly what. More to the point, though, was that keeping him there while they secretly searched for a replacement meant that they were effectively making the fire/no-fire decision over and over again each day! For each person they interviewed, they had to decide not just whether that person was a good hire, but whether he was good enough to enable them to actually go through with firing the current VP. Months later, the VP was still there and the problems at the company were much worse.

When you make a decision and then find excuses to not implement it, either it's a bad decision in the first place, or the reason you don't want to implement it is due to decision fatigue. Either way, you are facing the choice again and again. In one way or the other, you need to execute that decision. When you let it linger in some shadowy twilight world between life and death, you only suck the energy and morale out of everyone.

Ugly Picture? Get a New Frame!

Part of how an organization builds and maintains an optimistic culture is how it treats negative news. It is very easy to be caught up in all the reasons something won't work; after all, those reasons always sound so logical and reasonable and it's always easier to decide to not take a risk.

When it comes to negative news, the important thing is to reframe it as something more neutral or even positive. This is actually less difficult than it sounds, mainly because the news frequently appears worse than it actually is. In Edwin Lefevre's classic, *"Reminiscences of a Stock Operator,"* he observes that the news media is always most excited and positive at the top of the economic cycle, and most dire and pessimistic at the bottom. Lefevre's book was written in 1923, and his observation remains true today. Just because it's easier to get the news doesn't mean that the psychology has changed. Rather than getting caught up in the negativity, develop the habit of reframing. For example, if some businesses are having trouble that means that their clients are available. How can you take advantage of the situation?

While most businesses viewed the Great Depression as a time to hunker down, cut everyone possible from the payroll, and hide under the bed until things got better, one CEO took a different perspective. He saw the Depression as an opportunity to find the best people, build their loyalty and commitment, and stockpile equipment and material against the day the economy turned. Tom Watson's confidence that things would get better propelled IBM into becoming the global powerhouse it remains to this day.

In another example, I hear frequent news reports featuring respected economists claiming that hyper-inflation and total social collapse are just around the corner. Is that likely? I'm no economist, but I have to wonder how many people today remember "Dow 36,000?" James Glassman's book was published at the height of the Internet boom: in October 1999, just a few short months before the market crashed in March 2000. The predictions of a rosy future stretching into forever were loudest, and most believable, at the top.

In a very real sense, it's not what we see that determines our reactions: it's what we say about what we see. Optimistic organizations don't close their eyes and ignore what's going on; rather, they develop the skill of finding the opportunities that others are afraid to seek out.

Nine Hundred and Ninety-Nine Light Bulbs on the Wall

Just as we have to reframe negative news, we have to reframe failure. As we've discussed throughout this book, failure is a form of feedback. In Thomas Edison's case, the feedback was that he learned a great many ways to not make a light bulb. This is easy to say, but hard to live: that's a big part of why innovation is so difficult. Without innovation, though, organizations become stuck: they lose the excitement and novelty that made them great. Just as individual growth is key to maintaining individual motivation, innovation is the organizational growth that is key to maintaining a vibrant, exciting organization. So why is it so hard?

Isaac Asimov wrote in his classic novel, *Foundation*, that the people who most fiercely defend the status quo today are the same people who yesterday most bitterly opposed it becoming the status quo. So it is with innovation.

Innovation involves disrupting the comfortable, familiar, safe ways of doing things. Although a culture may start out aggressive and entrepreneurial, if the organization is successful then, over the years, people learn to be careful. Partly, we've been taught since childhood not to make mistakes: mistakes are VERY VERY BAD. Mistakes mean a low grade and that Goes On Your Permanent Record. Remember all the talk about your permanent record from when you were in school? It's time to shake those habits; they are about as useful as worrying about a monster under your bed.

Another piece of the puzzle is that we start to measure all the different ways we can cut costs and we start thinking about how much better the business would do if all that wasted effort and misdirected work were just eliminated. We reward managers for staying under budget, not for taking bold steps in the service of the organization. As we discussed in Chap. 8, where there is no room for mistakes, there is no room for learning: the same is true about innovation. When we get too focused on counting beans, all we become good at is counting beans.

The challenge is distinguishing between exploration, which leads to new products and services, and actual waste. Exploration is a dirty business and a lot of it fails. That's only waste if you don't bother to learn how not to make those light bulbs.

Once a company knows how to succeed, it tends to get better and better at succeeding in that way: IBM with mainframes, Microsoft with Windows, Cicso with routers, Oracle with databases, Google with search, Amazon.com with shopping, Apple with iGadgets. Where the companies often fail, though, is in moving outside the box they just created for themselves. This is particularly striking with Apple, which once dominated the smartphone market. Apple is in the box that Steve Jobs built and other companies, notably Samsung, are moving beyond it. It remains to be seen whether Apple can jump ahead again.

Practically speaking, therefore, innovation is about optimism, risk taking, and effective decision making. It is not the province of one wild-eyed kid in a garage or the iconic lone inventor. No matter how much movies make innovation out to be the result of some crazy inventor having a sudden brilliant insight, innovation comes from the organization; it is about building the environment which fosters creativity and which gives people room to explore. In order to make that happen, we have to avoid four traps and make sure we institute four key elements.

The four innovation traps are:

- Perfection trap—making our products and services more perfect always feels like a worthwhile goal. Make no mistake, to a great extent it is worthwhile. However, each generation has less "gosh wow!" than the previous one. My iPhone 4 is a lot better than an iPhone 3G, but the iPhone 5 isn't enough better to convince me to upgrade. Pursuing perfection can blind us to alternatives, and it's the alternatives that defeat our "perfect" products. The perfect mousetrap is wonderful until someone shows up with a cat.
- To much to lose trap—we become focused on not hurting our existing products. Just remember, if you don't turn your cash cow into hamburger, someone else will.
- Identity trap—the company defines itself in terms of its products: "we're a database company" or "we're a hardware company." Specialization is great until your niche becomes irrelevant. IBM reinvented itself to have a life outside of mainframes and is doing quite well.
- The creeping box trap—it's great to think outside the box. The problem is, once you move outside the box, it eventually grows to surround you again. Yahoo thought it was outside the box until Google came along. As already mentioned, Apple is in the box that Jobs built. Organizations get so focused on their own cleverness that they forget that other people are looking to think outside their box.

As for what you have to do to encourage innovation, that's actually pretty easy. We've discussed all of these elements repeatedly throughout this book:

- Continuous learning—As we discussed in Chap. 5, continuous learning is key to motivation. It is also key to innovation. Innovation comes from putting together familiar things in new ways. The more you know, the more likely that is to happen. Steve Jobs knew nothing about building computers, but that didn't stop him from inventing the iPhone.

- Mistakes—At the risk of beating a dead horse, mistakes are feedback. How many light bulbs have you made?
- Take breaks—Another topic we've discussed at length. Creativity doesn't happen when you're exhausted. The "Eureka!" moment comes when you take a break and see things differently.
- Patience—Innovation is an ongoing process. If you wait until you desperately need a breakthrough before you start, your odds of success will be better in Vegas. Creativity takes time. Innovation is most important when it seems the least necessary.

I hear from many businesses that they'd like to be more innovative. What's stopping you?

Organizational Diagnosis

As we've discussed previously, when we set goals we need to know not just if we're on track, but if we're off track as well. We can't really trust a system that doesn't give us tools to recognize and correct problems. Just as this is true at the individual and the team level, it is true at the organizational level. It's not enough to know what you should do; you also need to know what to do when things don't work out as expected.

Fundamentally, Murphy's Law holds true in organizational development just as it does in engineering. Things will go wrong. Mistakes will happen. People will misunderstand, miscommunicate, misconstrue. Go back to our discussion of team development in Chap. 3: people have to learn how to talk to one another. This process takes time. While we certainly hope that problems will be small, localized, and easily dealt with, we need to be prepared to handle the situations where that's not the case. Remember, most teams get stuck somewhere along the way to high performance.

The goal of organizational diagnosis is to apply our skills at problem solving to understand what is going on in our organization and then apply the information we've discussed throughout this book to moving the organization forward. Organizational "problems" can take many forms, from obvious failures or outright disasters; to feeling stuck, meaning that you're expending a great deal of energy on something, but not seeing results; to strong performance that can't quite make the jump to extraordinary performance. This last can be particularly pernicious as management becomes complacent and becomes unwilling to take the risk of improvement. In any and all of these situations, the key is to be able to identify what is happening, propose possible courses of action, evaluate those proposals, form an action plan, execute it, and be able to evaluate the results. For something ostensibly so simple, why is it so difficult?

Back to the Symptoms

Earlier, we discussed the process of looking at symptoms as the route to finding the problem. The danger here is that we become too focused on the symptoms. Treating the symptoms will often make us feel better in the short term, but only serves to mask the real problem. For example, if your car is making a weird knocking noise from one wheel, you can simply deal with the symptom by closing the windows and turning the music up. As they said on *Car Talk,* this approach works great until your axle breaks and the wheel comes off.

Of course, knowing that we get focused on symptoms isn't the real question. The real question at this point is, why do we get focused on symptoms? The answer is because they're there. Symptoms are easy to see and they seem easy to deal with. Making a symptom go away feels good. For a short time, everything appears to be working.

In one technology company, one of the engineering teams couldn't make decisions. Now, we've looked at decision making from several different angles, and we therefore know that we're looking at a symptom. There are any number of factors that can cause this symptom to appear:

1. We could be looking at a so-called leaderless team. As we've discussed, leaderless teams don't work. This is one of the reasons why.
2. The team could be using wrong decision making method for the organizational culture or for the team's stage of development. Stage one teams that attempt to use voting systems often end up stuck. Stage two teams are particularly resistant to directive leadership.
3. Lack of engagement: if the team isn't committed, it isn't really taking the decision seriously. As a result, and note that this is an additional symptom, no one is asking questions or pushing back on ideas.
4. Perceived lack of control: if the team doesn't believe that their actions will matter, they won't try. Decisions are a ritual they go through even though they "know" it won't matter.

Indeed, even the basic problem, "can't make decisions," can mean different things: are decisions being made but not implemented? Are decisions not being made at all? Are they being made and then revisited and second-guessed? Each of these scenarios present different symptoms and point to different underlying problems.

Considering all this, however, is complicated. The company responded to the situation by bringing in a Decision Consultant, someone who specialized in teaching people to make decisions. After all, they said, we want someone who specializes in exactly what is wrong.

Did you ever notice that doctors who deal with respiratory illness are known as Ear, Nose, Throat doctors, not Achy, Coughy, Sneezy, doctors? You don't go to a doctor who specializes in coughs; you go to the doctor who understands the system in which coughs occur. Even when you go to a specialist, said specialist usually, or at least hopefully, has enough knowledge of the overall system to recognize when they are not the right person. We might go to a doctor because of our symptoms, but we do not go to Symptom Doctors.

In this case, the company was not addressing what was wrong; they were addressing a symptom. After their Decision Consultant finished working with the team on whatever it is that Decision Consultants do, things really did look better for a short while. It wasn't long, though, before other decision making problems cropped up. So they brought their Decision Consultant back again, and so it went. The problem never really got better, but the symptoms were periodically alleviated. There was no increase in productivity, but everyone did feel better about the team, particularly the Decision Consultant.

The problem with just treating symptoms is that we end up making ourselves feel better while the problem is constantly getting worse. However, when the solution to the problem is to bring in a Symptom Doctor, that's what ends up happening. Over time, this approach undermines morale and enthusiasm: not only are there clearly problems, but they must be very big problems because the organization is spending lots of money trying to fix them and they are not going away! Eventually, some organizations come to believe that the problems are simply part of doing business; at that point, the business becomes a very unpleasant place to work!

Remember that the symptoms are only the symptoms. World class organizations don't hire Symptom Doctors; they bring in people who understand the system and who will identify and help them solve the real problems. They're also more likely to be able to help you make your organization more resilient and successful as well.

What Did You See?

Sherlock Holmes on more than one occasion told Watson that it was foolish to speculate until all the facts were available. One of the most difficult aspects of organizational diagnosis is separating what you see from what you think about what you see. I've conducted exercises in which people are asked to do something, for example ask to cut into a line, and then describe what the reaction is. Many people tell me that, "She didn't allow me to cut in because she was in a bad mood," or something similar.

The observation is only whether or not the person let you cut in the line. Everything else is interpretation. We don't know why she didn't let him cut in the line; perhaps he didn't say please. The point, though, is that it's hard to separate what we see from what we think about what we see. This can pose a challenge in organizational diagnosis: instead of acting on what is in front of us, we act on what we think about what is in front of us. For example, earlier we discussed the case of the passive aggressive manager. By interpreting the behavior instead of simply observing it, the person making the complaint created chrome out of thin air. No amount of fixing of this mythical passive aggressiveness would have solved their very real problems, whereas merely observing the situation quickly led to the solution. As we discussed in Chap. 9, managers observing employees working late rated those employees as more productive, even though what they were really doing was surfing the web. The observed behavior was "in the office late." The interpretation was, "productive." The employees who didn't stay late were rated as less productive and no one could figure out why productivity was always so low.

Observing without interpreting is difficult, but if we don't learn to do it, all we really do is create chrome.

Enough of What Not to Do! What Do I Do?

As we can see, successful organizational diagnosis starts with effective problem solving. Of course, there's more to it. You have to look at the big picture and see how the system is working. The exact details will vary from organization to organization, but there are a few tells that are true virtually anywhere.

For example, how are your employees behaving? Are they happy, enthusiastic, motivated by enjoyment of their jobs? Or are they tired, irritable, always trudging through the day, motivated by fear of being fired? If it's the latter, or if you can't tell the difference, that's a bad sign.

Is hope your dominant strategy? In other words, do you just hope things will get better? Do you hope the problem will go away? Hope is not a good strategy. It leads to false economies: at one company, they hoped to increase their revenue by $100,000 per month, but weren't willing to spend the money to make it happen. Instead, they just hoped that "things would work out favorably." They didn't. More than hope was required. Their false economy cost them over $1,000,000 of lost revenue the next year. "I hope we'll" is a warning sign.

What do your hiring results look like? Are you really getting the best people, or are you getting the people who couldn't find a job anywhere else? Are you turning your new hires into top performers or are they sitting around collecting a paycheck and doing little? When you hire top talent, can you retain them? If you can't, try looking at the organization from their perspective. What are they seeing and experiencing? Don't assume the problem is them: that's interpretation. The observation is that they leave after a few months on the job. One high tech company tied itself into knots trying to hire a particular engineer: they offered him money, stock, perks. He wasn't interested. They kept raising the ante until he accepted. Three months later he was gone. Was it due to some flaw in his character? Nope. It was a symptom of a deeper problem that the company chose to ignore, hoping it would go away. It didn't. Their profits did though.

Is everything a crisis? Unexpected bumps in the road are a normal part of doing business. How you respond to them, however, can tell you a great deal. If everything is a crisis, that's a red flag. When everything turns into a crisis, you're already in hot water. The converse, a complete lack of urgency, can also tip you off to impending trouble: it's easy to get complacent when things are going well, but that's often the best time to build the organization.

What do outsiders think? Sometimes, it helps to solicit the opinions of trusted outsiders. Bring in someone you can trust to be frank with you and ask for feedback. If the person thinks the work environment is unacceptable, bring in one or two more people. If all of them agree, odds are that you need to make some changes. If necessary, bring in an expert who can see the system. Avoid the Symptom Doctors like, well, the plague.

Finally, practice. Diagnosing organizational systems and developing your business is really about learning to use a set of tools and practicing them until you can use them under stress. They will feel awkward and unnatural at first: jujitsu students always tell me that "I'd never do that technique!" because it feels so awkward when they first learn it. By the time they reach black belt, that same technique is now as natural as breathing.

You will make mistakes along the way: expertise is often less about making fewer mistakes and more about recognizing mistakes early and knowing when to change strategies. It's been said that, "We start by trying to make a profit, move to cutting our losses, and end up by trying not to lose (face)." All too often, we get caught up sticking to a failing strategy in the hopes that it'll work well enough for us to not feel like we've wasted time, energy, or other resources. We don't want to look foolish. In fact, if we pay attention to the feedback we're getting, we haven't wasted anything. It's when we ignore the feedback that we start to dig ourselves deeper and deeper.

The key to making organizational diagnosis a useful tool for making and keeping your organization optimistic and success focused is being willing to learn from our mistakes.

Wrapping It All Up—The Success Mind

Building a success mind is not something that just happens. Nor is it the province of a few exceptional or particularly talented individuals or organizations. Rather, it is the result of training and developing the skills that lead to an optimistic, effective mindset in individuals, and an optimistic, entrepreneurial mindset in organizations. Giant businesses like IBM can become more optimistic and entrepreneurial, and tiny startups can be weighed down by a focus on negative outcomes and failure. It all depends on which habits and mindsets you allow to dominate and become part of your culture. Building a world class organization isn't something that happens by accident: it's the result of knowing the right things to do and practicing them until they work. And it is the result of taking intelligent risks, focusing on success, not failure.

Good luck!

Questions to Consider

1. What automatic routines exist in your organization? What mindset are they producing?
2. What does failure mean in your organization?
3. In what ways are members of your organization given control of the little things?
4. In what ways is the feeling of control undermined?
5. When do decisions made by your team come back like Dracula from the grave?
6. When was the last time you stopped to admire your progress?
7. Why will Symptom Doctors make problems worse?
8. What are three things you can change to make your organization more optimistic and success oriented? What's stopping you?

Recommended Reading

Balzac, S. (2010). Reality from fantasy: Using predictive scenarios to explore ethical dilemmas. In D. Gibson & K. Schrier (Ed.), *Ethics and Game Design: Teaching Values Through Play*. New York: IGI.

Ethics and Game Design is a worthwhile read for anyone who wants to understand more of how to use games as teaching tools. My chapter focuses on the use of predictive scenarios, a powerful technique for building skills and identifying employee strengths and weaknesses through the use of scenarios that are fun, exciting, and appropriately stressful.

Benson, H. (1975). *The Relaxation Response*. New York: HarperCollins.

Benson, H., Proctor, W. (1984). *Beyond the Relaxation Response*. New York: Berkley.

For a discussion of the physiology of stress and practical techniques for dealing with it, these two books are hard to beat. Benson is an MD at Harvard Medical School and founder of the Harvard Mind-Body Institute.

Benson, H., Proctor, W. (2003). *The Breakout Principle*. New York: Scribner.

More of Benson's work, discussing the physiology of creative breakthroughs and inspiration. Again, an excellent work for anyone who is serious about increasing business performance.

Cox, R. (2002). Sport Psychology, Concepts and Applications (5th Ed). New York: McGraw-Hill.

I've used a lot of sport examples in this book. The similarities between sports and the business environment should be quite clear by now. If you're interested in understanding mental skills training for producing high performance under stressful and competitive conditions, this book provides an excellent overview.

Csikszentmihalyi, M. (1990). *Flow: The Psychology of Optimal Experience*. New York: Harper Collins.

Flow is one of the most powerful motivational tools available. It's something that can be used to dramatically improve employee performance and happiness in the workplace, provided, of course, that you are willing to create the conditions necessary for it to occur. This book discusses the nature of Flow and goes into depth on how to create it. Well worth reading if you want to understand more about this amazing motivational force.

Fisher, R., Ury, W., & Patton, B. (1991). *Getting To Yes (2nd Edition).* **New York: Penguin Books.**

Ury, W. (1991). *Getting Past No.* **New York: Bantam**

The classic works on a negotiation technique that actually works. If you want to truly master the fine art of letting other people have your way, these books are a must. Both books are based on the work of the Harvard Negotiation Project, and include examples of negotiation techniques applied in a variety of business and diplomatic settings.

Miller, W., & Rollnick, S. (2002). *Motivational Interviewing* **(2nd ed.). New York: Guilford Press.**

All about the psychology of preparing people for change, from getting them interested to developing confidence, to actually planning and making the change happen.

Pentland, A. (2008). *Honest Signals: How They Shape Our World.* **Cambridge MA: MIT Press.**

Pentland's work on body language and the study of the subtle signals we send is both comprehensive and comprehensible. Unlike mythological claims such as looking up and to the right, Pentland's signals actually work. They're also very hard to notice. This book discusses what to look for and what to do. It also makes it clear just how hard it is to fake body language!

Schein, E. (2004). *Organizational Culture and Leadership (3rd Edition).* **San Franciso: Jossey-Bass.**

For those who want to fully understand organizational culture and its influences, this is the classic work by the man who invented the term "organizational culture." Ed Schein is a professor emeritus at the MIT Sloan School of Management and is widely viewed as the father of organizational psychology.

Schein, E. (1999). *The Corporate Culture Survival Guide.* **San Francisco: Jossey-Bass.**

For those who don't have the time to work through *Organizational Culture and Leadership*, this book contains much of the same information although in less depth. *The Corporate Culture Survival Guide* is a fast read, and provides a great deal of perspective on the psychology of how people interact in an organizational setting.

Schein, E. (2009). *Helping: How to offer, give, and receive help.* **San Francisco: Berrett-Koehler.**

Ed Schein is also an incredibly prolific writer. *Helping* is an analysis of the dynamics of the helping relationship between individuals and within teams. Schein explains the importance of that relationship to team dynamics and successful team performance, and shows you how to build it successfully.

Useem, M. (1998). *The Leadership Moment*. New York: Three Rivers Press.

An excellent, and extremely enjoyable, description of nine famous examples of extraordinary leadership. It's worth reading to see just what really works... and what doesn't.

Wheelan, S. (2005). Group Processes: A developmental perspective (2nd Ed.). Boston: Allyn & Bacon.

Susan Wheelan is quite possibly *the* expert on group dynamics and the psychology of team formation. Her book is a valuable read for anyone who is interested in developing an in-depth understanding of the psychology of group processes. A strong background in psychology is a must for really understanding this book though!

Zimbardo, P. & Boyd, J. (2008). *The Time Paradox*. New York: Free Press.

An excellent discussion of how we perceive time and the historical and cultural roots of our beliefs, attitudes, and uses of time. Poor time perspective is the bane of many an individual and an enterprise; this book lays out the different ways we have of dealing with time and provides instructions for developing a more balanced and effective time perspective.

About the Author

Stephen R. Balzac is a consultant, author, and speaker. He is the president of 7 Steps Ahead (www.7stepshead.com), an organizational development firm focused on helping businesses get unstuck and turn problems into opportunities.

Steve has over 20 years of experience in the high tech industry as an engineer, manager, entrepreneur, and consultant. He is a popular speaker on topics ranging from leadership, innovation, learning, organizational change, and motivation.

In additional to publishing over a hundred articles on different aspects of organizational performance, Steve is the author of *The 36-Hour Course in Organizational Development,* published by McGraw-Hill, and *Organizational Psychology for Managers.* He is a contributing author to *Ethics and Game Design: Teaching Values Through Play.*

No stranger to the demands of maintaining peak performance under highly competitive and stressful situations, Steve is a fifth degree blackbelt in jujitsu and a former nationally ranked fencer.

Steve appears in *Under the Boardwalk: The Monopoly Documentary* movie, and has the distinction of being the only guest personally panned by a New York Times movie critic.

S. R. Balzac, *Organizational Psychology for Managers,*
Management for Professionals, DOI: 10.1007/978-1-4614-8505-6,
© Springer Science+Business Media New York 2014

Bibliography

Balzac, S. (2010). Reality from fantasy: Using predictive scenarios to explore ethical dilemmas. In D. Gibson & K. Schrier (Eds.), *Ethics and game design: Teaching values through play*. New York: IGI.

Baumeister, R., & Tierney, J. (2011). *Willpower: Rediscovering the greatest human strength*. New York: Penguin Press.

Benson, H. (1975). *The relaxation response*. New York: HarperCollins.

Benson, H., & Proctor, W. (1984). *Beyond the relaxation response*. New York: Berkley.

Benson, H., & Proctor, W. (2003). *The breakout principle*. New York: Scribner.

Bueno de Mesquita, B., & Smith, A. (2011). *The dictator's handbook*. New York: Public Affairs.

Cialdini, R. (2009). *Influence* (5th ed.). New York: Pearson.

Cox, R. (2002). *Sport psychology, concepts and applications* (5th ed.). New York: McGraw-Hill.

Csikszentmihalyi, M. (1990). *Flow: The psychology of optimal experience*. New York: Harper Collins.

Dixit, A., & Nalebuff, B. (2008). *The art of strategy: A game theorist's guide to success in business*. New York: W. W. Norton.

Fisher, R., Ury, W., & Patton, B. (1991). *Getting to yes* (2nd ed.). New York: Penguin Books.

Gollwitzer, P., & Brandstatter, V. (1997). Implementation intentions and effective goal pursuit. *Journal of Personality and Social Psychology, 73*, 186–199.

Gollwitzer, P. (1999). Implementation intentions: Strong effects of simple plans. *American Psychologist, 54*, 493–503.

Hater, J., & Bass, B. (1988). Superiors' evaluations and subordinates' perceptions of transformational and transactional leadership. *Journal of Applied Psychology, 73*, 695–702.

Kark, R., Shamir, B., & Chen, G. (2003). The two faces of transformational leadership: Empowerment and dependency. *Journal of Applied Psychology, 88*, 246–255.

Kirkpatrick, S., & Locke, E. (1996). Direct and indirect effects of three core charismatic leadership components on performance and attitudes. *Journal of Applied Psychology, 81*, 36–51.

Koestner, R., Lekes, N., Powers, T., & Chicoine, E. (2002). Attaining personal goals: Self-concordance plus implementation intentions equals success. *Journal of Personality and Social Psychology, 83*, 231–244.

Latham, G., & Locke, E. (2007). New developments in and directions for goal-setting research. *European Psychologist, 12*(4), 290–300.

Locke, E., & Latham, G. (2002). Building a practically useful theory of goal setting and task motivation: A 35-year odyssey. *American Psychologist, 57*(9), 705–717.

Mandell, B., & Pherwani, S. (2003). Relationship between emotional intelligence and transformational leadership style: A gender comparison. *Journal of Business and Psychology, 17*, 387–404.

S. R. Balzac, *Organizational Psychology for Managers*, Management for Professionals, DOI: 10.1007/978-1-4614-8505-6, © Springer Science+Business Media New York 2014

Marsh, R., Hicks, J., & Bink, M. (1998). Activation of completed, uncompleted, and partially completed intentions. *Journal of Experimental Psychology: Learning, Memory, and Cognition, 24*, 350–361.

Miller, W., & Rollnick, S. (2002). *Motivational Interviewing* (2nd ed.). New York: Guilford Press.

Pentland, A. (2008). *Honest signals: How they shape our world*. Cambridge: MIT Press.

Peterson, R., Smith, D. B., Martorana, P., & Owens, P. (2003). The impact of chief executive officer personality on top management team dynamics: One mechanism by which leadership affects organizational performance. *Journal of Applied Psychology, 88*, 795–808.

Schein, E. (1990). Organizational culture. *American Psychologist, 45*(2), 109–119.

Schein, E. (1996). Three cultures of management: The key to organizational learning. *Sloan Management Review, 38*(1), 9–20.

Schein, E. (1999). *The corporate culture survival guide*. San Francisco: Jossey-Bass.

Schein, E. (2003). Five traps for consulting psychologists or, how I learned to take culture seriously. *Consulting Psychology Journal: Practice and Research, 55*(2), 75–83.

Schein, E. (2009). *Helping: How to offer, give, and receive help*. San Francisco: Berrett-Koehler.

Seijits, G., & Latham, G. (2000). The effects of goal setting and group size on performance in a social dilemma. *Canadian Journal of Behavioural Science, 32*(2), 104–116.

Sheldon, K., & Elliot, A. (1999). Goal striving, need satisfaction, and longitudinal well-being: The self-concordance model. *Journal of Personality and Social Psychology, 76*, 482–497.

Stone, D., Patton, B., & Heen, S. (2010). *Difficult conversations: How to discuss what matters most*. New York: Penguin.

Turner, N., Barling, J., Epitropaki, O., Butcher, V., & Milner, C. (2002). Transformational leadership and moral reasoning. *Journal of Applied Psychology, 87*, 304–311.

Ury, W. (1991). *Getting past no*. New York: Bantam.

Useem, M. (1998). *The leadership moment*. New York: Three Rivers Press.

Wheelan, S. (2005). *Group processes: A developmental perspective* (2nd ed.). Boston: Allyn & Bacon.

Yukl, G. (2002). *Leadership in organizations* (5th ed.). Upper Saddle River: Prentice-Hall.

Zimbardo, P., & Boyd, J. (2008). *The time paradox*. New York: Free Press.

Index

A

Accreditation, 37, 150, 157–160, 166, 168
Artifacts of culture, 3, 20
Automaticity, 151
Autonomy, 28, 30, 31, 48, 144, 146, 156,
    166–168, 171, 177, 186, 239
  employee feedback, 31, 32
  in organizational narrative, 23–25, 27, 28,
    31, 37, 139, 154, 164, 166, 172, 186,
    217, 238
  leadership, 21, 27, 30, 42, 44, 46, 48–53,
    55, 128, 140, 144, 152, 156, 161–164,
    171, 174, 186, 219, 233, 246, 251
  motivation, 24, 27, 28, 30, 31, 36, 57, 58,
    126, 132, 140, 146, 159, 163, 165–167,
    171–174, 180, 186, 188, 217, 221, 241,
    248, 249, 235–238

B

Blame, 60, 127–129, 133–135, 137, 139, 142,
    146, 177, 245
Boredom and high performance teams, 53
Brainstorming, 33, 218, 243, 246
Breaks, 53, 157, 183, 185, 188, 218, 228–231,
    250, 251
  innovation and, 79, 230
  motivation and, 129, 166
  performance and, 42, 53, 126, 133, 188,
    214
  stress and, 216, 218, 219, 232

C

Challenges, 21, 32, 38, 49, 160, 168, 170, 214,
    221

Change

Change, 36–39, 45, 54, 55, 58, 126, 132–134,
    138, 139, 143, 145
  culture, 22, 23, 26, 30, 33–35, 37, 39, 44,
    51, 133, 136, 140, 141, 154, 157, 159,
    160, 180, 213, 236, 245, 247, 248, 251,
    254
  motivating employees, 84
  organizational learning, 157, 160, 165,
    166, 168
  questions to ask, 57
Chrome, 242, 252, 253
Coercive power, 159
Competence, 37, 60, 140, 146, 156, 158, 159,
    163, 166, 167, 171, 186, 188, 213, 239,
    244
Conflict, 21, 22, 30, 44, 47–50, 54, 56, 144,
    217, 222
Control, 23, 27, 30, 31, 54, 56, 126, 129, 134,
    137, 145, 150, 151, 164, 172, 166, 172,
    174, 175, 189, 237–239, 246, 251
Counterculture, 13, 14, 111
Cultural immune response, 54, 159, 218

D

Decision making, 45–47, 49, 50, 52–54, 56,
    57, 162, 174, 185, 245–247, 249, 251,
    252
  fatigue, 226, 246, 247
  in teams, 53, 55
  will power, 235, 245, 246

E

Enthusiasm, 25, 132, 138, 172, 180, 187, 236,
    252

S. R. Balzac, *Organizational Psychology for Managers*,
Management for Professionals, DOI: 10.1007/978-1-4614-8505-6,
© Springer Science+Business Media New York 2014

CPSIA information can be obtained
at www.ICGtesting.com
Printed in the USA
LVOW13*1302190917
549269LV00009B/21/P